Money Mammoth

Money Mammoth

Harness the Power of Financial Psychology to Evolve Your Money Mindset, Avoid Extinction, and Crush Your Financial Goals

by

Dr. Brad Klontz

Dr. Ed Horwitz

and

Dr. Ted Klontz

WILEY

Published by John Wiley & Sons, Inc., Hoboken, New Jersey.

Published simultaneously in Canada.

For general information on our other products and services or for technical support, please contact our Customer Care Department within the United States at (800) 762-2974, outside the United States at (317) 572-3993, or fax (317) 572-4002.

Wiley publishes in a variety of print and electronic formats and by print-on-demand. Some material included with standard print versions of this book may not be included in e-books or in print-on-demand. If this book refers to media such as a CD or DVD that is not included in the version you purchased, you may download this material at http://booksupport.wiley.com. For more information about Wiley products, visit www.wiley.com.

Library of Congress Cataloging-in-Publication Data

Names: Horwitz, Ed, author. | Klontz, Brad, author. | Klontz, Ted, author.
      | John Wiley & Sons, Ltd., publisher.
Title: Money mammoth : harness the power of financial psychology to evolve
      your money mindset, avoid extinction, and crush your financial goals /
      by Dr. Ed Horwitz, Dr. Brad Klontz, & Dr. Ted Klontz.
Description: Hoboken, New Jersey : John Wiley & Sons, Inc., [2021] |
      Includes index.
Identifiers: LCCN 2020028689 (print) | LCCN 2020028690 (ebook) | ISBN
      9781119636045 (cloth) | ISBN 9781119636069 (adobe pdf) | ISBN
      9781119636052 (epub)
Subjects: LCSH: Finance, Personal—Psychological aspects. |
      Money—Psychological aspects. | Financial security.
Classification: LCC HG179 .H598 2021 (print) | LCC HG179 (ebook) | DDC
      332.024001/9—dc23
LC record available at https://lccn.loc.gov/2020028689
LC ebook record available at https://lccn.loc.gov/2020028690

Cover Design: Wiley
Cover Images: (Wooly Mammoth): © CSA Images/Getty Images
(Money Bag): Wiley

SKY10024448_012621

Dr. Brad Klontz

Dedicated to you, the reader, for having the courage to tackle the most stressful topic in the lives of three out of four people. IF you evolve your money mindset, you CAN transform your financial life.

Dr. Edward Horwitz

I would like to dedicate this book to my wife, Chris, for her love, support, and insights throughout the writing process, and along our road in life together. I would also like to dedicate this book to the millions of people who struggle with money issues. Over decades of seeing the generational financial devastation caused by mishandling personal financial decisions, my passion for finding a solution burned. Too many families and children have been destroyed by bitter divorce simply because their parents didn't know how to engage in positive money discussions or guide their children with correct financial wisdom. Therefore, I dedicate this book, and a lifetime of thoughts, reflection, research, and experiences, to all of you. I sincerely hope you find the insights and solutions to discover financial security and contentment for you and all your financial relationships.

Dr. Ted Klontz

To my friend and wife, Margie, and to my children, who remain my best teachers, and to the countless folks who have allowed me to walk with them on their journey of finding peace in their relationship with money. To all those who wonder if they are the only ones who don't "do well" with money: The answer is a resounding "NO." May this book help you find your way.

Contents

About the Authors

DR. BRADLEY T. KLONTZ, Psy.D., CFP®

Bradley T. Klontz, Psy.D., CFP®, is an expert in financial psychology, financial planning, and applied behavioral finance. He's an associate professor of practice at Creighton University Heider College of Business, co-founder of the Financial Psychology Institute, and Managing Principal of Your Mental Wealth Advisors. In addition to *Money Mammoth* (Wiley, 2020), Dr. Brad Klontz is co-author/co-editor of *Facilitating Financial Health* (NUCO, 2008; 2016), *Financial Therapy* (Springer, 2015), *Mind Over Money* (Broadway Business, 2009), *Wired for Wealth* (HCI, 2008), and *The Financial Wisdom of Ebenezer Scrooge* (HCI, 2005; 2008).

Dr. Klontz is a Fellow of the American Psychological Association, and a former president of the Hawaii Psychological Association. He was awarded the Innovative Practice Presidential Citation from the American Psychological Association for his application of psychological interventions to help people with money and wealth issues and his innovative practice in financial psychology for practitioners across the country.

Dr. Klontz has been a columnist for the *Journal of Financial Planning*, On Wall Street, and PsychologyToday.com. His work has been featured on ABC news shows *20/20, Good Morning America*, and in *USA Today, The Wall Street Journal, The New York Times, The Washington Post, The Los Angeles Times, Time, Kiplinger's, Money Magazine*, National Public Radio, and many other media outlets and professional magazines and journals.

In 2019, he was appointed to the CNBC Financial Wellness Council and in 2018 received the Montgomery-Warschauer Award from the *Journal of Financial Planning*, honoring the most outstanding contribution to the betterment of the financial planning profession. He has partnered with organizations including Capital One, JP Morgan Chase, Mutual of Omaha, and H&R Block in efforts to help raise public awareness around issues related to financial health and financial psychology.

Learn more about Dr. Brad Klontz at www.BradKlontz.com, his Money Mindset channel on YouTube www.YouTube.com/c/drbradklontz and @DrBradKlontz on social media.

DR. EDWARD HORWITZ, Ph.D., CFP®, FBS, ChFC, CLU, CSA

During his 35-plus-year career in the financial services industry, Dr. Horwitz has educated tens of thousands of agents, financial planners, wealth managers, and consumers in the field of personal finance and risk management. He holds a Ph.D. from Kansas State University, an MBA from Creighton University, and an undergraduate degree in finance from the University of Iowa. In addition to his academic degrees, Dr. Horwitz also holds numerous professional designations in the fields of insurance risk management, financial planning, and applied financial behavior. Dr. Horwitz currently serves as the chief risk and compliance officer for Creighton University, holds the Inaugural Mutual of Omaha Endowed Chair in Risk Management, and is an associate professor of practice in the Economics and Finance Department at the Heider College of Business at Creighton University. Dr. Horwitz serves as the program director for Creighton's finance programs in enterprise risk management and was the developer and director for programs in financial planning and financial psychology and behavioral finance.

Dr. Horwitz is a regular industry speaker, author, media contributor, and applied financial psychology intervention researcher. His contributions have appeared in numerous national and local media outlets, in-print and online, including *Money* magazine, *The Wall Street Journal*, CNBC, and MSNBC. He is considered a creative leader, educator, and financial behavior futurist who brings his experience and academic research perspective to find unique solutions to consumer and organizations. Dr. Horwitz has provided advice and counsel to all likes of individuals from lower-income people struggling with debt issues, to Rock and Roll Hall of Fame musicians, members of the entertainment industry, professional athletes, and professional sport teams.

Dr. Horwitz's published research is focused on applied financial psychology-based solutions. He has authored several chapters in leading industry text books including *Client Psychology* (Wiley, 2018) and *Financial Therapy—Theory, Research, & Practice* (Springer, 2015). Dr. Horwitz is considered a leading industry contributor in the field of financial planning, behavioral change, financial psychology, and strategic enterprise risk management, both in his research and the breadth of his experience and practice. His insights and creative approaches to breaking through financial behavioral issues are highly respected.

DR. TED KLONTZ, Ph.D.

Dr. Ted Klontz is an associate professor of practice at Creighton University's Heider College of Business and founder of the Financial Psychology Institute. He was a founding official of the Financial Therapy Association.

Ted has an extensive international private practice, including troubleshooting, strategic planning, advising, and consulting. He is a pioneer of and has been working in the field of financial psychology for over two decades, authoring six other books on the topic.

Foreword

Our attitudes toward money and wealth have a far-reaching influence on how we live and lead our lives. Perhaps more so than any other aspect of our social development. In my case, as a boy growing up on a farm in northeast Nebraska, I saw my parents wrestle with farmland debt, soaring prices on farm equipment, and bankruptcies that made it nearly impossible to keep the family business afloat. Though we made it through, the impact of seeing that struggle forever changed the way I thought about money. It changed the way I foresaw achieving financial security and led me to a career as a financial advisor. Nearly 40 years later, I've built a top-ranked financial services firm serving tens of thousands of clients around the country, teaching them an undeniable truth about their financial behaviors: They underestimate the extent to which emotion plays a defining role in the success of their financial future.

Chances are you have your own story with your own unique values, life lessons and attitudes toward money. They've taught you some valuable lessons and probably exposed a few mistakes along the way, too. It's a relationship, really. We have our own connection with money that influences how we save it, invest it, or spend it. What is so profoundly powerful about this book is that it shines a light on how you develop these postures toward money and, more importantly, what you can do to adjust your own habits so you can make your financial situation work for you.

At Carson Wealth (carsonwealth.com), we help our clients pursue True Wealth™, which is what we define as "all that money can't buy and death can't take away." Using a holistic approach to financial planning and aided by technology, we discuss the emotions behind the decisions being made in a financial life. This experience connects the dots between life and wealth, making their financial situation easier to understand.

A top client of ours recently came into the office for her annual review and, as she and the advisor were getting caught up, she seemed flustered. Long-time friends, the advisor's and client's children went to school together. The advisor picked up on her uneasy position and asked if she was feeling okay.

She responded, "You've known me for a long time and we've trusted each other, so I'm going to be direct with you," she replied. "I'm more scared coming in to see you than I am seeing my doctor." Surprised, the advisor asked why.

"I just get nervous about money," she continued. "At least with the doctor, I know my results are either positive or negative. When it comes to money, I don't know exactly where I stand, and I feel intimidated by this area of my life because of how little I know. I want to do what's best for my kids, but I don't understand any of this and it makes me really nervous."

There are tens of thousands of stories just like this one. It underscores a scary reality about the psychological component interwoven into the fabric of our financial lives. Our anxiety over money is an issue that's as old as money itself.

So, where do you go from here? Start by recognizing that financial psychology is the future of financial planning. The author's make a solid case for this and brilliantly outlines how this issue is no longer simply an academic one. It's a personal one, and it will impact each of you in your own unique way. With every chapter, you'll be carried into a deeper layer of understanding of your own financial habits and, more importantly, equipped with an action plan on how you can make smarter decisions for your financial future.

Think about the numerous beliefs you have about money. How have they influenced you up to this point in your life? What healthier habits can you adopt going forward? How can you go about building a more secure financial life for yourself and your family, equipped with this knowledge? These are all questions that will be answered in-depth in *Money Mammoth*. My advice, as a financial advisor who sees just how far we've fallen when it comes to financial literacy, is to take these concepts and share them with everyone you know.

Really, that's what I see being so powerful about this book. It forces you to not only look at yourself holistically but also opens your eyes to the multi-faceted way money infiltrates your thinking, your desires, your attitudes and your future. If we intend to make smarter financial decisions and raise financially savvy children, this book makes it clear we must first start with ourselves. The more holistic your planning, the better your ability to make the right financial decisions.

Whether you're a saver, spender, or investor, we are fortunate to have so much opportunity sitting in front of us. If you get nothing else from reading this book, know this: Every piece of who you are, whether psychologically, spiritually, emotionally and physically, subtly intertwines with your feelings about money and shapes the way you see the world.

The good news is the tools, concepts and exercises in this book put the power in your hands to better understand your belief system and your habits and how adjustments can be made to live more fully. As an advisor, I wish all my clients came to the table with the knowledge this book provides.

A tip before you dive into the book. Stop defending what you think you know and embrace the unknown. Open yourself to the realization you have much to learn, and often it's sitting within the depths of who we are, the people we associate with and the environment in which we grow.

What I'm talking about here is a lesson we often share with our clients. Let us help you live your life by design, not by default. As you read on, use the principles in this book to be purposeful in your approach. To move forward in a smarter way. Because the future favors the prepared.

Ron Carson
CEO/Founder
Carson Group

Introduction

YOUR MONEY MAMMOTH

Mammoths ruled their domain. Enormous creatures and majestic in their being, they lived at a time long after the dinosaurs were gone. Mammoths roamed the land of Western Europe and Northern America, eating grass, raising their young, and enjoying life. Changes in the mammoths' environment were happening all around them, but they failed to see and adapt to the effects. Over their time, the earth cooled, and as the tundra started to freeze, their food sources began to disappear. The mammoths started to migrate to find more sources for food, but they encountered new challenges. Neanderthal cave dwellers learned to communicate within tribes and learned to work together to hunt. Prehistoric humans evolved from the scavenger to the hunter and quickly ascended the food chain. The mammoths were slow moving, large sources of meat protein, and sadly, easily killed. In the end, early human's social hunting skills, a changing environment, and their species' failure to evolve and adapt was the source of the mammoths' eventual extinction.

OUR EXTINCTION LEVEL EVENT

Throughout history, species adapt and evolve over time to changing conditions or they become extinct. It is a cruel truth of nature and natural selection of survival of the species. However, don't be fooled into thinking these events only occurred millions of years ago. In fact, they are happening every day on our planet; you just may not be aware that they are occurring. While we instinctively look to environmental changes, like climate change, for examples of these events, they are not the only signs. Historically, environmental changes were the source of many early excitation events, but they aren't the only source of excitation level changes.

Some theorize that the extinction level event that will impact humans may come from social versus environmental changes. Is it possible that the social phenomenon of not being able to properly handle our personal finances could lead to enough social unrest to cause a civil war? Can the underlying divide, or political exploitation, between the "wealthy" and "poor" grow to the point that the inequality destroys our social environment, leading to a quantum shift in our lives and society? In fact, it might not be the warming earth, pandemic disease, carbon emission, or a giant meteor that wipes us out. Consider the real possibility that our inability to address financial inequality and the number of people living in poverty as the foundational sources of our ultimate demise.

TODAY'S REALITY

When it comes to our relationship with money, we are stuck in the Stone Age.

- According to the American Psychological Association (APA), money is a significant source of stress for three out of four Americans.[1]
- Forty-five percent of Americans have no savings whatsoever.[2]
- The average person age 60 or older who does have savings has about $150,000, certainly not enough to stop working.[3]
- Almost 40% of American adults wouldn't be able to cover a $400 emergency with cash, savings, or a credit card charge they could quickly pay off.[4]
- The median American household has only $11,700 in savings.[5]
- Among elderly Social Security beneficiaries, 48% of married couples and 69% of unmarried persons receive 50% or more of their income from Social Security. In 2019, the average monthly Social Security retirement benefit for a new retiree was about $1,500.[6]
- The level of credit debt in the United States during the height of the most recent economic expansion (2019) was over $35,000.[7]

It's painfully obvious that the average American is in terrible financial shape. Despite the relentless barrage of information and warnings from financial experts that saving for the future is not a luxury but a necessity. In our society, people who don't save are looked down on. We blame them for being irresponsible without realizing that today's bad financial behaviors were our ancestor's essential survival behaviors.

SO WHO ARE YOU?

Ask yourself if the environment you were raised in was one of financial independence or one of interdependence. *Independence* in this case means that every family unit within your tribe was expected to, and generally did, take care of itself. Or was it interdependent, meaning that everyone shared, when necessary, financial resources. If the latter, you may find it very difficult to save while others close to you have significantly less.If your case is the latter, you may feel a great sense of responsibility for people who are in need. You may find that they expect you, if you have more, to share what you have, and if you don't, they may cut you out of their lives.

YOU ARE WIRED TO SPEND

You are wired to share and not save. That makes it a significant challenge to deal with modern personal finance. But we have another significant challenge: We are also hardwired to spend. Not all that we gathered is given away. We use it; we spend it now; we don't invest in our future. So why do we have that impulse? It's the same reason we have a problem with obesity. We can blame our DNA.

Your ancestors did not live long by engaging in moderation.When there was something to eat, they ate as much of it as they could.They didn't say, Oh, I think I have had enough, I'll quit now, and save some for later.They didn't avoid eating fatty or sugary foods; they thrived on them. There were probably those who thought they should eat in moderation, but in prehistoric days, when people didn't know when or where their next meal would come, they were less likely to survive to pass on their DNA. So, the survivors, our ancestors, were consumers.

Consuming as much as they could, even beyond when they were full. They did so because the next meal was not a guarantee and any food that went uneaten would quickly spoil.

This consumer programming helps to partly explain our current obesity crisis in America. We are no better at managing our calorie intake than we are at saving money. In many ways, money is our food.We love to consume it as we find it!

If we get the chance, we will consume more than we need. But now we have the ability to consume more than we even have. We call this buying on credit. Businesses understand this human need and seduce us to consume our money, borrow more, and consume that too. They are just capitalizing on human nature. So modern society has created a situation in which our ancestral programming sets the stage for our becoming obese and broke.

YOU ARE WIRED TO TRY TO KEEP UP WITH THE JONESES

In tribal life, ancestors' status within a tribe was a matter of life or death. One of the greatest threats to their survival was finding that they no longer belonged in the group and they no longer had a community to help keep them safe. Our ancestors left on their own would not live long enough to pass on their DNA. So, today, we are incredibly sensitive to whether we belong in a group or not. We are wired to be on constant lookout for cues that we might have lost our place.

In the past, it was critically important that our ancestors kept up on the latest gossip and rumors.Tribes typically consist of 100–150 individuals, so it was a daily task for our ancestors to see where they stood. It was important to know who was mad at whom, and who was in good favor with the leaders of the tribe. Given that our current society is so much larger, we rely on social media and the news to make sure we are not caught by surprise. Watching the news, whether accurate or not, triggers our pleasure centers and gives us hits of dopamine similar to those we get from food and sex. Our brain rewards us for keeping up with the Joneses. For our ancestors, keeping up with the news was a matter of life or death.

ALL THE RULES HAVE CHANGED

Within the past two generations, there has been a dramatic shift away from this tribal social system. Part of the responsibility of the tribe was taking care of each other, including as older people. Over time, as we moved from small tribes to larger groups, this responsibility was passed on to institutions, corporations, and the government. Several decades ago, such entities were there to take care of the tribe. Your company would fund your retirement, and Social Security would step in to take care of the remainder. You saved a little for vacations and holidays, but when and how retirement would occur was not a concern.

What about all this debt? Our grandparents didn't have credit problems. They didn't struggle with credit card debt. Were they wiser? More disciplined? Perhaps, but that's not why they didn't carry massive amounts of debt. The fact is that they couldn't have gotten access to unsecured debt if they wanted it. There was no such money mechanisms as credit cards. The only unsecured credit they were likely to get was from the local grocer, who wasn't likely to extend it more than $100 or less. In the past few decades, we have been given access to easy and fast credit.

But recent cultural shifts have dramatically changed the landscape. Corporations have shifted from defined benefit plans, such as pensions, to defined contribution plans, like 401(k)s. These somewhat subtle shifts have changed the responsibility of saving for retirement from the institutions back to the individual. So we shifted the responsibility of taking care of our aging members from small tribes to the government. In the past few decades, institutions have been discharging this responsibility, but now there are no tribes left to fall back on.

So now it is all up to the individual. This has never happened in human societal evolutionary history, and it is significant to note. You heard this message if you remember the daily briefings after the corona virus outbreak, when self-reliance was called for and lack of government reliance became a reality. This dramatic shift alone helps explain, to a large degree, our society's current financial problems as well. Look at the total global economic impact of the corona virus–related disruptions for businesses, organizations, individuals, and government, and the unintended results from these shifts of societal personal responsibility. Who was most impacted? The poor and the elderly, those groups least able to take on the personal responsibility and who were more dependent on government systems.

WE MUST EVOLVE

So, what can we do? The first step is to move away from lecturing, scolding, shaming, blaming, judging, scapegoating, and treating ourselves or others as if we are flawed or broken. We describe *shame* as an emotional gluetrap that keeps you stuck. Shame is not helpful. Second, we need to develop strategies to overcome this basic wiring that was essential for our ancestors to survive in the ancient world but works against us in today's world. This book is designed to help you understand your financial psychology, why you do the things you do around money. But we don't stop there. In each chapter, we offer tools to help you both tame your inner Money Mammoth and harness its powers to help you achieve your own ideal financial mindset.

THE WINDS OF CHANGE

The message here is that, indeed, change is all around. Change is the one inevitable constant in our existence. Some change is for the better and helps us live happier and richer lives, but some change can threaten our literal existence as a species. How can we tell the difference and be prepared? After all, what doesn't kill us makes us stronger, right? However, if we become so smart as a species that we create automated workarounds to address these changes, will it make us weaker and softer? Will those changes sneak up on us like the proverbial lobster in the pot, unsuspectingly boiling us alive? Will we think we are living high and happy, relaxing in the hot tub of life, only to discover too late that we are becoming extinct?

A HISTORICAL MOMENT

Will we look back to this moment in time and identify these financial trends as the cause of societal collapse which foretold our future? Is this the cause of our extinction? Are we like the mammoths, living in a world that is changing faster than we can comprehend or address? Or will the smartest and most enlightened of our species lead the way to change the trends that threaten our existence? Make no mistake, making behavioral change is hard, and doing so while fighting your genetic instincts will take some expert guidance.

TIME TO EVOLVE

Let's learn from the woolly mammoth and early humanity, and adhere to the lessons evolution has provided. To avoid a life of pain and struggle, let's explore how to take action now through financial awakening and rewiring our financial behavioral actions. Let's evolve and become a new species, the Money Mammoth, who confidently roams the earth and thrives in this new, constantly changing world.

NOTES

1. American Psychological Association, American Psychological Association Survey Shows Money Stress Weighing on Americans' Health Nationwide, February 4, 2015, https://www.apa.org/news/pressreleases/2015/02/moneystress.
2. Kathleen Elkins, Here's How Much Money Americans Have in Savings at Every Income Level, CNBC, September 27, 2018, updated October 11, 2018, https://www.cnbc.com/2018/09/27/hereshowmuchmoneyamericanshavein savingsateveryincomelevel.html.
3. Kathleen Elkins, Here's How Much the Average Family Has Saved for Retirement at Every Age, April 7, 2017, updated July 31, 2017, https://www.cnbc.com/2017/04/07/howmuchtheaveragefamilyhassavedforretirementatevery age.html.

4. Federal Reserve Survey, Report on the Economic WellBeing of U.S. Households in 2018, May 2019, Board of Governors of the Federal Reserve, May 24, 2017, updated July 31, 2017, https://www.federalreserve.gov/publications/ 2019economicwellbeingofushouseholdsin2018dealingwithunexpectedexpen ses.htm.

5. Kathleen Elins, Here's How Much Money Americans Have in Savings at Every Income Level, CNBC, September 27, 2018, updated October 11, 2018, https://www.cnbc.com/2018/09/27/hereshowmuchmoneyamericanshavein savingsateveryincomelevel.html .

6. Social Security Fact Sheet, SSA.gov, https://www.ssa.gov/news/press/factshee ts/basicfactalt.pdf .

7. Bill Fay, Consumer Debt Grows as U.S. Economy Expands, August 27, 2019, https://www.debt.org/2019/08/27/consumerdebtgrowsasuseconomyexpands/.

SECTION I

YOUR ORIGINS

Your Ancestors

This is the story of James and Alex, both of whom grew up in wealthy families. Both have more money at their disposal than they could spend in a lifetime. Both are surrounded by conspicuous luxury, and they have had the best education that money can buy. They eat the finest foods; they wear the finest clothes, and they run in the most elite social circles. They are financially set for life. In terms of material possessions, they have it all. Their wealth is not only profound, it is generational. Both come from families that have been wealthy for generations. Even though they come from similar places, they are very different people.

James is a spoiled brat. His life consists of parties late into the night and sleeping in almost every day. He doesn't do anything productive. He doesn't work. He mistreats service providers. In fact, he can be downright cruel. Even though his parents have given him everything he wants, he resents them. He drinks too much; he eats too much, and he gambles incessantly. Inside, he feels bad about himself. He feels lost, purposeless, depressed.

Alex, in contrast, lives a very different life. He wakes up early each morning, and spends much of the day strategizing how he can leverage the financial gifts he has been given in ways that are consistent with his and his family's basic value of making the world a better place.

He feels a sense of responsibility to be a good shepherd of the gifts he has been given. He is interested in knowing how he can increase his wealth so that he can do even more good things. He exercises rigorously to keep himself in peak physical condition. He is a practitioner of meditation and yoga. Though he didn't have to, he joined the military service, risking life and limb for his family and his country. He has spent years forgoing all of the pleasures that his family's money could have provided for him in an effort to make a name for himself and enhance the family legacy. He hopes to gain prominence as an officer and return home to enter politics. He is deeply connected to his family history. He appreciates what his parents, grandparents, and great grandparents have done for him and his family. In fact, he knows all about each of them: how they each made a living, what they worked at, and what they accomplished. He is driven to elevate his family's wealth and its status, and to pass this legacy down to his own children and grandchildren as he helps make the world a better place.

These two young men come from similar wealth, but have developed into very different people. Both were given every opportunity. One is passionate, appreciative, and ambitious. The other is depressed, resentful, and purposeless. It is human nature to seek pleasure and avoid pain. So it's easy to understand why someone like James, who has everything, might sit back and enjoy it.

So this begs the question: Why would an incredible rich young man, someone who has more money than he could ever need, someone who is living in the lap of luxury and comfort—why would he join the military, forego comfort and pleasure, risk his life, and be so utterly focused on growing his family's wealth and status?

THE ANCESTOR ROOM

To answer that question, we will visit ancient Rome. Two thousand years ago, Rome was the most powerful civilization in the world. Its aristocrats were incredibly wealthy. They lived in sprawling estates, had slaves to do their manual labor, and received the best education and health care available. The story of Alex mirrors that of many of the children of Roman aristocrats. The clearest path to wealth and status was political, and the quickest path to political office was a resumé of military accomplishments. To this end, these young men would sacrifice all the luxury and comfort that Rome provided to travel thousands of miles away and risk health, life, and limb in the pursuit of military distinction.

The short answer as to why young men behaved that way: It was all about their ancestors. Roman aristocrats had a tradition of making wax masks of the men in their families. The masks were usually made when someone reached the age of 40 and only if he had achieved a noteworthy political rank. The mask was a sign that he had achieved the minimal level of social status needed to be recognized as successful within the family. The mask showed that he was on a similar path to achievement and social prominence as his ancestors who were similarly recognized. These masks were stored in the reception room of their atriums and were arranged next to labels of the highest political offices held by each person. They were worn by actors during funeral processions, but were also shown to visitors.

Next to the collection of wax masks was a chart illustrating the family tree, with painted portraits of the ancestors. Nearby would also be a collection of armor and weapons captured by their ancestors, prominently displayed family achievements that would be seen by anyone who visited the home.

Located in the entryway and near the center of the villa, these tributes to the family's history and accomplishments were displayed for all to see. It would not have been uncommon for the family to walk visitors through the space, showing off the military trophies and political distinctions and telling stories about the trials, tribulations, and achievements of their ancestors.

Imagine what it would have been like to have been a child growing up in such a home, hearing stories about the various artifacts, pictures, and accomplishments of your ancestors, which were so prominently displayed. What must it have been like to have been shown a sword taken from a Carthaginian officer by your great-great grandfather in the Battle of Agrigentum in Sicily or hearing about how your grandfather helped restore Roman honor as a general in the Battle of Carthage in North Africa?

This deep connection to the past would help you make sense of the privilege you were now enjoying, and more important, the sense of duty and responsibility that accompany your privilege. Imagine how your self-esteem would be bolstered as you were told that you, as a direct descendent, have the same blood coursing through your veins. That the traits of courage and wile are built into your very being. You would believe that the highest levels of accomplishment for you are not only possible but are expected. That your ancestors are watching you, supporting you, and encouraging you to take the family to the next level. It is not hard to imagine that growing up in this way, you might develop an intrinsic motivation to do your part to maintain and grow your family's wealth and status and the belief that you could do it.

SO WHAT'S IN YOUR ANCESTRY ROOM?

When was the last time you visited someone's home and saw busts and portraits of their ancestors lining their walls? Interestingly, some of the most generationally successful families do have pictures of their ancestors displayed prominently, but for most of us, this is just not the case. It makes sense though, because, for rare exceptions, many of our ancestors never achieved significant fortune or status and few could afford an artist to paint a portrait. Many Americans are the descendants of immigrants. Aside from the occasionally wealthy adventurer, no one in their right mind would choose to leave a life of wealth and privilege to get on a boat and travel across the world to start over in a country where they knew no one and often didn't even speak the language.

If there were busts of your ancestors, with the possible exception of your parents or grandparents who may have been able to capitalize on the opportunities for socioeconomic advancement, the busts would likely not be of those who accomplished great things as measured in our culture or by ancient Roman standards. Instead you would see pictures and artifacts of refugees, indentured workers, slaves, and immigrants.

For most Americans, you would be looking at the historical legacy of poverty. Many of our ancestors came to America in an attempt to escape the depredations of political upheavals, poverty, calamity, disease, and natural disaster, or were forced to come here against their will. For many of us, our more recent ancestors would be represented by the tools and artifacts of farmers, auto workers, government employees, cooks, or laborers.

So, if you closed your eyes and imagined the hall of fame for your ancestors, what would you see? What financial legacy did they pass down to you? What beliefs about money did they pass on to you? What beliefs about what is possible did you inherit?

WHY AREN'T YOU RICH?

If you are like many Americans, your family has been in the land of opportunity for generations. So why weren't more of us born into an ultra-wealthy families? Take a moment to answer this question for yourself. Your most valuable answer in terms of truly understanding yourself will be the first thought that popped into your mind. You may be tempted to modify this so that it sounds more rational. Resist the temptation and stay with the image that first popped into your mind. Let the implications of that belief unfold. Just let it flow.

If your ancestors achieved financial success, congratulations! Now that doesn't mean that they passed this down to you, but hopefully, you have benefited from either the resources they were able to build or the mindset that allowed them to become successful. But if you are like most of us, ask yourself this question: Why weren't your ancestors rich?

So why aren't you rich? The answer is simple: You and/or your ancestors didn't successfully hoard enough money or valuable objects. Of course, there are a plethora of other considerations, but in strict behavioral terms, that's pretty much it. Rich people have amassed a bunch of money for themselves. Poor people have not. It turns out that high financial net worth is not about how much money you make; it is defined by how much money you save.

Here are two possible causes for your ancestors not becoming wealthy. The first is that they were dedicated to the concept of saving money, but they were unable to do so because the money or the opportunity to learn about money was not afforded them. This would include having been the unfortunate victims of oppressive governments, discrimination, or any number of atrocities throughout human history from which they were not able to recover.

The second possible cause is that they didn't buy into the concept of hoarding. According to Dictionary.com, *hoard* is defined as "a stock or store of money or valued objects, typically one that is secret or carefully guarded."[1] There are several key elements to this definition. First, it requires someone to stock up and save money or valuable objects. Second, it requires someone to protect, preserve, and safeguard the hoard.

The great news about this is that if you are reading this book, you likely live in a free society where people just like you have been able to create financial success. So while institutional and/or cultural barriers exist, it is possible for you to overcome them.

Today, we honor hoarders of money and resources. If you are not among them, it would be normal for you to feel bad about yourself. You may ask: Why were they able to do it, and me and my ancestors failed to do it? But here's the thing: While today we honor hoarders of money, thousands of years ago we killed them.

DEATH TO SAVERS

The majority of us are just not wired to save. In a 2018 study published in *Nature Communications* titled "Differential Temporal Salience of Earning and Saving," researchers Kesong Hu, Eve De Rosa, and Adam K. Anderson found that we are wired to pay more attention to earning than saving.[2] They noted that "savings" are for future use, are currently inaccessible, and are abstract, which decreases our attention and motivation to save. In contrast, we are wired to focus more on earning or gaining money and possessions now, which is much more concrete. Not only are we wired to pay attention to immediate concrete gains versus long-term abstract savings, our ancestors survived by sharing what they had when they had it. Those who didn't share were sanctioned by the tribe, often quite dramatically—sometimes banished, sometimes publicly executed. The ultimate sanction was to be thrown out of the tribe, which was a prescription for certain death. The sharers survived, and so they passed on their sharing genes and became the dominant group with the trait of sharing.

In many contemporary settings, the bias toward sharing instead of saving for oneself is very much predominant. For example, this approach to resources is quite prominent in Appalachia, Native American tribes, many African American communities, poor neighborhoods, and others. Those members of the community who share what they have with others are venerated while nonsharers are sanctioned. An underlying premise is that "If I look out for you when you need help, then you will look out for me when I need help." Each generation had its share of hoarders, but the majority of our ancestors, those individuals who survived, were those who had a sharing bias.

At this point, you may be wondering about your money beliefs. Where did they come from? Did they evolve from my ancestors thousands of years ago? How much of my financial behavior is hardwired and on auto pilot, and how much can I really control? Can I really fight genetic tendencies against saving, and if so, how? Can I become aware of my tendencies and correct them or am I doomed for financial extinction too? In the next chapter, we begin to explore those and many other questions, but first we need some Mammoth Insights to lead us on our journey.

Chapter 1 Mammoth Mindset Insights

1. Wealth can be a tool for happiness, but not the only source.
2. Setting expectations for greatness can occur through ancestry education.
3. Ancestral expectations can help build intrinsic motivation to achieve.
4. Sharing understandings and expectations of wealth can be generationally powerful.
5. Our early ancestors who evolved and survived had a sharing bias.
6. Setting an expectation for savings and financial independence is very important.

NOTES

1. Dictionary.com, "A supply or accumulation that is hidden or carefully guarded for preservation, future use, etc.," https://www.dictionary.com/browse/hoard?s=t.
2. Kesong Hu, Eve De Rosa, and Adam K. Anderson, "Differential Temporal Salience of Earning and Saving," *Nature Communications* 9, no. 1 (2018): 2843.

CHAPTER 2

Your Parents

You are a product of your parents, and so is your relationship with money. Take a moment to think about your parents and their experiences around money. Did they grow up wealthy? Poor? Middle class? What was that like for them? Were they satisfied with their socioeconomic status as kids? Were they dissatisfied? Did they feel shame about having too little or too much money compared to those around them? Were they raised knowing that they would have family financial support when they needed it, or were they cut loose at an early age knowing they had to sink or swim on their own? What lessons did your grandparents teach them? What cultural and/or historical events impacted their relationship with money? How would you rate their satisfaction with their financial status in adulthood? Were they happy with their achievements? Did they feel remorse or despair?

Don't be surprised if you don't know the answers to these questions. After all, money is a taboo topic in our culture. Many of us feel shame around money, and it can be difficult to think about, let alone talk to your children about. However, your parents' experiences around money have had a dramatic impact on your relationship with money. Shedding light on their experience can help you make sense of your own financial beliefs and behaviors. If your parents are still alive, we encourage you to sit down with them and interview them about their relationship with money. If not, try to interview aunts, uncles, or cousins. Ask them questions about your grandparents and any stories about your other ancestors. In terms of understanding and mastering your own financial psychology, uncovering the details of your family history is pure gold.

Now think in terms of how your parents raised you around money. How was money handled in your home? How was it talked about? Did your parents agree about financial matters? Was money a topic of disagreement or conflict, or was it avoided altogether? What did your parents teach you about money, either overtly through instruction or by example?

When you take the time to explore your parents' experiences around money, you will make better sense of your own financial beliefs and decisions. As a child, you watched them closely. They created the universe in which you were raised; they created the initial structure on which you built your money mindset. Their beliefs about money have had a powerful impact on your own financial psychology—for better or worse.

YOUR PARENTS

As you think about your parents, their relationship with money, and what you learned, what feelings emerge? Our relationship with our parents is complicated, made up of a mixed bag of feelings and experiences over the years. Due to the nature of our species, we rely on the care, feeding, and protection of our parents longer than any other animal. As a result, we are more influenced by our parents than any other species. This is also where we get most of our socialization—how we make sense of relationships, our sense of self, and the various roles we play. For better or worse, you entered the world as the socialized and behavioral result of what you saw your parents say and do when you were very young. Typically, by the age of 7, your personality, behaviors, and social beliefs are fairly well cast.

When it comes to our beliefs and behaviors about money, research has supported a similar pattern of learning. What we see, hear, and overhear about money and relationships can influence us for our entire lives. These early childhood experiences create our money beliefs, which are hardwired into our subconscious. Our money beliefs drive our financial behaviors, and in many ways, determine our level of success. The subconscious representation of your financial beliefs, which greatly influences your money behaviors, decisions, and relationships, is known as Money Scripts®. They are what informs our day-to-day interactions, decisions, discussions, relationships, filters, and behaviors regarding all things financial.

Since Money Scripts® are so integral to our financial outcomes, it makes sense to know as much as we can about them. We dedicate Chapter 9 to understanding and assessing your Money Scripts®. For now, we are going to explore what roles your parents played in shaping your money beliefs.

Essentially, it could be fair to blame your financial problems, and possibly your relationship problems, on your parents. Most likely your financial beliefs and behaviors have sprung directly from your experiences in your childhood. Of course, you are ultimately responsible for your behaviors, but the fact is, your financial behaviors are rooted in your Money Scripts®. Research on Money Scripts® and their influence on financial outcomes is one of the fastest-growing areas of research in financial psychology. Financial professionals realize that understanding financial behavior is the future of helping clients with their financial needs.

BECOME YOUR OWN ANTHROPOLOGIST

Anthropology is the study of human societies and cultures and is a fascinating field. In studying a culture, anthropologists often immerse themselves into the culture, spending months or years living among the inhabitants. There, they both participate in the culture and observe the inhabitants, looking for insights into people's behavior from a cultural perspective.

Since you probably can't afford to hire an anthropologist to live with your family for a year to study you, you need to do your own research. This is where interviewing your parents, siblings, and other family members can be so valuable. In this process, it is not uncommon to discover stories you have never heard. Sometimes these stories shed light on your parents' behaviors around money. Take the opportunity to interview your family members, asking some of the following questions:

- What was it like for you growing up around money?
- How was money handled by your parents?
- What was it like for grandparents growing up?
- How did you feel about your socioeconomic status?
- What beliefs about money were passed down to you?
- What were your biggest financial mistakes? Successes?
- Do you have any memories that stand out?

Often, these prompts will start an extended dialogue about their money memories. This is a good opportunity for you to listen. Take the time to let them share their memories and experiences around money. You might want to record the conversation and/or take notes. After your interviews, take some time to see if you can see any patterns. Did you notice any recurring themes? What beliefs did they have about money? Did you notice any differences between the childhood experiences of your parents? How did this impact their relationship with money? Do you recognize any of these beliefs passed down to you? How did their upbringing impact the development of your relationship with money?

This type of study can be quite valuable and will give you tremendous insight into your own psychology of money. You might begin to better understand why your parents raised you the way they did. Your parents are as much a product of their parents and early environment as you are a product of yours. Keep in mind that your children are the next in line to inherit this family financial legacy. The great news is that it is not too late to make "edits" to your family legacy.

WHEN MONEY HELPS

Having disposable income and using it to help friends and family can be a wonderful resource. Money can be used to help in times of opportunity, transition, or need. Financial support can be used to help loved ones with a down payment for a first home, education, weddings, moving expenses, or starting a business. Having parents or other family members there to help can provide a deep sense of safety, security, and confidence, even if the help is never asked for or received. As a parent who is able to help financially, the opportunity to help can provide a tremendous feeling of importance, dependence, and connection to an older child or grandchild's life. We all know that early on in our lives, we have built very little financial savings, wealth, or independence. Having a parent there to give us a leg up with life's initial financial challenges can be a real benefit. Whether this help comes in the form of a gift or a loan, having support helps satisfy that deep, tribal need we have for connection.

WHEN MONEY HURTS

But not all financial help is good. There are many circumstances in which financial help, or the promise of financial help, can hurt. For example, there are times when financial support enables a pattern of irresponsible financial behaviors, encouraging bad spending habits, a lack of saving, a lack of motivation, or other self-destructive behaviors. In our research, we refer to this as *financial enabling* and *financial dependence*, which is discussed in detail in Chapter 3.

Sometimes money is used within family systems to hurt or control. Sometimes the power money can have to create a connection in the lives of those close to us becomes so important that we use money to enable those feelings. This can lead to a pattern of financial enmeshment.

FINANCIAL ENMESHMENT

Financial enmeshment is a blurring of boundaries among family members around money. Our research has found that financial enmeshment occurs more commonly with higher income males,[1] but it can afflict anyone. One example of financial enmeshment is when parents give children too much financial information or involve them inappropriately in adult financial matters. Common examples include:

- Using children to pass along financial information between divorced parents (e.g., "Please tell your mother to pay me the $100 she owes me").
- Sharing your financial stress with a child (e.g., "I don't know how we are going to pay rent this month").
- Having children answer the phone when creditors call.
- Talking poorly about a child's parents around money (e.g., "You can't have braces because your father won't pay child support").

Involving children in adult financial matters can have a negative impact on their own relationship with money. While some children may feel a sense of importance that they are being involved in adult matters, they are not psychologically able to cope with and process the information. As such, the experience often leaves them feeling anxious and insecure. It is very important to talk to your children about money, but it is not okay to share too much financial information with them. A great litmus test on what is "too much" is to ask yourself this question: "Am I feeling negative emotions around this issue (e.g., scared, guilty, or anger)?" If so, you are best not to share it. A better idea is for you to share those concerns with another adult, possibly even a professional. There is no shame in having financial stress or concerns, but you need to be careful not to burden children with your issues, as it can hurt them.

A FAMILY STORY OF FINANCIAL DESTRUCTION

The Allen family came from humble financial beginnings. Fred, the father and sole breadwinner, was a science professor at the local university. The family had to stretch Fred's meager salary across the entire family, which consisted of his wife, Jane, their two daughters, and one son. As with many fathers of his generation, Fred was not very close with his children. He was a bit of a mad scientist type who was always working on some ideas in his office or in his home laboratory. The Allen family lived a typical lower middle-class existence throughout the 1950s, 1960s, and 1970s.

Then in the 1980s, Fred's line of research led him to develop something revolutionary. After splitting the rights to the idea with the university, Fred quit his job and went into business. Fred took his innovation and built a business that became worth hundreds of millions of dollars. The company was held entirely by Fred and Jane as it grew organically. The Allens became very wealthy later in life when they were well into their 60s. But Fred and Jane, never having any real money, had no idea how to manage their new-found wealth. They wound up giving all their children tens of millions to help make their lives "easier and more enjoyable," and so that their grandchildren would "not need to struggle like they did." One of the three children joined Fred in the business to learn, and ultimately take over some day.

Twenty years later, Jane passed away and left unequal portions of her wealth to each child. The two kids who were not involved in the business received assets and cash of a hundred million dollars each. The child working in the business received far less in dollars than the other two by half, but inherited Jane's shares of 50% ownership in the business. At the time, the two receiving cash were very happy and had no interest in the business at all. All three felt the division of assets was reasonable and fair. The other sibling worked hard to build up the business and succeed Fred as his days actively involved in the business were drawing to a close.

After another 10 years, the kids who got money had spent an overwhelming amount of their inheritance and battled personal relationship issues and substance abuse. When the money was running low, the other two siblings saw how successful the business had become and felt they were shortchanged on their mom's estate settlement. This kicked off a series of lawsuits and resentment among the siblings. The one sibling was deeply hurt and angered that the hard work and dedication he had contributed to grow the organization was believed to be "owed" to the other two siblings who "partied away their money." The two siblings co-opted Fred, who had become severely afflicted with dementia, and ganged up against the single sibling who was now controlling and running the organization. Finally, to save any remnants of their family, and to help reconcile while Fred was still alive, the one sibling agreed to sell the company and settle. Unfortunately, they began fighting about the valuation and at what price to sell the business.

Fred passed away years ago, and his 50% of the business was divided among the children, who are now in their 60s and 70s. However, the three siblings are still embroiled in ongoing lawsuits. The one sibling still has a controlling interest in the business and runs the organization very successfully. The kids have now been fighting in the courts for over 15 years, and their families never speak. They have been fighting for so long and their bitterness is so deep, it's doubtful they can even remember what exactly they are fighting about. All three families should be set for life each with hundreds of millions of dollars. However, instead of enjoying their wealth and the time they have left, they waste time and money fighting over a few million here or there.

Fred and Jane's children had children of their own, all of whom were exposed to exceptional levels of wealth growing up. The family had many private jets, anything the children wanted they got, and their children's weddings were like royal affairs. Fred and Jane's children provided everything for their kids, so they never wanted or felt deprived. New York townhomes, Hollywood apartments, sports cars, and a healthy allowance were all lavishly provided to them. Almost all of Fred and Jane's grandchildren have subsequently struggled with failed relationships and substance abuse as well. Very soon they will have children of their own. How do you think their life stories will unfold?

This story is not that unusual for situations like these. Do you think the Allens were happier when they were middle class or super wealthy? Do you think that having more money will really make life better and make your family happier? Research would beg to differ. Studies consistently show that above middle class, there is no significant correlation between money and happiness.

PARENTS KNOW BEST?

When we are young, we see our parents as people who always know the answers. That's probably why as soon as we can think independently, around the ages of 4–5, we start asking a lot of questions. Parents try to answer these questions in a way that a young mind can comprehend and in a way that is likely to end the barrage of questions. However, when it comes to learning lessons about money, our parents' answers to these questions get written into a money blueprint. Even worse, a passing comment about money in the kitchen or at the dinner table can have a lasting effect. For example, a common phrase used by parents in response to a child's request for something is "No, we can't afford that." Think for a moment about how a young mind might interpret that. The message could be interpreted as "we don't have enough money" or "there isn't enough money." These Money Scripts® can lead to an entire life designed around making sure there is always enough money through an obsession around work. It could lead to someone feeling deprived and a propensity for overspending in adulthood to avoid the feeling of deprivation. It could also lead to a sense of learned helplessness; the logic being that since there isn't enough money, why bother trying to save or get ahead?

Innocent answers and simple reasoning can become the basis for our financial decision-making well into adulthood. Since money is not talked about overtly in many families, these simple misunderstandings or misinterpretation can often go unexamined. Probably not the best way to base sound financial decision-making for generations. Our parents' money beliefs and behaviors are, of course, shaped by their parents and so on. These Money Scripts® get handed down generationally, influenced and shaped by the financial experiences of each generation. These flashpoints leave their mark and can change the path of family Money Scripts®.

THE 2008 HOUSING CRISIS

An example of a recent shared financial flashpoint was how many parents struggled to make ends meet in the wake of the 2008 housing crisis. Many parents probably exposed their children to new beliefs about banks, the stock market, and home ownership. In fact, studies have shown that Millennials are less likely to desire or seek home ownership and are less trustful of the stock market compared to previous generations.[2] The reasons given were not student debt levels, as some would have thought, but rather a belief that home ownership was not a reliable way to build wealth. However, for the previous two generations, equity built through home ownership was a major source of wealth creation. At the time of this book's writing, home ownership is at or near all-time high, and property values in most markets have recovered to near pre-2008 levels or higher. Additionally, all three major stock market indexes are at or near record high levels and more than recovered from pre-2008 levels.

The lesson here is that you must accept the fact that your parents may not know best when it comes to money management and money relationships. Don't be too hard on them; they were only doing what they had learned. Some of you have already recognized that fact as you got older. Are you able to recognize your parents' money beliefs and behaviors that you share?

As parents, many of us struggle with how much we should expose to our children. On one hand, we want them to respect a hard day's work and the value of a well-earned dollar. On the other hand, we don't want them to worry about money and spoil their childhood innocence. However, good money lessons are important to learn and establish. Kids are bombarded through social media and living in a highly materialistic society to consume and assimilate into society. Debt is advertised on TV and everything seems to be connected to money. Wealth, success, fame, and celebrity are front and center in our culture, and our kids see it everywhere. Parents have a near impossible task to educate their kids about money and good financial savings habits versus societal and peer pressures. What makes it even harder is most parents don't have it all figured out either. The advice you received may have been flawed or inaccurate. It's okay to still love your parents and ignore their money and money relationship advice. Sometimes you need to be okay with that idea for you to move ahead and rewrite those incorrect beliefs.

In the next chapter, we explore in greater detail how to help children develop a healthy money mindset. Remember, nobody is born knowing and understanding everything they need to know about money and proper financial management. Healthy money mindsets must be learned. If the money mindsets handed down from your parents need some correcting, it's time to fix them for your children.

Chapter 2 Mammoth Mindset Insights

1. In terms of understanding and mastering your own financial psychology, uncovering the details of your family history is pure gold.
2. Your children are the next in line to inherit your family financial legacy. The great news is that it is not too late to make "edits" to your family legacy.
3. There is no shame in having financial stress or concerns, but you need to be careful not to burden children with your issues, as it can hurt them.
4. Studies consistently show that above middle class, there is no significant correlation between money and happiness.
5. Innocent answers and simple reasoning can become the basis for our financial decision-making well into adulthood.
6. It's okay to still love your parents and ignore their money and money relationship advice. Sometimes you need to be okay with that idea in order for you to move ahead and rewrite those incorrect beliefs.

NOTES

1. B. Klontz, S. L. Britt, K. L. Archuleta, and T. Klontz, "Disordered Money Behaviors: Development of the Klontz Money Behavior Inventory, *Journal of Financial Therapy* 3, no. 1 (2012): 2.
2. Jamie Lenz, "Millennials Are Buying Homes Far Less Often Than Older Generations Did, and That Puts a Large Sector of the U.S. Economy at Risk," BusinessInsider.com, The Conversation, May 21, 2019, https://www .businessinsider.com/millennials-are-buying-homes-far-less-often-putting-economy-at-risk-2019-5.

CHAPTER 3

Your Children

How far would you go to protect the life of a close family member who was in mortal danger? If you had no other choice, would you kill to protect them? If you are a parent, how far would you go to protect your own child? How far would you go to protect a child's emotional well-being? How far would you go to give your child a leg up in the world? While it is easy to criticize others for going too far with their children, it's important to recognize that the desire to help children—especially our own children—is hardwired and is in a large part responsible for the survival of humanity. Human offspring are immobile, defenseless, and totally dependent for years after they are born.

We are wired to perpetuate our genes. This is the origin of sexual behavior and the natural protective instincts we all have. Even if we are not parents, we are wired to feel empathy and protective toward children. Childlike features trigger a protective impulse in most of us. It is why you see total strangers often immediately soften, smile, or otherwise change their demeanor when a small child makes eye contact with them. The typical social distance and emotional reservation will often instantly melt away, and many people will tilt their heads, lean over, or even squat down to engage a child—even when they are total strangers. When it comes to our own offspring or that of close family members of friends, this instinct is intensified.

If your child, or a close family member, was in mortal danger, would you kill to save him or her? The majority of human beings have a strong inhibition toward killing other human beings. However, when the lives of our family members are threatened, this inhibition can be overridden. This is one of the reasons that in training soldiers, the military works hard to facilitate the creation of a family. The soldiers in a platoon, for example, consider each other brothers and sisters. Many accounts from combat reveal that soldiers are able to override their inhibition to killing not for patriotism or political causes, but out of a desire to protect their brothers and sisters.

So while we are prone to self-preservation, this impulse can be easily suppressed when we feel like the lives and/or well-being of our family members are threatened—especially our children. This natural impulse helps explain a variety of destructive financial behaviors. They are all done from a place of love, worry, and concern, but they can backfire quite dramatically. It is important to be aware of these impulses so that we can engage our analytical brains to think through the long-term consequences of our behaviors.

CAN MONEY MAKE YOU INSANE?

Ethan is 16 years old. One evening, he and his friends got a little bit wild. On an impulse, they stole some beer and had an impromptu party at his parents' house. But these decisions were not the worst ones he made that night. Later that evening, Ethan and his buddies decided to go for a drive. Tragically, Ethan's drunk driving led to the death of four pedestrians and left one of his passengers brain damaged and paralyzed. Ethan's blood alcohol level was tested at 0.24 several hours after the crash, which was about three times the legal limit in Texas.

Due to the horrific nature of the crime, the prosecutor pushed for 20 years in state prison. Ethan pleaded guilty to four counts of manslaughter and received 10 years of probation from the juvenile court. Many were outraged by the verdict. They thought that his family's wealth afforded a defense that allowed him to receive a reduced sentence. However, the sentence isn't what makes this story so remarkable.

The unusual part of the story came at Ethan's trial when his mother and attorney asserted what has now become known as the "affluenza defense." A psychologist called in for expert testimony made the argument that Ethan's socioeconomic privilege was actually a mental disorder. The defense argued that Ethan was afflicted by his wealthy upbringing and environment, which resulted in criminal insanity. Due to his wealthy upbringing, the argument went, he was unable to distinguish between right and wrong. Ethan became known as the "affluenza teen."[1]

While nobody can say for certain whether this line of defense impacted the judge's verdict and sentencing, it raises several interesting points. Can growing up in a wealthy environment, spoiled with materialistic possessions and luxuries, warp your sense of reality to the point where you can't function as a normal member of society? Could wealth so warp your sense of reality that you could be classified as insane and not be held legally responsible for your actions? Is it the wealth that can lead to a disconnect from "reality" or is it more the result of bad parenting?

You can imagine how someone could be raised in an environment that puts him or her out of touch with the experience of the average person. For example, imagine you grew up in a world where you got everything you wanted, where you could do whatever you wanted without consequence, and where your parents would use their money and influence to fix whatever problems you created for yourself. Don't you think that after years of living in that environment, your sense of reality and personal responsibility would be skewed? While fair-minded people would agree that this experience would be detrimental to a well-adjusted upbringing, it certainly wouldn't excuse drunk driving.

WERE YOU A SPOILED CHILD?

It's easy to point fingers at people who are wealthier than you and argue that they are spoiling their children. However, the concept of spoiling is really a matter of perspective. To the average European in the Middle Ages, we as adults today were all spoiled as children. In fact, we were living in the lap of luxury. We had our own room (or only had to share it with one or two other people); we had indoor plumbing; we didn't have to start working until we were teenagers (or even adults); we got to go to school, we probably weren't beat on a regular basis (sorry, if you were); we probably had more than one set of clothes or shoes; we were regularly given a bath with warm water; and we were probably taken to a doctor or dentist for "check-ups" when there was nothing major wrong.

So, rather than putting people into categories of good/bad, right/wrong, it can be helpful to look at the concept of "spoiling" along a continuum. Certainly, Ethan would have been on the outer edge of our modern spoiling analysis, but in historical terms, so were we and so would our children be. But when does spoiling cross the line? At what point does a little spoiling and protecting of children go too far and risk doing real damage?

THE COLLEGE ADMISSIONS SCANDAL

In 2019, over 50 people were charged in a multimillion-dollar scheme revolving around William "Rick" Singer, a college admissions consultant.[2] It was alleged that, for a fee, Rick would help your child get admitted into a prestigious university. Reportedly, Rick had a network of people inside many of these universities, including one or more college athletic coaches and admissions administrators who could help facilitate the admissions either directly or indirectly. The network also involved admissions exam proctors, who in some cases changed students' answers to increase their scores.

His services allegedly also arranged for creating fake academic and athletic student profiles of participation to help gain admissions, sometimes working directly with athletic coaches and officials inside the universities. Of course, cooperation and help with admissions came at a price, depending on the university desired and how much help was needed.

There were several celebrity cases that were heavily featured surrounding this scandal. For example, actress Lori Loughlin and her fashion designer husband Mossimo Giannulli allegedly paid over

$500,000 to Rick so that their two children could gain admission to University of Southern California (USC) as student-athlete rowers, even though neither were rowing athletes.

In another case, actress Felicity Huffman paid $15,000, disguised as a charitable donation, to increase her daughter's SAT scores post-exam. There were other stories like these reported, where there were bribes, corruption within the admissions system, and test-taking integrity was compromised. To date, none of the students were charged, as their parents were seen as the "principal actors" in these cases.

After sentencing, Huffman confessed, "I am deeply sorry to the students, parents, and colleges impacted by my actions. I am sorry to my daughters and my husband. I have betrayed them all." Huffman said her daughter asked why she didn't believe in her. "I had no answer," Huffman said. "I can only say I'm so sorry. I was frightened, I was stupid, and I was so wrong. I am deeply ashamed of what I have done. I have done more damage than I could ever imagine. I realize now with my mothering that love and truth go hand in hand. I take full responsibility for my actions."[3]

Many were quick to pile on and condemn the actions of Huffman and others who were clearly trying to game the system to give their children an advantage. After all, isn't it totally unfair and outrageous? Not only is it cheating, it also seems to be the worst kind, where wealthy people use their advantage to elevate their children at the expense of people who couldn't afford to hire college admission consultants—let alone one who had the ability to game the system. This feeds into the worst stereotypes of the wealthy and famous.

However, ask yourself this question: If you were able to help your child get into an "elite" university, would you do it? Set aside the cheating aspect for a moment. If you had the money to do it, would you hire tutors and/or a college admissions consultant if you thought it would help your child have a better life?

It's easy to say that you wouldn't go to the extent that Huffman and others went. If she could go back in time, she would almost certainly make a different choice too. But what if a consultant told you that's what all the other wealthy people are doing? What if he sold you on the idea that the other children your child was competing with were also receiving similar advantages, and if you didn't do the same, you would be hurting your child's chances at a better future.

Parents will go to dramatic lengths to provide a better, happier, and safer life for their children. Many would sacrifice their lives for their children, not to mention their time and money. If it seemed like there was no other way, many of us would be tempted to become involved in questionable or even illegal acts if we felt it would give our children a leg up in life. Many of us might be tempted even if it involved illegal acts. Put aside these more dramatic stories for a moment and consider the impact that too much family support can have on the development of a child. What happens when parents go too far?

MONEY IS A POWERFUL REINFORCER

Money is a powerful reinforcer. In psychological terms, a *reinforcer* is anything that increases the likelihood that a specific behavior will occur. For example, when you promise a child a cookie if he or she eats all the vegetables on the plate, it will likely increase the chances that the child will eat all of the vegetables. As such, the cookie is a reinforcer since it increases the vegetable-eating behavior. In many ways, money is like this cookie.

For most people, there are days when we are just not looking forward to going to work. Perhaps it's cold outside and your bed is so comfy and warm. Perhaps you're tired, you've got a hangover, or you would rather just go hiking. So what makes you push through your resistance and go to work even though it would feel so much better to play hooky? The answer lies in the powerful reinforcing nature of money.

When you think about it, money is incredible! You can trade it for food, shelter, and warmth. You can use it to adorn yourself in beautiful attire and to display your relative status to attract and secure a mate. You can use it to provide safety for you and your family. You can use it in the service of your most important values. For many people across the world and throughout history, having money was often a matter of life or death. So we want money. We need money. And for most of us, the more money the better.

HUMANS ARE LAZY

Human beings are lazy. We are designed for the conservation of resources. Consider the example of muscle building. Building muscle is an easy concept that requires two ingredients: muscle overload and being hyper caloric. Essentially, you take whatever muscle you want to grow, and you give it more than it can handle. Then you eat more calories than you need. Then your body makes the muscles bigger. Repeat this process and you can become a muscle-bound freak. But muscles take energy to maintain, so the moment you stop loading the muscle with weight, your body takes that energy back to use elsewhere and the muscle atrophies. Essentially, if the resources aren't needed to get the job done, then the body self-corrects in favor of atrophy.

Psychologically, humans are wired to seek pleasure and avoid pain. Inevitably, work becomes difficult or boring and becomes a source of pain, while non-work activities can hold the promise of pleasure. So unless we are properly motivated and reinforced for our work efforts, just like a muscle that is no longer needed to carry a heavy load, our motivation to work at tasks that can be painful will naturally atrophy in favor of activities that require less effort and provide more immediate pleasure.

Money acts as a powerful reinforcer to help us push through the inevitable discomfort we experience at work. It keeps us getting up and doing our job even on those days when we would rather be golfing or fishing. The promise of pay increases may further reinforce keeping us focused and engaged.

What happens when we get a cookie whether we eat our vegetables or not? Or what happens if you get a cookie for NOT eating your vegetables? What happens when we get money for nothing; when we get paid for not going into work? What happens when we get money whether we put ourselves in challenging, uncomfortable, or painful situations or not? If you would get paid the same amount whether you slept in on Monday and then spent the day doing your favorite activity or dragged yourself out of bed early and worked an eight-hour day at your job, which would you choose?

How many days in a row would you maintain your work ethic if you realized it made no difference because you were going to get paid either way? If you accept the arguments that humans are lazy and money is a powerful reinforcer, we would argue that working when work is unnecessary to support oneself is more difficult to explain than someone who decides not to work because they are getting paid regardless.

FINANCIAL ENABLING AND FINANCIAL DEPENDENCE

When we get paid for doing nothing, the act of doing nothing gets reinforced. When getting paid for doing nothing becomes a habit, it can lead to a syndrome of financial dependence.

Financial dependence is the reliance on nonwork income to meet one's financial needs. Our research has found that financial dependence is associated with some devastating financial and psychological consequences that seem to emerge regardless of where the money comes from.

Whether financial support is coming from the government in the form of public assistance or from a family trust, dependence on others for financial support has consequences. On the psychological side, dependence on nonwork-related income is associated with a lack of passion, drive, motivation, and creativity. Financially, it is associated with lower income and lower net worth. While financially dependent people rely on the income, they also tend to resent the source of the income. Clearly, it should come as no surprise that money can be used to manipulate and control others, especially as their dependence on nonwork money grows over time.

In many ways, financial dependence is a debilitating condition that can destroy a person's drive and passion. As such, it is something to be avoided, especially when considering how we are raising our children around money.

Financial enabling is the other side of the financial dependence equation. *Financial enabling* is essentially financial help that hurts. It is almost always done with the best intentions, such as when a parent wants to support a child's goals or passions. However, in the case of financial enabling, the enabler may report having a hard time saying no to requests for money. Our research has shown that financial enablers also tend to have lower income, higher credit card debt, and may feel feelings of resentment or anger after giving away money.[4] Financial enabling behavior can get complicated and very emotional when it involves friends and/or family members.

CUTTING THE FINANCIAL UMBILICAL CORD: FIVE STEPS

We have worked with many families stuck in the financial enabling–financial dependence cycle. We have also worked with financial professionals who are worried about clients who are putting their financial health in jeopardy by financially enabling their children. In our work, we have identified five steps to help cut the financial umbilical cord.[5]

1. **Recognize that financial help can hurt**. The first step in breaking the enabler-dependent cycle is recognizing how your attempts to help someone via financial support can actually be harmful. Financial enabling is almost always done from a good place. You see someone you love in need and you want to help him or her. But by definition, financial enabling hurts. It can hurt you, the giver, financially. If you are reinforcing irresponsible or harmful behaviors then you are hurting the receiver. Financial dependence can be quite psychologically crippling, robbing the dependent of drive, motivation, passion, and/or creativity. You may also be hurting your relationship as financially enabling often comes with strings attached from the giver, and feelings of resentment on the part of the receiver.

2. **Understand the curse of too many options**. Depending on the level of financial support being provided, you may be giving the financial dependent too many choices. For example, we know of many adult children who have earned multiple graduate degrees in different fields without ever settling on a career or getting a job. Others move around frequently, or start and quit jobs often, never allowing themselves the opportunity to establish themselves. When people need to depend on their own work efforts to fund their lives, the experience can be quite grounding and can give a deep sense of purpose. These people also grow psychologically as they learn to delay gratification and to stick out challenging situations and learn to navigate challenging relationships.

3. **Acknowledge the curse of unstructured free time**. Research on the concept of "flow" by Mihaly Csikszentmihalyi, found that it is much more difficult to enjoy unstructured free time than it is work.[6] Gainful employment brings with it the opportunity to have flow experiences, where you are being challenged and you lose yourself in productive efforts to meet challenges. Contrary to popular belief, we struggle much more to enjoy unstructured free time, like during weekends and on vacation. With too much free time, we tend to dwell on our problems and feel isolated and uneasy. Work has many built-in social and emotional benefits, even if we find parts of our job distasteful. This is another way that financial enabling can hurt someone.

4. **Rip off the financial band-aid**. Since money is such a powerful reinforcer, threats and warnings that aid will end unless certain behaviors occur are typically met with failure, especially if the financial enabling has been going on for years. It is very difficult if not impossible for the financial dependent to change until the money stops flowing. Set a date by which the financial support will end and stick to it. You might want to brainstorm other ways to assist that don't involve giving money, which could include paying for therapy, career counseling, life coaching, or financial planning.

5. **Establish ongoing support**. It can be very difficult to stick to your guns as you are withdrawing financial support to a loved one, as it is not uncommon for the person to become angry or depressed. Financially dependent people may even engage in an adult version of a toddler's temper tantrum, which could involve crying, yelling, or making threats. As such, it is very important for the financially enabling to have an emotional support system to help keep them strong and encourage them to stay the course and not give in to adult temper tantrums.

RAISING FINANCIALLY HEALTHY CHILDREN

Children are born into a world of money like fish are born into water. Children are raised in a particular socioeconomic environment and have experiences common to that environment. This becomes their reality—their type of food, clothes, transportation, school, home, and so on. As they grow older, they will become increasingly cognizant of money and its implications. They will become curious about it. They will see the value that others place on money. They will pay more and more attention to it. They will begin to notice that their experiences of money are not the same as everyone else's.

Children will learn very powerful messages about money. They receive these messages from their parents, their extended family members, their culture, their peers, and from society at large. Sometimes these messages are overt and explicit, but many times, they are much more subtle.

For example, consider the lullaby "Hush Little Baby." Have you ever really thought about the explicit money messages this seemingly innocuous song delivers, embedded in gentle, soothing tones and oxytocin-fueled cuddles? So what does a loving parent do when your bird won't sing, your diamond ring turns out to be a fake, your mirror breaks, your mode of transportation breaks down, and you've got a stubborn goat? Don't worry, all problems can be solved with the purchase of something. Papa is going to just keep buying you stuff until you feel better.

Early in life, children develop a conceptualization of money, and their formulation will set them on a financial course. So parents have two choices. They can let children make up stories about what money is and how it is to be used with the help of social media and their peers. Or parents can consciously teach children what money is, what it does, what it can't do, how it should be used, how it can cause joy or pain, and the values they want associated with it.

IT'S NOT SO SIMPLE

Money is an incredibly complex subject akin to issues like time, death, sex, and God. Except there is no money Bible. Even if there were, there would probably be no more agreement about the true meaning of money than there is about God between the Torah, the New Testament, or the Koran.

So, the challenge is to become clear about what money means to you and how it fits in with your values, goals, and worldview. We can't teach what we don't know. And then, of course, there is your child's other parent. Are they reading from the same script as you? How about grandpa and grandma?

It is also important to remember that children learn more from what they see around them than what those around them say. Are you modeling your own beliefs about money in your daily life—about what you believe is possible? Your actions will teach them whether you say anything or not. Remember, your actions will be much more powerful a teacher than anything that you will say to them about money. This is one of those critical times in life where your parenting message cannot be "do as I say and not as I do." Your children will interpret that as "do as my parents did and not blah, blah, blah...."

So what do your behaviors reveal about your relationship with money? For a quick look, spend a few minutes examining where your money went last month. Want to take a quick look at what you actually value? How much money did you save? How much money did you spend? How much money did you give to charity? Look at how much you have saved. Warning: This can be an "ouch" moment for many of us.

A BIG HEADS-UP

Beware! Your children will be learning about money long before you think you need to teach them. From birth, they have been exposed to money. At some point in time, they witness the magic. They may not know what happened, but they noticed something big happened, and money was involved. By the age of two, they will begin becoming aware of its magic-like qualities. It's power to bring, or take away, happiness or sadness, and that it often arrives around birthday time with other gifts and attention.

For example, imagine walking through a mall with a young child when he or she notices one of those coin-operated mechanical horses that when you drop a coin in, it magically starts moving, providing an instant adventure. Your little one is enraptured by the sight and sound of the horse rocking and his or her awareness that another child is mounted on it bouncing up and down, squealing with delight. As you approach, your child sees that the other child is dismounting with an incredible look of satisfaction.

Your child begins pulling on your hand, looking up into your eyes with a pleading gaze that says, "Please, please, please!" You're in a rush, but you weigh the costs of saying, "No," and decide to consent in order to maintain the peace you need. You dig into your purse or wallet, fish out some quarters, and insert them. From now on, when your child sees something that he or she wants to do, he or she has learned that you carry magic coins with you that bring fun and happiness. If you didn't have any coins with you, you might have to deny your child that experience, and he or she would quickly learn the consequences of not having money.

QUICK START TIPS FOR HEALTHY FINANCIAL HABITS

Entire books have been written on how to raise financially healthy children. One of our favorites is written by the *New York Times* columnist Ron Lieber, titled *The Opposite of Spoiled*.[7] We cover some key considerations for creating healthy financial habits.

ALLOWANCES

Allowances can provide wonderful teaching opportunities. There is some debate over whether allowances should be a basic right that a child has simply by being a member of the family or if allowances should be tied to a list of chores, responsibilities, or behaviors that are rewarded monetarily. Regardless of your opinion, allowances can be used to reinforce values and to teach basic money management skills.

A common mistake is to give children an allowance without any strings attached. Don't be surprised if they mismanage it. Of course they will! Their prefrontal cortex, the part of their brain responsible for planning, controlling impulses, and delaying gratification is not fully developed until early adulthood. The best approach is to build structure around the allowance in accordance with the values you wish to instill. For example, you could teach the concepts of buckets, where the allowance is divided into four portions: 1) saving, 2) spending, 3) giving, and 4) investing, as follows.

Saving

Saving is important. In fact, a discipline around saving money is the framework that creates wealth. If you spend all you make, you will never get ahead. Saving for intermediate goals is a much-needed value and skill. So a portion of the allowance should go into a savings account. Children are encouraged to save for a desired object or experience, one which they couldn't afford with their allowance alone. They are taught the experience of delaying gratification and the thrill that accompanies being able to achieve a savings goal. As much as possible, allow children to determine when and for what the savings account is allowed to be tapped. Research has found that people save more when accounts are given inspiring names, so utilize this tool accordingly.[8] As such, the savings account could be titled "Lorrie's American Girl Shopping Spree" or "Hunter's Rock-Climbing School."

Spending

Another important lesson for children is the experience of spending. We must not forget that it is important to allow yourself to enjoy your financial resources. With the spending portion of the allowance, children are given the freedom to spend it as they wish. Money can and should be used to enhance experiences of life. What's the point of a lifetime of sacrifice if you are unable to allow yourself to enjoy your life.

Giving

Money can and should be used to make the world a better place. An allowance gives parents an opportunity to pass down their philanthropic beliefs. For example, you could choose three to five charities and have your child select from them, perhaps after a discussion or visits to the charities. Then after several months or even a year of saving, you can give your child the experience of giving to the chosen charity. It can be fun and reinforcing to take your child in person to the charity and have him or her hand over the funds. You could set up a meeting ahead of time with a staff member of the charity to make sure your child has a wonderful experience. The staff member can thank your child and share all the ways that the money will be used to help others. Your child could also help engage in the good the donated money will do, such as helping to distribute food or sort clothing that the donated money may have helped provide. In this way, your child can see and experience firsthand the joys of giving.

Investing

While opening and feeding a traditional savings account is a way of saving, the ideas of investing and the long-term effect of compounding can easily be integrated, and in our opinion, probably should. As such, we encourage the inclusion of an investing bucket. This could be called a "financial freedom" account or something of that nature. The teaching opportunity here lies in the concept of delaying immediate and intermediate gratification for a long-term goal. Ideally, this goal would be that of financial freedom, where the money is kept in an investment account in perpetuity with the eventual goal of having it spin off income so that your child could be free from the need to work for money at some time in the future. Given the research on actively managed accounts and index funds, you might want to be conscious about how you are teaching your children to invest when they become old enough to consider such information. Given that index funds outperform actively managed funds 80% of the time, unless you are a professional investor, you might want to teach your children to put their investments in a diversified index fund approach versus teaching them to pick individual stocks of companies. The articulation and reinforcement of financial best practices can go a long way to laying a solid financial foundation for your children into adulthood. Since they are going to remember and store beliefs about money, it's best to make sure those beliefs are founded in best practice.

A FAMILY ALLOWANCE

In addition to personal allowances, some families have a "family allowance." This is a pool of money about which all family members help make decisions. Since most people end up in personal or business situations in which they need to share resources, this gives them the experience of negotiating and cooperating around money. The pool of money can be tracked and eventually used for the purchase of a family-centered household item, furnishing, entertainment, vacation, or even the decision on what type of vehicle the family will eventually purchase. The family allowance gives children another opportunity to see the benefits of delaying gratification and saving money. It can also be used to help them learn important personal financier skills such as comparison shopping and price negotiations.

TALK ABOUT MONEY (BUT NOT TOO MUCH)

A big mistake parents make is *not* talking to their kids about money. Talk to them about money. If they ask a question such as "How much money do you make," tell them. Ask them what prompted them to ask. If they say something to the effect of "We're rich, aren't we?," ask them what *rich* means to them, and then tell them what it means to you. If you must take some time to figure out what to say, do that, but answer their question. If you don't, someone else will. Maybe TV will; maybe a friend will; maybe a book will; or maybe they will decide for themselves what is real. Like the subject of sex, most parents want to have the chance to at least give their children their input, share their values, their dos and don'ts. That won't just happen on its own; parents must make sure it happens on their terms as much as possible.

Many parents make the mistake of not talking to their children about money. However, it is possible to make mistakes in the other direction: that of sharing too much financial information. In our research, sharing financial information that may make a parent feel better, but the child feels worse, is referred to as *financial enmeshment*.[9] One of the incredibly injurious, but all too common, ways kids learn about money and its power to build and destroy is for parents to involve their children in money issues that are not appropriate.

If you and your partner have unresolved issues around money, especially those in which you are not in agreement, get some help and come to an agreement—the same as you would if you had differing ideas about how to raise your children. Find agreement. If you have secrets around money, either work those out with your partner or don't tell your children about them.

Raising financially healthy children starts with you. You need to understand your own financial psychology: your beliefs, your worries, your feelings, your hang-ups. Your personal insight is critical. Also, don't forget to think about the other people in your life and what they are teaching your children about money. You may need to politely ask their grandparents, for example, to hold off on teaching them about money, especially if you aren't happy with what they taught you.

Remember, your children are learning about money from you, from what you say or from your silence. Take some time to think about what you want your children to know, and then think about the messages you want to pass down to them in your discussions and, more important, by your examples.

Chapter 3: Mammoth Mindset Insights

1. It is important to be aware of emotional impulses so that we can engage our analytical brains to think through the long-term consequences of our behaviors.
2. Recognize that financial help can hurt.
3. Recognize the psychological value in the need for individuals to generate their own income stream.
4. Acknowledge the curse of unstructured free time on the mental health of the financial dependent.
5. Help the enabler develop, implement, and stick to a plan to stop the financial aid.

NOTES

1. Daniel Victor, "Ethan Couch, 'Affluenza Teen' Who Killed 4 While Driving Drunk, Is Freed," *New York Times*, April 2, 2018, https://www.nytimes.com/2018/04/02/us/ethan-couch-affluenza-jail.html.
2. Gregory Korte, "The Rise of Rick Singer: How the Mastermind of College Admissions Scandal Built an Empire on Lies, Exploited a Broken System," *USA Today*, June 24, 2019, https://www.usatoday.com/in-depth/news/nation/2019/06/19/college-admission-bribery-scandal-rick-singer-exploited-broken-system-loughlin-huffman/1133729001/.
3. Associated Press, "Huffman Gets 14 Days Behind Bars in College Admissions Scam," Fox 61 News, September 13, 2019, https://www.fox61.com/article/news/local/outreach/awareness-months/huffman-gets-14-days-behind-bars-in-college-admissions-scam/520-af5bbafe-c4c9-4f3c-93ef-4ab4dc5de5f5.
4. B. Klontz, S. L. Britt, K. L. Archuleta, and T. Klontz, "Disordered Money Behaviors: Development of the Klontz Money Behavior Inventory," *Journal of Financial Therapy* 3, no. 1 (2012): 2.
5. B. T. Klontz and A. Canale, "When Helping Hurts: Five Recommendations for Planners with Financial-Enabling Clients," *Journal of Financial Planning* 29, no. 3 (2016): 24–28.
6. Mihaly Csikszentmihalyi, "Eight Ways to Create Flow According to Mihaly Csikszentmihalyi," Positive Psychology.com, https://positivepsychology.com/mihaly-csikszentmihalyi-father-of-flow/.

7. Ron Lieber, "The Opposite of Spoiled." *New York Times*, March 22, 2015, https://www.nytimes.com/2015/03/22/books/review/the-opposite-of-spoiled-by-ron-lieber.html.

8. B. T. Klontz, F. Zabek, C. Taylor, A. Bivens, E. J. Horwitz, P. T. Klontz, and D. Tharp, "The Sentimental Savings Study: A Double-Blind, Randomized Control Experiment to Increase Personal Savings," *Journal of Financial Planning* (October 2019).

9. R. Kemnitz, B. T. Klontz, and K. L. Archuleta, "Financial Enmeshment: Untangling the Web," *Journal of Financial Therapy* 6, no. 2 (2015): 32–48.

Your Mate

If we are to extrapolate mammoths' mating and social behavior from their descendants, the elephants, we can assume that mammoths lived relatively separate lives. Females birthed, cared for, and protected the young, while the males were absent except during the mating season. Some have suggested that traditional human gender roles in many cultures throughout history share some similarities with elephants.

While little is known about the mating habits of the mammoth, we do know all their lives depended on finding the resources necessary to sustain life. The same is true for humans today. Traditional marriage ceremonies often include vows to maintain the marital bond through times when life is better or worse, times of sickness and health, and times of bounty and scarcity. In other words, ideally, the marital bond is stronger than any of the aforementioned circumstances.

Despite our vows to remain together, issues of bounty and scarcity are a primary threat to modern marriages and families. Money issues remain one of the greatest areas of conflict in couples and are a major cause of divorce, especially in the first few years of marriage. Proactive money conversations are typically rare, and when they do happen, they can often be quite stressful. In this chapter we explore how conflicts around money arise from genetic differences, how different environments result in varied beliefs about money, and how couples can navigate these differences effectively.

GENETIC DIFFERENCES?

One of the conditions that make financial conversations difficult is our genetic wiring. Research has found that some of us are naturally more prone to be savers, while others are more prone to be generous or spenders. For example, neuroscientists have observed individual differences in attitudes around the division of resources. It appears that some of us are prone toward an individualist orientation, while others are more socially oriented. Mashiko Haruno from the Tamagawa University Brain Institute and Christopher Firth from the University College London found these differences appear to be hardwired.[1] People who have a social value orientation don't necessarily think through situations of inequity; instead, they have an automatic aversion to inequity. This aversion can be seen via emotional arousal in the brain, while more individualistically oriented people do not have a response in the brain.

Some of us are prone to save for ourselves, while others are more prone to give away money. Under ideal conditions, these differences create a balance between total self-absorption and unbridled caretaking of others to an extent detrimental to everyone involved. These different orientations are not necessarily bad, but they can lead to conflict.

THE GIVER VERSUS THE SAVER

Consider the example of Todd and Mary. They have argued for decades about giving money to others. Todd is the giver, so when he sees people who have less than he does, especially in circumstances where he believes that unfairness or injustice are involved, he feels compelled to provide financial assistance. In fact, when he sees inequality, he feels a sense of guilt around all that he has and wants to use his resources to help make things better. In contrast, Mary, while a caring and generous person in her own right, does not feel nearly as compelled to give, nor does she struggle with feelings of guilt for the resources she has been able to acquire.

When looked at in the worst light, we might call Todd over-generous, an enabler, and an easy mark. In a similar light, we might describe Mary as selfish. At least, that's what they called each other when the topic would come up. Arguments ensued, and the conversation devolved from there. In light of recent research, we now know that Todd's instincts are not so much triggered by high-minded generosity as much as by feelings of emotional distress. When he sees economic disparity, he experiences a strong activation of the amygdala, which is associated with feelings of emotional distress. Under such stressful conditions, he feels compelled to take action to relieve the distress, which for him involves giving money. For Mary, although she notices economic disparity and feels compassion, her pain centers are not triggered, so she is not driven by her emotional brain to give.

Todd and Mary have been married for over 30 years and have argued about this issue for decades. In their efforts to convince each other that one is correct and the other is wrong, they have resorted to years of confirmation bias in action. They each seek out people, studies, and examples that prove their point and show that the other person is wrong and needs to change.

When they learned about the reality of the recently discovered genetic differences around giving, they began to see it was not that either one of them was defective or wrong, it is just that they are wired differently. They very quickly worked out the difference by creating a "Todd Give-away without Any Questions Asked Fund." It's a separate bank account with a separate checkbook. They determined what percentage of their yearly income they were able and willing to "give away." Now, this required some negotiation for sure, but they were able to arrive at an agreed-upon number. That's how much Todd can give away to help "ease the pain" he feels when he sees what he believes is economic injustice and/or inequality. Mary could have a fund for her "give-aways" too, but said she really didn't need one, especially in light of Todd's commitment to give from their household resources. They still contribute as a couple to those causes that they both want to support.

After a great deal of seething resentments toward each other and decades of clashing, tension, ill-will, casting subtle and not-so-subtle aspersions toward each other, for the last few years they have experienced and appreciated each other in a new and unique way. Recognizing their differences as being the result of genetic variation allowed them to stop fighting, mostly to justify to each other there is nothing wrong with them. Todd has a deep appreciation for Mary and her willingness to allow his "generosity" to express itself without judgment. Mary appreciates the boundaries around the amount that Todd gives, which she helped establish. They both now share in the joy, pleasure, and sense of connection that came from being able to resolve this long-standing irritant.

INTERDEPENDENCE VERSUS INDEPENDENCE

The Story of Carla and Cody: Opposite Sides of the Tracks

Socioeconomic class can have a profound impact on a person's beliefs and experiences. At the extremes, these can represent entirely different cultures, with different philosophies, values, norms, and experiences. The wider the gap between two members of a coupleship, the more stress it can put on the relationship. Navigating these differences often requires insight, conscious effort, and in many cases, consultation with a third party to help gain perspective, navigate challenges, and negotiate solutions. Research we conducted with Farnoosh Torabi for her book *When She Makes More: 10 Rules for Breadwinning Women* calls attention to how financial disparities can be even more challenging when a woman makes more money than her husband does.[2] These challenges include internalized beliefs about gender norms and pressure, opinions, and judgments from others.

Carla came from a remarkably wealthy family. She left home after college, and using her own wit and wisdom, developed a successful business of her own. In a few short years she had amassed a fortune. Carla was loved and renowned in her community as someone who cared, was a smart businesswoman, and who could get things done. She had deep compassion for her community and those who struggled. She knew how to get large groups of people together and organize them in amazing ways. She was a darling of the social world. She was an "A" lister." More than one suitor was left with his hands in his lap, always kindly rebuffed, but rebuffed all the same.

Carla fell hopelessly in love with her furrier Cody—that's right, the guy who came every six weeks or so to shoe her horses. Cody was a simple man of humble means who was carrying his family's trade into the fourth generation. Everything Carla was— extroverted, socially active, and high profile—Cody was not. Nor did Cody have any interest in any of the trappings of wealth and high society. This stark difference enchanted Carla, and Cody shared her affections. Marriage resulted.

We met them four years into their relationship. By this time, Carla's parents had passed and left her another huge sum of money. Carla had sold her business interests and wanted to spend the rest of her life traveling the world with Cody, seeing places and doing things that many could hardly imagine. The problem was, Cody began feeling emasculated. He was still working shoeing horses because he wanted to. It gave him a sense of purpose. He wanted to feel equal in the relationship, but because of the enormous wealth disparity, he felt more like a kept man. It wasn't that he didn't want to travel the world with Carla; he just wanted to feel like he was contributing equally to what they did. So, if a high-end ski trip was going to cost $40,000, he felt like he should be contributing $20,000. It had gotten to the point where he wouldn't even attend meetings with her financial advisors so that they could talk about their financial plans as a couple. He said, "Why should I come, it's all your money anyway, and I'm just a pretender."

The problem is, of course, that a furrier could never make enough money to match the wealth that Carla had at her disposal. Specifically, his gross income was $50,000 per year while the interest income from her investments alone topped $3.5 million per year. After some discussion, we arrived at what turned out to be an elegant solution that was acceptable to both of them.

Rather than matching each other in dollars, they moved into the realm of percentages. So, if a trip were to cost $35,000, that amount would represent 1% of her income for that year. He would also contribute 1% of his income. When that was proposed, his eyes lit up, tears began to flow (quickly followed by hers), and he said, "This is what I have been looking for, a way to do things together." At last report they were living this plan and were doing well.

The Story of Jerry and Martha: What Would You Do with $1 Million?

While it sounds like a dream come true, a sudden influx of money can be stressful for couples. In a recent presentation, we asked for volunteers to help us demonstrate the point. A gentleman by the name of Jerry raised his hand. We handed Jerry a heavy bag of money and said: "This is yours. What are you going to do with it?" He said, as you might expect, "I'm going to put it away and keep it." His wife, Martha, looked at him and said, "What do you mean, you're going to keep it?" Jerry smiled and very quickly said, "We'll keep it," smiling as he handed the bag of money over to her.

Then we asked them to imagine that one of their loved ones had called and said that they had just been diagnosed with a serious medical condition and were asking them for financial support. Jerry very quickly said, "I don't have to imagine at all; this happens all the time, and the way I see it, their problems are theirs, not ours. I would say 'No.'" Martha looked at him as if he were an alien being and said,

> *Over my dead body. Money will never be more important than my loved ones. If they need help and I can give it, I will! If they needed all that we just received, it's theirs; I couldn't live with their blood on my hands.*

Jerry's response comes from a place in his mind that says everyone is and should be responsible for their own welfare and care. It is no one else's responsibility to take care of him, nor is it his to take care of them. We are and should all be financially independent. Martha's response comes from a place in her mind that we are all here to help each other, so if we have and another person doesn't, we give. If they have and we don't, they give. We are and should be financially interdependent.

It is obvious that Jerry's and Martha's positions were polar opposites. For them, this situation represented a significant area of financial stress. We had stumbled into a real issue with them and offered to meet with them after the presentation to see if we could help. In our post-presentation follow-up, we discovered that Jerry and Martha were both relatively high-income earning professionals, while each of their families-of-origin were not. There were huge disparities of incomes within their families. We learned that the attitudes both had expressed during the presentation had been a sore point in their marriage of 17 years. Jerry had discovered more than once that Martha had been "slipping" family members money without his knowledge, after she had agreed not to.

The solution that we worked out was to create a special "Friends and Family Support Fund." Jerry and Martha agreed that if and when relatives would ask for financial support, they would let them know that they, Jerry and Martha, had allotted a certain amount each month to be able to support their friends and family while maintaining the ability to take care of themselves and their own family and their future. Once a month, Jerry and Martha sit down and go over the requests and determine who and what they want and can support. Seven years later, this one-time irritant has disappeared.

If you come from an interdependent family and your partner comes from an independent family system, you can expect that there will be some tough moments. Studies have shown that even when controlling for things like income and proximity to family members, some cultures carry much more mental responsibility for the financial care and support of family members than others do. If your partner hails from a different culture and/or socioeconomic class than you do, we suggest that you expect to have passionate differences of opinion arise and prepare yourselves for this eventuality. It can help to preemptively discuss issues related to family and money. You could make general guidelines, if not actual decisions, before one or both of you get emotionally flooded in the midst of a conflict.

BOOBY TRAPS

Money is a hot topic in relationships. Imagine you are talking with your partner and he or she says one of the following:

> *We'll have to take a look at our cash flow to see if we can afford that.*
> *We need to take a look at the budget.*
> *I want to talk to you about money.*

If you are like most people, these statements will initiate the emotional flooding launch sequence. Your heart rate increases; your body tenses up; you might become irritated or angry. You could also "get big" and raise your voice or "get little" and clam up, retreat, or change the subject. This happens instantaneously, regardless of your partner's intent.

Perhaps you know from previous experience that your partner will likcly havc a ncgative reaction to initiating a discussion about finances, so you don't say anything at all.

Something we have found very helpful is for people to discover their sensitivities and then share them with their partners. These sensitivities are not right or wrong, they are just that, sensitivities. Like being sensitive to sunlight or peanuts or watermelons. Rather than to try to change each other's sensitivities, find a way to talk about the subjects using different words, or discovering times that are better. Some couples find it helpful to enlist a third-party professional to help talk about their money situation together.

WHERE FROM HERE?

The ability to productively talk about and resolve money issues is directly related to a couple's ability to tackle other challenging issues, topics, and problem-solving skills. The better the skills, the easier it is to work with the money issues because there is an established pattern of success dealing with other difficult topics of relationship.

Often, when couples are in conflict around money, there are other underlying issues of concern. These can include equity in the relationship, different childrearing philosophies, history of betrayals, and so on—all are visitors whispering in the ears of two people who are trying to reach a financial resolution. The ghosts of our past relational misgivings haunt our ability to have deep and meaningful dialogue with our partners. If you have difficulty talking about important issues in your relationship, you'll more likely than not have trouble resolving money issues as well. Here, again, it may be helpful to enlist a third-party professional to help with your important talks about money.

HOW ARE YOU DOING WITH MONEY?

Looking at the way you and your partner interact with money, how is it working for you? There is no right or wrong way to do money within a relationship. What's important is that it's working for both of you. Don't be surprised if what works for you now doesn't work as well in the future. That's predictable. Changing beliefs, priorities, and circumstances are inevitable. Promotions, role shifts, children, switching jobs, illness, success, losses, opportunities, and other life events stir the financial pot. As we mature and our relationship develops, we will often experience different needs and wants.

Important values may change as well as some of our priorities. Circumstances may force us to do things differently. All this can be considered positive growth rather than being judged as a problem. To make things even more complicated, it will be unusual if you are both ready to change some of these things at the same time. It is the exception rather than the rule that both people in a relationship are ready to change in the same way at the same time.

If your answer is that you are not satisfied with how things are going or that they even feel impossible or intractable, take heart: Things can get better for you. Talk to your partner. If that doesn't work out well, get help. Enlist a professional third party to help talk about your problems together.

FINDING THE RIGHT KIND OF HELP

What does good help look like? While any good marriage counselor can help with basic communication skills, one that also has some expertise and experience working with couples and families on money issues is a huge plus.

You will hear pundits giving specific advice on how couples "should" do money. For example, consider the debate over whether couples should pool their money or keep separate accounts. There is no right or wrong answer. We have seen highly successful couples doing it in many different ways. Every relationship is unique. There are no cookie-cutter, one-size-fits-all programs that will answer your unique challenges. Make sure that those professionals you go to for help are open to and capable of customizing solutions for you. Ask them for examples of couples that have been successful working through their problems. Pay close attention to how well they listen to you—both of you. If they are doing most of the talking, look elsewhere.

The key take-away is that if you are not happy with how money is being dealt with in your relationship, talk about it. We know this is easier said than done. Your impulse will be to avoid talking about money because you are fearful of the emotions and conflict that will follow. But ignoring this issue could be fatal to the relationship, and facing it head on, together, can bring you closer together. If your partner has said that it is not working for him or her, listen. Assume that such a discussion is a sign of growth. Get creative about it. Respect the differences. Know the unique sensitivities to the subject that each of you have. Remember to listen as if it were the most important discussion of your life, because at that moment it actually is!

THE CONVERSATION INTERVENTION

Money is the No. 1 source of stress in the lives of Americans, and one of the most common sources of conflict for couples. Most money conversations between couples are "drive-bys." During the course of the day, one or both members of the couple will bring up money concerns in passing: a sarcastic comment here, a frustrated remark there. These types of money conversations rarely solve anything. In fact, they make matters worse, leaving the couple feeling resentful, disrespected, and misunderstood.

Like a stick of dynamite, money conversations need to be handled with care. Entering them without the proper respect increases the chances these conversations will explode and hurt somebody. The *Conversation Intervention* is designed to help couples have a different type of money conversation.

In our work with couples, the Conversation Intervention has helped couples have a different conversation around money, setting the stage for increased empathy. The conversation can also enhance the ability to negotiate solutions to money conflicts that were previously at an impasse.

SETTING THE STAGE

Six instructions for having a conversation about money with a spouse, partner, business partner, family member, or friend follow. In fact, these instructions are useful for conversations around any potentially emotionally charged topic.

1. **Set an appointment**. Agree not to engage in "drive-by" money conversations. Set a time and place to talk. Show up ready to listen. Your readiness to listen can be enhanced by taking a few moments to breathe deeply and set aside the stress of the day. Remove all distractions, devices, and items that could potentially distract you.

2. **Sit "knees to knees."** Set up two chairs facing each other with nothing in between. Sit with your knees anywhere from a few inches to a few feet away from your partner, according to your comfort level.

3. **Pick a speaker and a listener.** In order to avoid an early argument, flip a coin, do rock/paper/scissors, cut a deck of cards, or pick odd/even. The winner is the first speaker.

4. **Use reflective listening.** The speaker talks for one to two minutes. The listener listens, then summarizes what he or she

has just heard, without analyzing, interpreting, asking questions, or arguing. This is a very challenging task for most people, especially when the issue is a hot topic and/or the couple has a history of conflict around the topic. The listener reflects back what he or she thinks was said. The speaker listens and replies: 1) "Yes, that's it," or 2) clarifies his or her previous statement. If the speaker offers a clarification, the listener reflects back what was said and asks for the speaker's reply again. This listening and reflecting continues until the time period ends.

5. **Switch roles and repeat as needed.** For this exercise, each person can take turns sharing his or her answer to each question in turn.

6. **Take a time out.** Emotional flooding is poison to a relationship. When we are flooded, our thinking brain goes offline and we end up doing or saying something we regret. If your anger or frustration reaches a level 6 on a scale of 1–10, take a 10–20 minute timeout, during which you both examine YOUR ROLE in where the conversation went bad. Then come back together and start again.

Chapter 4: Mammoth Mindset Insights

Money Dialogue Facilitation Questions for Partners

What follows are 12 questions designed to facilitate a different type of money conversation. In our work with couples that are in conflict about money, we have found this intervention to be highly effective in "softening" the often rigid and exaggerated defensive postures and stances that people take when they feel misunderstood. Take time to reflect on these questions. This can be done in the moment as you are conversing or in the days or hours before the conversation.

1. What is your earliest money memory?
2. What is your most joyful money memory?
3. What is your most painful money memory?

4. What was the socioeconomic status of your family of origin? How did this impact your relationship with money?

5. What was the original socioeconomic status of your parents growing up? How do you think this impacted their relationships with money?

6. Name three things you learned from your mother about money either directly or indirectly.

7. Name three things you learned from your father about money either directly or indirectly.

8. What are your financial goals?

9. What are your biggest financial fears?

10. Name one or more things you are willing to do differently in order to improve our relationship.

11. List three values that you would like to guide your family's life.

12. Name three things you appreciate and admire about your partner.

NOTES

1. Mashiko Haruno and Christopher Firth, "Activity in the Amygdala Elicited by Unfair Divisions, Predicts Social Value Orientation," *Nature Neuroscience* 13, no. 2 (2011): 160–61, https://www.ncbi.nlm.nih.gov/pmc/articles/PMC3145100/pdf/ukmss-35966.pdf.

2. Farnoosh Torabi, *When She Makes More: 10 Rules for Breadwinning Women* (New York: Penguin, 2014).

CHAPTER 5

Your Tribe

YOUR EXTENDED FAMILY

Historically, your tribe would take care of you. For most of our development as a species, we lived in small groups of closely related individuals. We were members of the same extended family. We lived together; hunted together; ate together; slept together; fought together; celebrated together; mourned together; raised children together. Anyone who was not from your tribe was a stranger, someone not to be trusted, a potential threat.

In your tribal life, you didn't need to worry about a lot of self-directed, individualistic behaviors such as saving. Your tribe would meet your needs. In many indigenous communities, the young and old are taken care of by the people in between. The children are treasured for the hope for the future they provide, while the elders are revered as the keepers of wisdom.

THE HILL

The Hill in St. Louis is a great example of a modern tribe. The Hill is an Italian enclave established in the late 1800s. In essence, it was a "Little Italy" where Italian immigrants gathered together to start a new life in America. They shared the same language, values, and culture. The community had each other's backs, and to some degree, still do. The community took care of each other. Because of extended life spans, industrialization, mobility, and work opportunity, these types of communities are nearly extinct in Western culture.

While most have melted away in form, "tribal" structures still exist as a mental orientation and have a profound impact on our psychology. We are all raised in an environment that has certain accepted and unacceptable behaviors around school, work, marriage, education, and money. They are the "norms" of the culture in which we are raised. They provide a foundation of expectations on which we build our lives. These norms are generally unspoken and for the most part go unnoticed until someone in the group tries to do something different. These structures are to us what water is to fish. We are submerged in them, and until we leave them, we are often not aware of their impact on our values, beliefs, and behaviors.

WHAT SAVES YOU MAY KILL YOU

For all the benefits of living in a tightly knit social group, there is a downside: It can be very difficult to go your own way. To leave would mean breaking a part of the support system and the energy you contributed to the tribe. The void created by your departure would have to be taken up by someone else. The result would often be a marriage outside of the group.

It can be extremely difficult to leave the support of your tribe on a practical and emotional level. Even if you are able to do it, the pressure to return home can be immense. A recent trip to Ireland made known the story of a son who came to America during the potato famine. He received a letter from his father begging him to return home because the father was aging and wasn't going to be able to take care of the farm and family much longer. The son did not return. His father ended up losing the farm and died a pauper's death. Upon the death of the son, the son's wife found the letter that her husband's father had sent. The son carried his father's "Please come home" letter in his pocket every day for the rest of his life.

RELATIVE DEPRIVATION

The preceding story helps make sense of why it can be so difficult to climb the socioeconomic ladder. For our ancestors, being exiled by our tribe meant certain death. Without the love and protection from our tribe, we would be exposed to the elements, predators, and other competing and potentially hostile tribes. There has always been a perceived strength in numbers to protect and defend against small groups of nomads. However, when we are on our own, the risk of being outnumbered makes it hard to protect ourselves and our family. That is why we have this subconscious pull toward groups as we are faced with fear, danger, and stress. When we are lost and afraid, we immediately look to the group to observe its behavior responses. We instinctively seek out the eyes of others to judge their fear of the conditions as a signal that we too must be afraid. We look and wait for the fight or flight instinctual behavior that will signal our response. When we are alone, we are exposed both physically and emotionally. We would rather follow the herd as it runs off the edge of a cliff to certain death than halt our charge and stand alone from our tribe.

Given the extreme consequences of social exclusion baked into our DNA, we are programmed to associate perceived negative judgment or dissatisfaction from members of our tribe as a threat to our survival. We want to belong; we want to dress like them, drive what they drive, and live where they live. We judge our well-being, not based on objective information but instead on how we are doing relative to people around us. In psychology, this concept is called *relative deprivation*,[1] and it is one of the reasons that people tend to resent those who have more than them. The bigger the gap between what we have and what others have, the more resentment and anger builds up, the worse we feel about ourselves. With this type of psychological pressure at play, it's no wonder people sabotage their financial success as the expectations and pressure from members of their tribe comes to bear on them.

HOW CAN WE KEEP THEM DOWN ON THE FARM

Paul was born into a large family of aunts, uncles, and cousins. The farm was the center of his family's life. The farm was the most important thing. Everyone was expected to contribute to the farm in whatever ways the farm needed. Its survival was essential. No one moved far away from the farm. When planting or harvesting time came, it was all hands on deck. If you were in third grade and grandpa needed you to work, he would come in front of the school and toot his horn. This was the signal that all his children and grandchildren were being called to the farm. Family members were fed in direct relationship to how much or how little you were contributing.

Three of Paul's uncles were drafted into World War II. Two of them returned to the farm and built the rest of their lives around it, with the exception of Uncle Jim. Instead of coming home, he moved across the country to pursue his own passions, never returning to live near the farm. Paul grew up listening to the derogatory comments about his Uncle Jim.

The message was clear: If you leave the farm, you are no longer one of us. Due to an unusual set of circumstances, Paul had an opportunity to go to college and took it. On his first visit back from college, two months after he first went, one of his uncles said, "I suppose you think you are too good for us now, don't you?" That comment was the severing of the cord of belonging for Paul. He knew it and felt it. He now rarely has any contact with the "clan," always getting the message that he abandoned them and had lost his place and right to be there.

WHAT THE TRIBE EXPECTS

We have worked with many individuals who come from extraordinary poverty, and through their talent, grit, and a bit of luck, make it big financially. We watch as they are tormented by wondering what to do with all of their newfound wealth. Their tribe expects them to share their success because that's how people in poverty survive. Their advisors, on the other hand, warn them against doing so. But their advisors represent a different tribe, and as such, they have a hard time trusting them. The feelings of anxiety around what to do, mistrust of their advisors, and pull from their family and community is so strong that many are penniless soon after they quit making the big money. There are numerous examples of famous actors, musicians, and athletes who end their careers broke and in debt. They were not able to violate the expectations of their tribe. Those who are able to buck the trend do so by conscious effort, support, and finding ways to both take care of themselves and their future while also giving back to their family, friends, and community.

The expectations in some tribes, more typically those of Western-oriented middle-to-upper-class groups, is that "we are all responsible for taking care of ourselves, so go do, explore, be successful, and we will celebrate you." Being raised in this group makes financial success so much easier. There is much less pressure to sacrifice your own financial well-being by propping up the financial status of others. These individuals tend to do much better financially than those who are raised in a group with the message "You are our hope; if you make it, we all make it." When the expectation is that you share all you have with the rest of your tribe, individual financial success is nearly impossible. It's the only way to stay connected after leaving the tribe, and unlike Paul, the ex-farmer, you are welcomed back when your wealth and fame are gone.

THE MODERN-DAY TRIBE—RISK SHARING

As society has changed, the duty to care for each other has drifted from networks of closely related individuals toward larger social structures. Medicare is a prime example. Medicare is essentially a risk-sharing community healthcare model for 60 million American seniors subsidized at approximately 75% of the costs by the federal government and funded through payroll taxes during our earning years, premiums, co-pays, and deductibles.

Informal risk-sharing models have been around in various forms for thousands of years. When early settlers formed small communities, like at Jamestown, they put together risk-sharing pools, enabling them to support each other. There was no insurance, just the tribe. If someone's fire got out of hand and his or her home burned down, neighbors chipped in to help build and furnish a new home for the person. This was long before the establishment of formal insurance policies, but the concept works the same way. As long as you were an upstanding member of the tribe and contributed a needed skill, the tribe would provide for your needs and share in your burdens.

The concept of insurance formalizes the informal tribal traditions of caring for each other. Table 5.1 is an example of how a more formal risk pool of medical expense sharing model might function. This example has been purposefully over-simplified to illustrate how risk pooling functions and does not include all the pricing factors involved with medical insurance delivery.

Let's say we have a tribe of 1,000 insurance group member units. Based on reliable past experience, we know that an individual is expected to have $1,500 of medical expenses in an average year; spouses are expected to add about $1,250, and $4,500 for the family (assumed to have four people on average, or $1,125 per person). Let's assume our 2,600-member group mix is as follows:

TABLE 5.1

Member Types (#)*	Total Units	# of People	Expected Claims	Total Claims
Individuals (1)	300	300 X	$1,500/Person =	$450,000
Spouse (2)	250	500 X	$1,250/Person =	$625,000
Families (4)	450	1,800 X	$4,500/Family =	$2,025,000
Totals	1,000	2,600		

Total Expected Medical Claims =	$3,100,000
Admin/profit (10%) = $3,100,000 X 10% =	$310,000
Claims Reserves (10%) = $3,100,000 X10% =	$310,000
TOTAL Expense for Group =	$3,720,000
Divided by total members/2,600	
TOTAL Estimated Annual Premium Per Member =	$1,430.77 ($119.17/Mo.)*

*Rates for Individuals would be $1,430, the Two Spouse Units would pay $2,860, and Families would pay $5,720.

The administrative and profit expenses are used to cover member services, like billing, claims, accounting and for generating statements, and so on. Claims reserve money ($310,000) is placed into an account to help cover years where claim costs run higher than average. In years where claims run less than average, those excess premiums are also placed into the future claims reserve fund. Once the tribe builds up enough in reserves to cover several years of higher-than-expected claims, the additional amount required of members for claims reserve can stop and premiums can be lowered. However, continued years of higher-than-expected claims can wipe out the reserve and cause a rate increase. Also, if the cost of delivering medical care (medical care expense inflation) rises faster than the amount of claims reserve (10% in this case), it can cause premiums to increase as well.

This is an example of how a risk pooling approach can be used to share medical expenses among a group of individuals. This model is a modern example of a voluntary needs-based tribe for medical sharing purposes. MediShare is a real-world example of how this model can actually function in modern society. There are some cases in which the responsibilities of the tribes have migrated out of the extended family unit and larger social structures have been developed to step in and fill the void. Medicare, a medical expense sharing tribe with 60-plus million members, funded and administered by the federal government, represents an example of a risk-sharing model in action. While the cost and funding related to Medicare seem in doubt, the viability of the model itself has been proven over the decades.

FEELING AT HOME IN OUR TRIBES

Making your way in the world today takes everything you got. Taking a break from all your worries should would help a lot. Wouldn't you like to get away? Sometimes you want to go where everybody knows your name, and they're always glad you came. You want to go where people see that troubles are all the same. You want to go where everyone knows your name.

— by Gary Portnoy,
Theme song from TV series, Cheers

For those of you old enough to remember looking forward to watching *Cheers* one night a week for half an hour, it felt like we were also transported to this special place in Boston. We were there each week, sitting next to Norm and Cliff, watching and listening like a fly on the wall. We felt like a part of this tribe and experienced the emotional joys and sorrows along with our fellow bar-mates. For many of us, the show was the best part of our TV week during a time when all we had was broadcast networks. In fact, if you were a regular member of that *Cheers* tribe, you probably felt a warm emotional memory just reading the above theme song words. Did you experience a nice memory?

Tribes are also represented in other popular TV shows, which reflect our cultural beliefs and reinforce the values of our own tribe. How many of you remember looking forward to watching your favorite show each week: *Friends, MASH, All in the Family, Hill Street Blues, LA Law, ER, Chicago Hope, Seinfeld, Entourage, How I Met Your Mother*—shows based on closely connected groups of nonrelated people who share in each other's struggles and triumphs.

A deep sense of loneliness and isolation is one of the underlying causes of depression. A big part of our subjective well-being relies on our ability to find our tribe, or multiple tribes, that center around a particular career, leisure activity, or area of interest. As we have migrated to this more disconnected "Tribe of Self," weekly TV shows and our streaming series have become replacements for our longing to find tribal connections. If you doubt this, try and remember how you felt when your favorite shows and streaming series came to a final end. We can experience emotional loss of connection and depression similar to breaking from a tribe. We long to see our fictional friends, and we feel a sense of loss as if they will no longer be a part of our lives in the future, similar in many ways emotionally as death. That is really powerful stuff!

YOUR TRIBES

We are all parts of modern tribes. Most of us can identify an affiliation with many tribes, including: 1) human beings on Earth; 2) Americans;

3) your race and/or culture; (4) your gender; (5) your sports teams; (6) your socioeconomic group; 7) your alma mater; 8) your company; 9) your professional associations; 10) your neighborhood, city, and state; 11) your religious affiliation; 12) your children's schools, teams, and activities; 13) your friends; 14) your extended family; and 15) your nuclear family. How many tribes can you list of which you are a member?

These were just a few examples of the many tribes we may associate with in our daily lives. Each of these tribes has rules, hierarchy, standing, behavioral customs, and shared beliefs. Our behaviors conform based on the tribe we are associating with at any given time. For example, people who visit family over the holidays find themselves slipping back into local accents and speech patterns by being around their family. They behave within their family norms and have their position and standing within the tribe.

The movie *Four Christmases* is a fun example of how being with different tribes with different customs and traditions is associated with different feelings and behaviors. The same holiday produces drastically different experiences, frustrations, and feelings. Often, holidays and weddings are when family members bring new guests home to meet the tribe and see if there is a potential fit. The tribe watches the new member and the interactions with the one who brought him or her. We wonder: Is this person like us? Will he or she fit in? What value will this person add to our tribe?

While we live in modern tribes, our brains function as if we are still in prehistoric ones, where the laws and customs are strong, and banishment feared. We will go to great lengths to maintain and advance our position within the tribe.

TRIBAL INFLUENCE

Tribes are critical to our existence and have many positive influences on our lives. However, in many ways, tribes can also be a limiting, negative, or even destructive influence on our lives. A tribe will seek its natural equilibrium among the leaders and followers and the roles played within the tribe. The tribe also works to maintain that equilibrium by keeping all members within their roles. If a member gets a new job and a huge salary increase, the tribal equilibrium may be thrown off and the leaders threatened for position.

Have you experienced a time when something potentially great might happen to you financially, maybe a career advancement, and you shared this news with your close group of friends or family members? Since they love you, you should expect a 100% positive response, right? But that doesn't always happen. Even though your tribe is filled with people you love the most, did anyone discourage your opportunity, perhaps in the context of worry or concern, that you might be making a mistake by moving into this new opportunity?

When a tribal member departs the group, the tribal balance and the roles within the tribe are tremendously impacted. That is why the tribe will self-protect and go to great lengths to keep that balance. Self-protection could be in the form of mild consternation around your plan to outright tears or admonishments. Psychologically, your desire to leave might feel like an existential threat to your tribe, and members might try to discourage you or threaten to disown you if you leave. Likewise, individuals can become self-actualized to the tribe and depend on the tribe for their identity and role in society outside the tribe. That is why banishment from the tribe is so impactful, and why we also go to great lengths to stay among the tribal members.

TRIBAL ENTITLEMENT

Our prehistoric survival depended on sharing. Sometimes relationships can get difficult when the tribe feels entitled to what the individual has acquired. From our prehistoric roots, the tribe owns all things and divides the food and resources. If one of the tribal members finds or kills something to eat, the food is shared among the tribe. Since the tribe is responsible for your shared clothing, shelter, food, and protection, the tribal members share everything in return. While that type of behavior might seem strange to many, the mindset is alive and well in many modern cultures and groups.

Consider an economically disadvantaged single mother who sacrifices everything, works two jobs, and drives her son all over for sporting events season after season. If her son makes the pros and signs a deal for millions, would mom be entitled to some of that money? After all, she supported, raised, and facilitated his talent development. Should there be a family return on investment? What is the expectation? Was it ever explicitly discussed? Did the child understand and respect the sacrifices his mother made? Is it right or wrong to have financial expectations of our adult children? The answer is (of course): It depends. These expectations are not necessarily right or wrong; they are culturally and tribal bound. Your instinctive response to this scenario reveals a lot about the rules and expectations of your own culture.

HOW TRIBES HANDLE SUCCESS

Consider the experience of James, a talented athlete who grew up poor. He worked hard to get a scholarship to play football at a Big Ten university. He became an All-American player and was drafted in the first round of the National Football League (NFL). He was there to enjoy the moment as they called his name; he put on his team cap and walked across the stage. The draft was one of the happiest moments of his life, and both of his parents were there to watch and share in the moment. A lifetime of hard work, effort, and sacrifice paid off. What an incredible moment.

Unbeknown to James, while he was backstage at the NFL draft event celebrating, his siblings, uncles, aunts, cousins, and friends were celebrating back home. They had gathered together to watch the NFL draft on television. They also had one more agenda item. After he was drafted, they held a meeting to decide how his signing bonus would be split among them.

James and his parents didn't know this was happening, nor was this signing bonus or potential salary ever discussed. When James learned about the plan that was hatched at home, he was surprised, insulted, and upset. When he informed his relatives that he was going to use the money to further his education, raise his children in an enriched and safe environment, and provide for them the best doctors and teachers and resources that he could, they disowned him. He was banished from the tribe.

Fast-forward 20 years, and he has never spoken to any members of his extended family with the exception of his mother and father, who refused to turn their backs on him. James's parents paid a price for their loyalty and were similarly shunned and never spoken to again by their relatives. He violated the expectations and norms of his "tribe" and was exiled as a result.

While James's story doesn't reflect how all tribes handle success, it is not atypical. The tribe also feels a sense of sharing in a member's accomplishments and success. Why shouldn't they? The tribe protects and watches over the members when they are young and most vulnerable. The tribe teaches and supports the growth and development of their members. So it's easy to understand why those who are so deeply invested in their members' success feel betrayed and slighted when cut off from the rewards. Our genetic wiring tells us that the spoils go to the tribe to be shared and consumed by all. In essence, wasn't the tribe gathering to divide James's kill exactly what had been genetically programmed over hundreds of thousands of years? That is why many professional athletes, artists, and performers who make it big often go through all their newly found wealth taking care of their tribe.

People look at this situation from the outside and say, "How could people be so stupid? If I had that kind of money, I wouldn't blow it all like they did." However, those people fail to recognize that those individuals are behaving exactly the way the tribe expects and playing the role in which they are most comfortable. After all, when their ride ends, they expect to go back to their tribe and need to make sure they will be welcomed. Tribal members leaving their tribe to go their own way is more of the exception than the rule. Such behavior in and of itself threatens the tribe. Remember: Where one can go, others can follow.

PROFESSIONS AS TRIBES

Every profession has its own set of cultural norms and expectations, for better or for worse. We focus on social work as an example. Our observation of the social work field, in general, has shown an expectation that if you want to join, you need to take a vow of poverty. University classrooms perpetuate this notion with the adage: "If you want to make money you're in the wrong profession; we are here to help people."

The norms and expectations of any particular group do not arise in a vacuum. Once established, they both attract like-minded students and shape the beliefs of those involved. So where did this money-avoidant set of beliefs in the mental health field emerge? Perhaps we can blame Sigmund Freud, the founder of modern psychology, who symbolically equated money with feces. Or perhaps it is because a segment of the mental health field was birthed in the New York School of Philanthropy, which was designed to teach students how to best help the unfortunate without regard for getting paid. In fact, taking money for helping others has always been a bit of a taboo. Regardless, the culture of money avoidance observed in the mental health profession (and likely many others, such as educators) can have a devastating impact on both the viability of the profession and on its members.

JIM'S REALITY MEETS PROFESSIONAL REALITY

Jim was a 48-year-old, mid-career-change guy. In his former job, he had been a highly successful businessman. As a result of the life-changing mental health help he had received, he wanted to become a therapist so he could, in turn, help others. Jim sold his business and went back to school. In one of the final classes he was taking for his graduate program in social work, he raised his hand and asked the professor: "When will we be learning how to make enough money to create a business and allow us to be able to support ourselves and our families as a social worker?" His question was followed by a hushed silence in the class. Jim's professor looked him in the eye and said in an icy tone: "If that is your concern, you should get up and leave now."

But it's not like Jim's concerns didn't have merit. A professor and chair of the social work department at a prodigious Mid western university told us, under conditions of anonymity, "Every year, as I stand before my 40 graduating social workers, I am aware that if they follow the normal path that social workers take, none of them will be able to make a living wage at what they do."

KILL DR. PHIL

Now, of course, in any tribe, there are those who stretch the boundaries and bend or even break the rules. But this always comes at a cost. Just ask Dr. Phillip C. McGraw.

An unwritten rule in the mental health world is to not draw too much attention to yourself. Dr. Phil didn't play by the rules, which is why you have heard of him. The therapist world has been playing a game of whack-a-mole with Dr. Phil for years now. He puts himself out there by showing his interactions with people on TV, opening himself up for ridicule or praise. He doesn't seem to get much praise from his mental health colleagues. In fact, many of them seem to take great delight in discrediting him with the following examples.

- Dr. Phil promotes "stereotypical gender roles" and "maintains a detrimental neutral stance with couples reporting violence in their relationships."[2]
- In referencing a show about people addicted to substances, a professor of psychiatry from the University of Southern California told the *Boston Globe*, "It is callous and inexcusable exploitation. These people are barely hanging on. It's like if one of them was approaching a lifeboat, and instead of throwing them an inflatable doughnut, you throw them an anchor."[3]
- In reference to one of his episodes, the National Alliance on Mental Illness referred to Dr. Phil's conduct as "unethical" and "incredibly irresponsible."[4]

- In a PsychologyToday.com article, "Dr. Phil's Very Bad Advice," a therapist wrote, "I think Dr. Phil often dishes out some very bad advice."[5]
- In a discussion in the magazine *Psychiatry*, the headline read "Is Dr. Phil Respected in the Psychology Community: The Dr. Phil on TV? Absolutely not."[6]
- In an article titled "The Scumbag Tactics Dr. Phil Uses to Populate His Human Zoo," a psychiatry professor was quoted as saying: "Once again, Dr. Phil shows us that there is no depth below which he will not sink to improve his ratings. His designation as America's 'psychologist' can't be taken seriously."[7]

But, there is another side to the story, which makes intuitive sense. There is some evidence that Dr. Phil's work on TV has actually had some significant mental health benefits for the country. For example, some researchers have found that viewers who regularly watch Dr. Phil are more likely to seek mental health treatment for themselves and their children.[8] Regardless of your opinion of Dr. Phil, he is just a great example of how your tribe can turn on you if you step out of line on the cultural norms.

WHEN SHOULD YOU SEEK A NEW TRIBE?

We feel safest when we are doing what others around us are doing. We feel most at risk when we act alone. Imagine this: Next month you quit your job, sell your house, sell your car, say goodbye to your family and friends, and move to another country where you don't know anyone and you don't speak the language. You know little about the people there, what they drive, what they eat, what they do for fun. All you know is what you have read about or seen online. Imagine what it would take for you to pull up stakes and do this. Imagine the mental and emotional fortitude needed to make this happen and to stick it out. Imagine the uncertainty and stress of feeling like a stranger. People seeking to increase their socioeconomic status can do so in one way by leaving their tribe and joining a new one. This new tribe functions very differently with its own unique set of different beliefs and norms.

Sometimes a particular tribe is too constricting and puts a ceiling on your success. This is a very difficult situation to encounter, and it takes a very strong, self-confident person who is willing to strike out on his or her own to find or create a new tribe. But sometimes leaving a tribe is necessary for individuals to realize their potential and achieve their goals.

The tribal-member relationship can be understood through the lens of social exchange theory.[9] Social exchange theory argues that relationships naturally seek a balance between giving and receiving. Each member within the tribe seeks to establish a relationship with the tribe where he or she receives value equal to or greater than what he or she gives or sacrifices to be there. When the balance is off, then discontent ensues. If your contribution or value to the tribe is significantly less than the tribe provides, then you risk having the tribe exclude you. However, when you feel you provide extensively more value to the tribe than you receive, it may be time for you to leave. This imbalance is often experienced as feeling like your family and friends are holding you back, keeping you down, or taking advantage of you.

People report experiencing these feelings quite often, especially when they are making progress in climbing the socioeconomic ladder. Rather than feeling the unconditional support and encouragement they desire, they experience disparaging comments, requests for financial support, and estrangement. Psychologically, it is much easier to just stay where you are or give away whatever money you accrue than to experience estrangement or hostility from your own tribe.

Another situation is when the tribe's values and direction are no longer ones you share or believe in, or when your tribe seems to be working against you and not supporting you as discussed earlier in this chapter. It can be very difficult to get ahead when you receive negative comments or energy, or you feel guilt at your success. You can feel like you're disappointing the people you love most. Such negativity can work like an anchor around your neck, pulling you to the bottom of the ocean. When you are looking to make changes to improve yourself and your situation, you need positive support to help succeed.

When you realize that your tribe is hurting you, it may be time to seek a new tribe. This doesn't mean you need to cut off the people you love in dramatic fashion. Perhaps, instead, you can just be more careful about what you share with them, particularly the things that feel most threatening to them. This, of course, can be painful and challenging. It hurts when you realize you can't share parts of yourself with the people you hold dear. The hope is that you can find a middle path to keeping your connections while removing the emotional roadblocks to achieving your goals while becoming your new Money Mammoth.

USING TRIBAL EXPECTATIONS TO EVOLVE

Tribal expectations can limit what you think is possible, but they can also set you free by helping you to evolve. Alex was the 17-year-old son of a blue-collar family. One day, he announced to his parents that he wanted to go to college. Going to college was never considered an option in his family. College was not even talked about with the exception of college football on Saturdays when they all watched the Ohio State University team. After making this declaration, Alex's father replied: "If you want to go to college, you'll have to find a way to pay for it because you'll get nothing from us." Alex had two younger siblings, and his parents could not afford to care for them and pay for Alex's college.

When Alex announced his intentions to his English teacher, the teacher roared with laughter. The teacher, who by his laughter had alerted the class that something hilarious had just happened, announced to the class, "Guess who says he is going to college?" The class then joined the teacher in his derision. For the next few weeks, he was teased mercilessly by the other kids about his "going to college" dream.

Few from his high school considered going to college. The path for most was farming or factory work. If you were lucky, your father worked for a big company and you had an "in" to getting a job. Most kids from his school could never hope to go to college. Their work life appeared to be predetermined. But Alex was stubborn. The more pushback he got, the more determined he was to go and prove every-one wrong. Alex was becoming his own Money Mammoth and nobody was going to stop him!

So, over the course of his senior year, he saved as much money as he could. He sold everything he had of value. The day after he graduated, he moved to another state to get a job. After the summer, he enrolled in college and got a job working maintenance for the college. Over the next four years, while going to school and playing sports, he worked in a dry cleaners, a pharmacy, a factory, an architectural firm, a summer camp, construction, and cleaned the kill floors at a meat packing plant. Alex graduated with three minors in addition to his major area of study.

Surprisingly, even to himself, Alex did well on standardized tests. He fell in love with learning; he excelled in the classroom; he finished college as senior class president and was awarded an all-expense paid fellowship at Michigan State University, where he earned his master's degree.

After college, Alex settled 300 miles from his family and created his own life. The first home he bought was nicer than anything his parents had ever lived in. He felt guilty about this, feeling that something just wasn't quite right. He never again felt a part of where he had come from. Alex had wandered from his herd and tribe.

ALEX HARNESSES HIS MONEY MAMMOTH

In Alex's case, even though coming from a very poor environment, there was no expectation that his family would support him, nor was there any expectation that he was to support them. He never felt any pressure to do so. The rule in his tribe was that when you are an adult; you are 100% on your own. Alex understood this and did what was needed to take personal responsibility for his well-being and finan-cial success. Alex evolved and avoided the extinction of his financial growth and opportunities. A tribal, herd animal developed the intrin-sic motivation and learned skills to break away and survive on his own, if needed. In this way, Alex evolved to a higher level of financial being and thrived in his new world—a world now filled with opportunity and boundless possibilities for growth, adventure, and happiness.

Chapter 5: Mammoth Mindset Insights

1. In the past, in your tribal life, you didn't need to worry about a lot of self-directed, individualistic behaviors, such as saving. Your tribe would meet your needs.
2. It can be extremely difficult to leave the support of your tribe on a practical and emotional level. Even if you are able to do it, the pressure to return home can be immense.
3. With this type of psychological pressure at play, it's no wonder people will sabotage their financial success as the expectations and pressure from members of their tribe comes to bear on them.
4. As society has changed, the duty to care for each other has drifted from networks of closely related individuals toward larger social structures.
5. When you realize that your tribe is hurting you, it may be time to seek a new tribe. This doesn't mean you need to cut off the people you love in dramatic fashion.
6. The hope is that you can find a middle path to keeping your connections while removing the emotional roadblocks to achieving your goals while becoming your new Money Mammoth.

NOTES

1. B. T. Klontz, P. Sullivan, M. C. Seay, and A. Canale, "The Wealthy: A Financial Psychological Profile," *Counseling Psychology Journal: Practice and Research* 67, no. 2 (2015): 127–43.
2. Sara B. Martinez, Toni Schindler Zimmerman, Jennifer Matheson, and James Banning, "An Analysis of Dr. Phil's Advice about Relationships," *Journal of Couple & Relationship Therapy: Innovations in Clinical and Educational Interventions* 10, no. 1 (2011): 53–68.
3. David Armstrong and Evan Allen, "Dr. Phil Says He Rescues People from Addiction: Others Say His Show Puts Guests' Health at Risk," *Boston Globe*, December 28, 2017.
4. Ken Hausman, "NAMI Leaders Issue Angry Response to TV Psychologist's Program, *Psychiatric News* (November 19, 2004).

5. Laurie Essig, "Dr. Phil's Very Bad Advice," PsychologyToday.com, February 10, 2011, https://www.psychologytoday.com/us/blog/love-inc/201102/dr-phils-very-bad-advice.

6. P. Gage, Psychiatry discussion started by Dr. Scorpiowoman, March 19, 2018, https://forum.facmedicine.com/threads/psychology-of-crime-why-do-people-become-criminals.28457/.

7. Jane Ridley and Doree Lewak, "The Scumbag Tactics Dr. Phil Uses to Populate His Human Zoo," *New York Post*, November 17, 2016.

8. Eric Rasmussen and David R. Ewoldsen, "Treatment via Television: The Relation between Watching Dr. Phil and Viewers' Intentions to Seek Mental Health Treatment," *Journal of Health Communication, International Perspectives* 21, no. 6 (2016): 611–19.

9. R. M. Emerson, "Social Exchange Theory," *Annual Review of Sociology* 2, no. 1 (1976): 335–62.

SECTION II

YOUR ADAPTATIONS

CHAPTER 6

Your Instincts

The alarm went off at 4:20 a.m. and jolted awake David and his wife. It was pitch black in the hotel room and outside. The dawn light had yet to show in the sky. They rose and dressed quietly by the light of a small desk lamp in their room. They were careful to be very quiet so as not to wake the other guests in the hotel, each donning white cotton pants, a white T-shirt, and the ceremonial red *Festival of San Fermin* scarf they had purchased the day before. They slipped on their running shoes and exited the room, making sure the door closed without a sound.

Once out of the room, they headed down the stairs and outside to the parking lot to find their compact rental car. They were in the town of St. Lo, Spain, a bit of a drive to Pamplona. After negotiating several roundabouts, they were onto the highway as the morning sun was starting to rise in the sky. They were still just waking up, but the adrenaline was starting to kick in as they got closer to their destination.

As they approached Pamplona, they crossed a bridge and entered town, where there were thousands of people: sleeping in the park or wherever they could and coming out of buses parked in the town center. Of course, like in most small European towns, few bathrooms were available and most store owners did not permit the use of their restrooms. There were simply not enough facilities for the thousands of people who were there for the festivities. People were voiding their bladders, defecating, and throwing up in open view. The smell was the worst they had ever encountered.

They drove through town and into the surrounding residential areas looking for a place to park. Finally, they found a spot next to a group of teenagers with green spiked hair, tattoos, and piercings. The young people were standing outside their car, the radio of which was blaring Rage Against the Machine's "Bulls on Parade," while they chugged beer, slamming the cans on the ground with a roar when they finished. This all appeared to be part of the pre-ceremony ritual as they built up their courage. David and his wife grabbed their map, trying not to look like tourists, and located the part of the route they had decided to occupy the night before.

As they walked down the street and cut through an alley, their shoes were sticking to the cobblestone streets and making Velcro-like sounds as they walked. The smell combined with the summer humidity created an overwhelming aroma they would never forget. They quickly strolled past a man urinating against a wall and another squatting against some stairs in an alley. They vowed to burn their shoes at the end of the day.

Finally, emerging from the alley, they came to the street they were looking for. They climbed several flights of stairs and crawled under the wooden fence barricade. They were now on the street where the bulls would soon be running, right before a spot known as the "Curve of Death," where the street takes a slight turn. They chose this spot because there was a wide opening and plenty of feet of wooden fencing. David's wife was scared to run with the bulls, but game. David assured her that if one of the bulls came close, they could simply jump up onto the fence and be safe.

The street—spanning a width of about 18 feet—as much narrower than they imagined and was already filled with hundreds of people. There were several open shops across the way that had wide openings that could allow people to tuck inside and get off the street. The couple wondered how all the bulls could make it down a street packed with people as far as they could see. People were dancing, eating, and drinking on the street, having the time of their lives.

Spanish police announced that all nonrunners must leave the course immediately. People started exiting the street in an orderly fashion, and David's wife wanted to go with them. She was scared; they all were. The couple looked for the fence behind them and the open shop doorways, and David reiterated the plan to jump onto the fence if the bulls got too close. She looked up and down the street and saw just one other woman on the street. David said, "You have come halfway around the world to be here at this moment; if you leave now, you will regret it for the rest of your life." He wasn't sure if he was convincing her or himself.

They were looking around and trying to figure out what to do when, suddenly, metal doors began to lower over the openings of all the stores on the street, cutting off the hiding places. The police again announced it was now or never to leave the street. They turned to inspect their bailout fence plan, but they now saw that it was covered with people. There was no room at all to jump up or under the fence. All their escape plans and exits were sealed and they were trapped. They also noticed that most of the people partying all morning and acting tough had left the street, and only a few dozen people stood with them in the path of the oncoming bulls. Hundreds of people looked on from the safety of their perches on the fence and from the balconies of buildings.

Then they heard the first rocket go off; the bulls were on the course. Next the second rocket sounded, indicating all the bulls had left the corral. David and his wife looked to their right and up the street where the bulls would come from. It was uphill for about a hundred yards from the start to where they were, the "Curve of Death." David noticed that behind the fences where the "chickens roosted" were paramedic teams with stretchers at the ready. Apparently, the danger was quite real.

In preparation for this moment, David and his wife had watched videos to understand the strategy they needed to use. They needed to hold their place and not try to run out in front of the crowd. They figured the bulls weren't as much of a concern as getting trampled by the crowd running in front of the bulls. Their plan was to let the six fighting bulls pass and run after them while keeping an eye out for the oxen steers following from behind. It was the part about letting the bulls pass that now had them worried. Since these bulls had never seen people and were likely to be quite frightened, the animals would probably keep running up the street. The section of the street in which the couple were standing opened into a wider area, allowing people to spread out.

The crowd began to yell, and David and his wife looked up the street for signs the bulls were coming. Like a rolling thunder, the mass began running up the street. A wave of fleeing people followed by six angry fighting bulls was headed right for David and his wife, and their hearts pounded as they were facing possible injury or death. David recalled the unforgettable feeling of every cell in his body screaming at him to run for his life, as he held in place for the crowd and bulls to arrive. He saw the front runners, their eyes wild with fear as they screamed and ran. He couldn't see the bulls but saw people being thrown up in the air toward the back of the crowd.

Time seemed to be moving in slow motion. The crowd of people arrived and fanned out into the wider area. The lead runners continued up the street, while several people peeled off from the front and tore past David diving at the base of the fence. They curled up in a ball with their backs to the street. It was like a free-for-all with no plans, just people running and hiding for their lives.

Then David saw an enormous black beast emerge directly in front of him. The horns were short and sharp, and the ground shook as the 2,000-pound bull spit snot from its nose. David knew he was about to get gored. However, he didn't sense fear; he was awake and fully in the moment. All of his senses and strength were firing in his body like he had never experienced before. He was mentally sharp and processing the situation at amazing speed. David was never more alive than in that moment.

They call it the "curve of death" because the street takes a slight turn and the surface is old brick cobblestone. As the giant black bull shifted his weight to his downward legs, his feet gave out on the slippery cobblestones, which were freshly watered earlier that morning. The bull fell on its side with a thud that shook the ground where David stood. As the bull went down, David quickly moved behind where the bull laid and struggled to get up, just 6 feet in front of him. He figured when the bull stood it would go straight ahead and not turn back up the street to chase him. David saw others in front of the bull luring it toward the street route. The bull sprang to his feet and headed up the road as David had hoped. He later recalled how clear his thinking and movements were, even though it all happened in seconds.

David turned to find his wife, who he had intentionally positioned behind him. He saw she had dove toward the base of the fence just after the bull had emerged. He helped her up, and they both ran up the street to chase the first group of bulls. They were full of adrenaline and seemed to float as they ran. Their bodies seemed light and quick. They stayed to the outside of the road and turned back every few seconds to check for any bulls approaching from behind. They heard the bells from the steers coming, so they moved to the side and let the steers run up the middle of the street just 2 to 3 feet away. Four steers with bells around their necks had been released to help move any straggler wild bulls along and up the street. The steers weren't wild and didn't seem dangerous. About 75 yards ahead, David and his wife made the final turn where the street entered the tunnel to the bullfighting arena. They did not enter the tunnel as it was already closed, since the bulls had arrived. The whole run seemed to last only a minute, but the memory will last a lifetime.

What David carried away from that day was the feeling of fighting his instincts. The sight of all those people running for their lives, being chased down by bulls heading directly toward him. His body cried out to run, and all his senses and instincts told him the same. Yet he knew if he did, he would probably get trampled, so he fought this instinct and held his ground. David recalled how it felt at that moment to listen to his logical sense and ignore his emotional responses building within him. Once David and his wife learned how to harness that same feeling when it came to compulsive spending, they were able to use that flashpoint to transform their relationship with money. That's when David and his wife evolved their financial mindsets, harnessed their inner Money Mammoths, and transformed their financial lives.

MARTHA AND HER INSTINCTS

Every morning, Martha's intention is to get up and go to the gym. She also wants to begin a new meditation practice. Despite these goals, it is almost like there is a part of her that is trying to sabotage her efforts. Most mornings as she is waking up, she finds herself immersed in the following inner dialogue: "Let's go to the gym tomorrow. You're tired and rest is important." But it doesn't stop there. This inner voice keeps countering: "In the big picture, what difference is not working out one day going to make?"

As she approaches her scheduled time to meditate, the inner dialogue continues: "Let's do it later tonight after you get everything else done. You had a hard day; you need to relax and watch some television. You deserve it." If Martha is going to get to the gym or establish a consistent meditation practice, she will need to override this inner dialogue whether it is by force of will or by an obligation or deference to someone else (e.g., a focus on health/longevity for her children). Martha will need to push past her natural tendency to keep doing things the same way, to not waste her energy, to seek pleasurable activities, and to avoid discomfort.

TOM AND HIS INSTINCTS

Tom's intention is to cut down on the amount of fat, sugar, and salt that he is eating, while increasing his intake of fruit and vegetables. Tom skipped breakfast this morning and feels good about his start to the day. He meets a friend for lunch, and the waiter hands him a menu. His eyes immediately go to the salad section. He knows he should order a salad, but he "wants" something else. When he walked into the restaurant, he saw another diner eating fish and chips.

He knows he shouldn't eat the fish and chips, but then again, he did skip breakfast and he does plan on working out this evening. After eating the fish and chips, Tom feels terrible. He promised himself he was not going to eat like that anymore. In fact, his doctor told him he needed to change his eating habits and he agreed. Overcoming his desire to eat wrong is tough. He knows he needs to do better, but it is just so difficult.

OVERCOMING MINDSETS

What's going on? Are Martha and Tom weak-willed? Are they lazy? Are they gluttons? Do they have some kind of character defect? They both know what they should be doing, so why aren't they doing it? What harsh words do you have for yourself when you are not executing on what you know you should do in some important area of your life?

We know what is wrong with Martha and Tom—the same characteristic that is wrong with you: They are human. They possess a mindset that has been developed over hundreds of thousands of years. This mindset represents a legacy of survival. Martha's ancestors did not start their day by meaninglessly exhausting themselves in useless activity. They didn't spend an hour running in circles or lifting the same heavy rock up and down for no purpose. They didn't go out into a forest of predators and sit against a tree with their eyes closed, trying to shut out the sights and sounds around them. And they certainly didn't stand still while a herd of wild animals charged toward them!

None of Tom's ancestors would have forgone an opportunity to eat a high-caloric food in favor of a low-calorie one. That would have been crazy. Much of human existence has been one of sustenance because resources were scarce and people were lucky to have their basic food, water, and shelter needs met. When a menu is placed in our hands, we will be automatically drawn to the foods that have the highest calories, fat, sugar, and salt content, just like our ancestors. The reason we find these foods delicious is because our preference for them was critical to our survival as a species. We are ill-equipped to deal effectively with abundance, and to do so requires us to work against and override our natural impulses. It goes against our genes to say: "I'll skip the breaded meat fried in fat and eat the berries and leaves instead."

OUR MONEY MINDSETS

When it comes to money, we are wired to manage it all wrong. We know what we should be doing with our money but have a tough time following through. Our brains have evolved over thousands of years to focus on short-term survival in a dangerous world with limited resources. They were not designed for today's optimal financial behaviors. In terms of our instincts, the question isn't why we do the wrong things with our money, which is normal. The real anomaly is why any of us do the right thing with it. It turns out that when we are doing what we should do with our money, we are overriding our natural impulses.

Many of our chronic struggles with money make perfect sense when we picture ourselves in the environment for which our brains have been optimized as a member of a small group of closely related migratory people in a world of scarcity and constant threat. That is the context in which our brains have evolved. Our instincts are designed to help us survive and thrive under those conditions. Our instincts simply do not line up and provide us with the money mindset we need to survive and thrive today. So, don't be tough on yourself if you struggle with money and money relationships.

OUR FINANCIAL INSTINCTS TOWARD SAVINGS

We can, in all honesty, blame our money mindsets on our ancestors. Thousands of years ago, our ancestors survived by sharing rather than saving. The notion of saving for your own good and for the good of your nuclear family is a relatively new concept.

The act of "saving" is a modern, positive spin on what historically was considered antisocial hoarding. Hoarding resources for your own use—saving more than what you needed to use today—would have been a serious breach of the sharing norm. Hoarding would have been threatening to the very survival of the community itself. Hoarders would have been heavily sanctioned to get back in line, and those who did not comply would have been expelled from the tribe, which in those times meant certain death. Hoarders were dangerous to the survival of the tribe, and as such, they would have been killed or exiled.

Based on the theory of natural selection, the exile or elimination of selfish hoarders means that the saving gene would not have been passed down to future generations. So, in essence, we are the product of our ancestors who shared all of their resources and were not savers.

It is not surprising that most of us aren't saving money. It is actually surprising that any of us are! In order to do so, we need to override our biological programming.

OUR ANTI-HOARDER BIAS

The evidence that we have a natural inclination to dislike hoarders of money can be seen in the general anti-rich sentiment in the United States. Once people move above the middle class, they face significant societal pressures and judgments that align against them. They get put into a less desirable social category. While we are jealous of what they have, we simultaneously disparage them as being greedy, selfish, or corrupt. This also has the added benefit of making us feel better about our own financial status as we can feel morally superior.

Consider the example of the domestic dog. The best chance for survival for its ancestors was to adapt their wild ways to the norms of human expectations and thus were favored as pets over those dogs that were too wild. In the same way, our ancestors were among the "sharers" in the tribe. Each generation was pruned of those who were least likely to share.

However, through the genetic lottery, each new generation produced another crop of hoarders. With the agricultural age, saving became more feasible and more important. Communities that were able to save some of their crops were able to invest it in next year's crop, thus improving its members' chances of survival. In evolutionary terms, the benefits of saving are quite new.

THE GIVE-AWAY

Based on contemporary notes taken by those first Europeans to encounter the native peoples of the Northwest, the entire indigenous culture and economy were based on the *give-away*. The greatest status was given to those who would give away the most. Many native people still survive through a culture of sharing what they have rather than saving it for themselves. Other accounts noted that if a member of an indigenous tribe stole something, he or she was punished as well as the person who was in possession of the object. The latter was being punished for failing to realize or notice that the thief needed or desired the object.

Many other contemporary examples tend to center on those groups of people that are severely financially disadvantaged. For example, in many less affluent cultures, such as in Appalachia, there is an emphasis on the needs of the collective over the individual. This is similarly true in many Latino and African-American circles, in which individuals who save for themselves and do not share what they have with family members and friends are often shunned. Often these communities have little, and the way they survive is by sharing what they have with those who need it. They share labor; they share food; they share medical expenses; they share trucks and automobiles.

THE MODERN SAVERS

There are people in our culture today who can and do save. Perhaps this inclination is a genetic variability or a learned behavior, but in any case, they are savers. In fact, some of them are driven to save. A few others save so much that it can reach the level of a hoarding disorder – saving to the point of sacrificing their relationships, their health, and their emotional well-being. They just can't spend money or let go of items they have acquired.

When families become great at saving over time and pass this mindset to their children, multigenerational wealth occurs. But savers, at least in the United States, are still in the minority. So what used to be a problem has now escalated in our times to a need.

Just as the hoarders were outliers in our ancestral histories, savers are outliers in our culture today. Instead of being punished, and possibly expelled from the tribe, they are now the heroes. They are still outliers, and these outliers tend to have little pity on the ones not like them. To the ones who don't save, they often say, "Just do it!" These savers don't realize they were the ones who would be punished to the point of death in their ancestors' days.

THE DRIVE TO SHARE IS HARDWIRED

In order to save, we have to contend with the existence of people who have far less than us. The easiest solution is to avoid them and not think about them. Problem solved! Or, we may notice them and rationalize why it is okay for us to have more: "I work hard and I deserve it." Or we may vilify them and justify that they are not as hard-working as we are. Or, as many do, we volunteer our time and/or money to charities or political groups that focus on helping the less fortunate. In essence, most of us need some cognitive coping strategies to override our ancestral programming toward sharing.

Studies over the last decade strongly suggest that most of us are DNA- "hardwired" to have compassion and a subconscious urge to help others and to share with other human beings who have less than we do. When we see inequality, 60% of us feel emotional pain.[1] The pain motivates us to relieve others' pain, so we do something to help. This results in a dopamine hit, and we feel better. We then see ourselves as altruistic, but in actuality, the charitable act relieves our pain and gives us pleasure. We see this phenomenon everywhere: people charitably responding to natural disasters, mass shootings, and tragedies by giving money, sending flowers, offering condolences, building monuments, and so on. It helps us reduce the pain we feel, while helping our fellow human beings, much like our ancestors did.

OUR SUBCONSCIOUS CO-PILOT

Consider the following two scenarios. If someone cuts you off in traffic—breaking the driving norm, acting as if you don't exist—most likely you will feel a rush of adrenaline and angry thoughts. On the other hand, if someone pulls up beside you with their turn signal on and looks your way—sort of saying, "I'm sorry, would you please let me in?"—most likely you will let them cut in, and you will have an entirely different physiological reaction: You will feel good.

In both cases, you are one space farther back than you were, but you have two totally different physical and psychological reactions. This is a gift of our ancestral heritage. In the first scenario, the unspoken message is: "You don't matter; you are of no consequence; I totally disregard your existence." In our ancestor' lives, this situation of being ignored was one of the most dangerous they could experience: not being seen, not belonging. In the second scenario, the person is acknowledging you as the "leader" of the road and is depending on your thumbs up or thumbs down. This leadership position is one of the safest roles to have in a tribal community.

These intense emotional reactions to a total stranger's behavior in a line of traffic make no logical sense. However, the scenarios perfectly illustrate how the subconscious, developed over eons, hasn't been updated for hundreds of thousands of years.

BEHAVIORAL FINANCE

The field of behavioral finance focuses on understanding people's instincts concerning money and why they are prone to making bad financial decisions. Behavioral finance is cognitive psychology applied to personal finance. It doesn't look at how our specific family, experiences, and beliefs impact our relationship with money. Instead, it focuses on our common, in-born instincts and how we perceive and make sense of the world around us. Much of the research in behavioral finance has focused on identifying cognitive biases that impact our financial behaviors. In this chapter, we explore several of the behaviors, including hyperbolic discounting, cognitive dissonance, confirmation bias, illusion of control, loss aversion, and status quo bias.

Hyperbolic Discounting: Why Is It So Hard to Save?

We just aren't wired to save for the future. Researchers have observed this phenomena in the laboratory for years and call it *hyperbolic discounting*. Essentially, human beings are wired to prefer a smaller immediate reward than a larger future reward. For our ancestors, there was little point in saving. After all, they could only save what they could carry with them, and saving one of their most precious resources, food, was nearly impossible because it would quickly spoil. So, in evolutionary terms, it was much better for our ancestors to consume as much as they could as quickly as they could. They lived in a feast-or-famine world where malnutrition and starvation were constant threats. Their instinct to consume as much as possible was passed down to us and helps explain our struggles around overspending (and overeating). Saving is a relatively new concept that requires us to consciously override our natural impulse to consume.

To be financially successful, we not only need to develop a habit of saving, but we also need to become hoarders of money. Financial security is not achieved by just saving some money for tomorrow, next week, or next month. Financial security requires us to create a hoard of money kept in a safe place where it can grow for decades on end.

Our prehistoric survival required our ancestors to share their resources, not to hoard them just for themselves. It was expected that when a hunter brought in some meat, it would be shared with the group. This, of course, also helped protect the hunter, who may not be so lucky in his or her efforts the next time. Our ancestors' willingness to share increased the chances of their own survival as it would inspire others to share with them in times of need. As such, the sharing mindset was passed down to future generations.

A huge hurdle for many savers is becoming okay with the idea that they are saving money while those around them—people they care deeply about—may not be doing so well financially. The instinct for most people, especially people from lower socioeconomic backgrounds, is to share what they have and not be "selfish" when others are in need.

To save for the long term, people need to find a way to temper the sharing instinct. Often, this requires dedicating a portion of one's income to charitable pursuits and/or adopting the mindset that even more can be done to make the world a better place if one is able to become wealthier. Regardless of the rationale, amassing wealth requires individuals to justify why it is okay for them to have money while others do not.

Cognitive Dissonance: Your Convenient Psychological Discomfort Escape Hatch

Life is complicated; there are few easy answers, and often these answers conflict with each other. Let's say you grew up in a poor household in which people talked openly about how terrible rich people are. Your parents were able to cite many examples of wealthy people taking advantage of others, engaging in ruthless tactics to grow their wealth, and seeming to have little remorse or concern for the harm they were causing. So the message is clear: Money is bad, and rich people are evil. On the other hand, if you and your family had more money, it would make life better: better food, better housing, more opportunities, and so on. Thus, on the one hand, money is bad, but on the other hand, it would be good if you had more money. How does it feel to live with these two conflicting beliefs about money? Not so good, right? Actually, it probably feels pretty darn uncomfortable. But don't worry, *cognitive dissonance* is here to save the day!

The theory of cognitive dissonance says that when we become aware of conflicting beliefs, we experience psychological discomfort and are driven to ease this feeling.[2] We will use any of a number of psychological tricks to make ourselves feel better. Often, we end up choosing one belief over the other, favoring the belief that is easiest to live with. For example, if our conflicting beliefs are that "money is bad" but "I want more money," getting more money can take many years of hard work and sacrifice. It might be much easier to just run with "money is bad." This belief will help you feel better about not having money while simultaneously easing the pressure of a lifetime of hard work, sacrifice, and saving. Another way we can ease our psychological discomfort is by picking a belief and going all in on it while ignoring any disconfirming evidence.

Confirmation Bias: You Know You're Right and You're Ready to Prove It!

Do you believe the world is a safe place or a dangerous one? Are people essentially good or evil? Are you fundamentally flawed or okay just the way you are? Do you believe that the future is bright or that things are bad and only getting worse? Your answers to these questions are the types of core beliefs that define your world. They create your experience of yourself and others.

In many ways, your beliefs are a self-fulfilling prophecy. For example, if you believe that people are essentially evil, you will have difficulty having open, trusting relationships with others. You will be suspicious of them and their intentions. When they do something good, you may write it off as evidence that they are just trying to manipulate you. You will be hyper-focused on their character flaws. In response to your mistrust and negative energy, people may try to avoid you, talk behind your back, or hide information from you in an attempt to avoid your displeasure. Later, when you find out that they have been purposely avoiding you or hiding information from you, it will just confirm for you that your belief that they people can't be trusted was indeed correct.

Confirmation bias is another mindset that can harm us. Confirmation bias is a mental filter that we use to confirm our preexisting beliefs. It describes our tendency to seek out evidence to support our beliefs while simultaneously ignoring or discounting evidence that challenges our belief. But it gets even worse than that. We will surround ourselves with people who think like we do—people who share the same core belief—and we will push away or avoid people who do not share our belief. We will consume media and join political, religious, and social groups that think just like we think. This just further entrenches our belief and our certainly that we are right.

Consider the belief "You can't trust banks." For many people who lived through the Great Depression, this was a very difficult belief to shake. Imagine going to the bank tomorrow, and there is a crowd of people shouting outside. You talk to someone in the crowd, and they tell you that the bank has closed and that all the money is now gone, never to be recovered. This happened to many Americans during the Great Depression. Even though the government began guaranteeing bank accounts up to a certain value in the wake of the Great Depression, many people were so traumatized that they avoided banks and the stock market altogether. There was also ongoing evidence, as there is even today, that financial institutions should not be trusted. If this is your belief, you will seek confirmation by filtering through the news for examples of financial institutions that are violating the public's trust. However, of course, this is only part of the story, and many financial institutions are trustworthy and acting appropriately.

It is important to know that your beliefs about "reality" are entirely subjective—a very difficult fact for most people to acknowledge. Once we have adopted a belief, it can be difficult to change. Beliefs become even more entrenched in our psyche when we have strong emotions associated with them, often based on a profound experience. We might build our entire lives around certain core beliefs. The difficulty with confirmation bias is that, in many ways, we become closed-minded. While being certain about our beliefs gives us a sense of safety and self-satisfaction, open-mindedness has been found to be associated with higher income, net worth, and success in life.

Illusion of Control

What do Michael Jordan and the ancient Mayan Culture have in common? They both suffered from an illusion of control. Jordan had a fabulous career at the University of North Carolina (UNC), where he led the Tar Heels to a national championship in 1982. In the wake of this success, he thought his college shorts were lucky. When he began playing in the National Basketball Association (NBA), he had wider and longer shorts designed for him, under which he wore his UNC shorts. He wore his lucky shorts under his uniform for his entire NBA career! Since he was the world's best basketball player, a trend away from tight and short shorts to longer and baggy shorts began. Thank you, Michael Jordan!

The Mayan culture at the peak of its power engaged in blood sacrifice. Like all cultures at the time, it struggled to make sense of natural disasters, drought, and death. The Mayans' belief in deities helped give them a sense of security. To please their gods, the Mayans would engage in human sacrifice at times of difficulty, new building construction, or a change in rulers. These sacrifices gave them a sense of control and predictability.

Studies have found that we are all vulnerable to overestimating our ability to influence or control events. Psychologists have termed this cognitive error the *illusion of control*. The term was introduced by Dr. Ellen Langer in a 1975 paper in the *Journal of Personality and Social Psychology*.[3] Dr. Langer showed how people have an instinct to overestimate their part in successful outcomes and underplay their role in failures—all while not taking into account how chance comes into play. This phenomena occurs in many ways in our financial life. For example, despite evidence supporting the efficient market hypothesis, which suggests that people just aren't able to consistently beat the market, people continue to try. The more time and effort people expend picking a stock, the more they believe that they have insight into the future direction of the stock and the stock market.

Loss Aversion

"The thrill of victory, the agony of defeat" was the memorable opening for the *Wide World of Sports* TV show that was popular in the 1990s. This catchphrase describes an important aspect of human nature. We are wired to seek pleasure and avoid pain. It feels so good to win and absolutely terrible to lose. *Loss aversion* is the technical term describing our natural aversion to experiencing loss. For example, studies have found that the psychic pain of losing money is approximately twice as powerful as the experience of an equivalent gain.

Loss aversion plays itself out in our financial lives in many ways. We don't want to admit that we have lost, and we can be vulnerable to holding on to a losing investment much longer than we should. This is also commonly seen in business ventures that have failed. To avoid the psychological pain of admitting defeat—which could include loss of capital, embarrassment, shame, guilt in having to let go of staff, and so on—many are inclined to go down with the ship. In trying to avoid experiencing a loss, entrepreneurs may keep borrowing money, robbing their retirement plans or even selling off assets to try to keep the business afloat. In our studies on the psychology of wealth, we have found that ultra-wealthy individuals have significantly less loss aversion tendencies than do middle-class individuals.[4] As such, they are much more willing to admit when they have failed, take their losses on the chin, and move on.

Status Quo Bias

Let's face it: You're lazy. It's okay; you can't help it and you're not alone. It turns out that we are all wired to be lazy. When given the chance, we will naturally be drawn to finding the easy way. In other words, we prefer to spend the least amount of physical and mental effort needed to get the job done. We are wired to conserve energy and to avoid exerting ourselves unnecessarily. This tendency, the *status quo bias*, was passed down to us from our ancestors, who lived in a world of limited resources. This strategy helped them survive. Often, they didn't know when they would get their next meal, so it made sense to conserve their energy to maximize their ability to survive during times of scarcity.

Our tendency to conserve energy manifests itself in many ways in modern society. Take working out, for example. We need to override our natural laziness to exercise, and it takes conscious effort to build this habit. It's just not natural for us to burn a bunch of unnecessary calories lifting weights, jogging in circles, or pedaling a bike that doesn't move. So, we need to push past our mental resistance, which is often quite tough to do.

We are also wired to conserve mental energy. We employ a host of cognitive shortcuts to this end. One of the ways we conserve our mental energy is to stick with the status quo. We have a natural bias toward keeping situations just the way they are. If you've ever tried to change a habit, you know how challenging it can be to institute a new behavior. It is so much easier to just keep doing things the way we have been doing them.

So, given that we are lazy and we prefer to keep situations the way they are, how can we maximize the likelihood that we will reach our goals? The key is to capitalize on your mental laziness and harness it to your benefit through automation. For example, let's say that your goal is to start investing or to invest more for your retirement. You've named this as an important goal, and you are excited about taking action. You've also decided how much you want to contribute each month.

At this point in the process, one of the worst actions you can take is to count on your future self to keep writing checks or transferring money each month. It will only be a matter of time until something unexpected comes up that requires money—something ALWAYS comes up—or you forget to make the transfer. Saving money is easy to put off, fall behind on, or quit altogether. Given our propensity toward keeping situations the way they are, a much better strategy is to set up automatic contributions. You can do this through automatic monthly transfers from your checking account to your IRA or salary deferrals in the case of your 401(k) or other employer-sponsored retirement plan. These strategies will allow you to set the stage for a status quo of success.

When you automate, you will need a conscious effort to sabotage your achievement of your savings or investing goal. Sabotaging yourself will require extra mental energy and several actions—none of which you will be excited about doing—to stop the automatic transfer. By automating the achievement of your goal, you will guarantee your success by harnessing the power of your mental laziness in service of your financial health. Overriding your natural impulses is needed to meet the financial demands of modern society, which require you to delay gratification, save money, and build wealth. We are hardwired to take all the wrong actions when it comes to money. Financial success requires ongoing conscious efforts to override our impulses to allow ourselves to save money. Our financial health depends on it!

Chapter 6: Mammoth Mindset Insights

1. Be aware of the harsh words you have for yourself when not executing on what you should do in some important area of your life.

2. Our instincts simply do not line up and provide us with the money mindset we need to survive and thrive today. So, don't be tough on yourself if you struggle with money and money relationships.

3. We are the product of ancestors who shared all of their resources and were not savers.

4. In essence, most of us need some cognitive coping strategies to override our ancestral programming toward the financially destructive aspects of over-sharing.

5. To be financially successful, we not only need to develop a habit of saving, but we also need to develop a money hoarder mindset.

6. To save for the long term, we will need to find a way to temper the sharing instinct.

7. Regardless of the rationale, amassing wealth requires you to justify why it is okay for you to have money while others do not.

8. While being certain about your beliefs may provide a sense of safety and self-satisfaction, open-mindedness has been found to be associated with higher income, net worth, and success in life.

9. We are all vulnerable to overestimating our ability to influence or control events.

10. Those with an ultra-wealthy mindset have significantly less loss aversion tendencies than middle-class individuals and are much more willing to admit when they have failed, take their losses on the chin, and move on.

NOTES

1. J. Fields, M. Copp, and S. Kleinman, "Symbolic Interactionism, Inequality, and Emotions," in *Handbook of the Sociology of Emotions* (Boston: Springer, 2006), 155–78.

2. A. J. Elliot and P. G. Devine, "On the Motivational Nature of Cognitive Dissonance: Dissonance as Psychological Discomfort," *Journal of Personality and*

Social Psychology 67 (1994): 382–94; L. Festinge, "Cognitive Dissonance," *Scientific American* 207 (1962): 93–106.

3. Ellen Langer, "The Illusion of Control," *Journal of Personality and Social Psychology* 32, no. 2 (1975): 311–28.

4. B. T. Klontz, P. Sullivan, M. C. Seay, and A. Canale, "The Wealthy: A Financial Psychological Profile," *Consulting Psychology Journal: Practice and Research* 67, no. 2 (2015): 127–43.

CHAPTER 7

Your Environment

When it comes to financial behaviors, what is normal? How much should you save? How much should you spend? Your environment plays an enormous role in the development of what you consider normal in the world of money. Environmental factors that help shape your relationship with money include your country, your city and state, your neighborhood, whether you are in an urban or rural environment, your culture, your religion, your socioeconomic group, your family-of-origin, your profession, and many others. We are wired to survive and adapt to the environment in which we live.

Some beliefs and behaviors lead to positive financial outcomes. Other beliefs, such as those associated with overspending and credit card abuse, can be destructive to your financial life. Your money beliefs and financial behaviors have a deep and meaningful impact on your life, and the way in which these beliefs are formed are not always based on accurate information.

For example, some environments encourage outward displays of wealth at the expense of retirement savings and financial security. If you live in one of these environments, you will feel a strong desire to also show outward displays of wealth, even if you can't really afford to do so. You may feel pressure to lease a car you can't afford, wear designer clothes, and buy the biggest house a bank will approve a loan for. These types of overspending behaviors, of course, negatively impact a person's net worth. Other environments support more modest lifestyles, even among the ultra-wealthy. In these environments, outward displays of wealth are seen as tasteless, tacky, and unsophisticated. In these environments, it is much easier to save for the future because there is significantly less pressure to demonstrate your social status through consumerism.

DEMOGRAPHIC COMMUNITY

Think about the geographical location in which you were raised. Did you grow up in the Midwest, in the South, or on the East Coast or West Coast? Did you attend public school or a private prep school? How would those different community environments impact your beliefs about money and your norms around spending? If you were raised in a rural community, how might your financial beliefs and behaviors differ from someone who was raised in an urban setting? Our perspectives around money differ based on the lifestyles we are exposed too. Perhaps those who live in a city setting are exposed to more marketing and materialism, which leads to an overrepresentation of outward displays of status. Do the greater number and closer proximity to others require a higher level of attention to fitting in or just the opposite? Is the need for materialistic items to be different, or fit in, change your beliefs and behaviors around money? If you grow up in a rural setting, do your purchases for items like transportation and housing become more based on utility and less on status?

Do you ever notice that when you travel to different cities or countries, you are drawn to signs of affluence or poverty? It seems like we are preconditioned to quickly assess where we would fit in or how this new environment differs from what we are used to. We may tend to look for and notice the size and types of housing or cars we see. Does it look better or worse than what we have? We are constantly judging and assessing what is happening around us, especially when we enter new environments.

SCHOOL SIZE AND DIVERSITY

What about the size and location of your school? How does that impact your relationship with money? Do the kids who attend Beverly Hills High School (90210) have the same money beliefs as kids who attend high schools in a small Midwestern town? The number of students, the diversity of the student population, the socioeconomic status of the families in the school district, public versus private school, and the financial behaviors of the faculty—all contribute to the formation of students' financial beliefs and behaviors.

The truth is, by the time you get to high school, your financial beliefs are likely well established. Social pressures of school may change perceptions of money and its role in social status and acceptance. If you are not wearing the right clothes or driving the right kind of vehicle, you are at risk of being resented or disdained. In some cases, having money may be needed to fit in socially, while in other cases, having money may be viewed negatively and cause you to be an outcast. If you come from a wealthy family surrounded by less affluent classmates, you might develop a sense of guilt around money. This could lead to a negative association with money. If you come from a less affluent family and are surrounded by wealthy classmates, you may feel a sense of inferiority. This could lead to a pattern of overspending trying to fit in.

COMMUNITY JOB ENVIRONMENT

The primary industries and jobs in your community also play a role on what feels normal when it comes to money. If you grew up in an agricultural or rural environment, perhaps you were raised to be more conservative with money. Much of the net worth in such communities is sunk into farm equipment and land. In contrast, if you grew up in an urban finance district, where many people work in finance or accounting, you might have a very different set of beliefs about money.

JASON'S STORY

Jason grew up in a small Midwestern town of less than 500 people. His father was a farmer as was his grandfather and great grandfather, making the family farm in its third generation. However, in the early 1980s, the combination of low grain prices and high interest rates threatened many family farms. No matter how much the family cut corners trying to make ends meet, keeping the family budget afloat was seemingly impossible. Jason knew this by the endless fights his parents had about money and his dad's rants about how the bankers were all corrupt. Jason couldn't remember how many times he would be in the pickup with his dad on a drive into town or to the field when his father would say, "Whatever you do son, don't ever let yourself be in debt to any banker. If you don't have the money to buy something, then save and wait!" Those were some of the last conversations Jason remembers with his dad. The following fall, the bank foreclosed on the property and they lost the farm that had been in their family since the 1880s. Just after the farm sale, unable to face the humiliation or deal with the local gossip uptown, Jason's father took his life in the days before Christmas.

With no family farm left to fulfill Jason's heritage, he went to technical school to learn a trade. He had trouble adjusting to this new life for which he was unprepared. He spent his upbringing in the fields and among the animals, up before dawn and working until the last of the daylight faded. He had never pictured a life that didn't involve farming. Living in an apartment and working in an office cubicle was not very comfortable for him at first, but Jason learned to adjust.

Jason lived in a way perceived by many as meager. He saved as much as he could each week and kept the cash in an old, plastic, ice cream container in the back of his freezer. He remembered this trick from his grandmother who lived during the Depression and didn't trust banks either. After she passed, they found the container in her freezer storing rolls of tens and twenties with rubber bands around them. He remembered the rubber bands were all frozen and cracked, and it made the money look like roses all opened up in the container. They found several other stashes of cash in old coffee cans, cookie jars, and old cigar boxes all over her house. Everyone said she was the richest lady in town, but nobody ever knew the extent of it. Jason thought that was a pretty cool way to go, having all that money and never needing a bank.

Jason was required to have a checking account to cash his paycheck, pay rent, and complete other transactions, but other than that, he avoided banks and paid for everything in cash. As such, he never participated in his company's 401(k) plan, which sounded too technical and too much like banker-talk for him. Jason lived frugally and saved as much cash as possible. He never really cared much about buying a house as his dream was to save enough to buy back the family farm and fulfill his family destiny.

The deep-seated trauma Jason experienced growing up stuck with him throughout his life. While he steered clear of debt, he also missed out on opportunities to build greater wealth through investing and diversification. Not having learned basic money management skills and the proper use of debt, his money beliefs guided his behaviors in his adulthood. In a way, even though Jason was no longer living on the family farm, prior generations were still guiding his daily life through subconscious money beliefs. Jason's story mirrors the financial behaviors of most adult Americans who are subconsciously playing out Money Scripts® that was written generations ago.

ECONOMIC TIMING

Timing has a huge impact on our relationship with money. In times of economic prosperity, people are more optimistic and more willing to take financial risks. In times of economic struggle, people tend to me more pessimistic and risk averse. The impact of broader economic conditions can impact an entire generation. Reflecting on the economic context in which your parents, grandparents, and you were raised can be very useful.

THE STORY OF RICK AND CARRIE

Rick and Carrie both graduated in 2004 from a well-respected, southern, business college. They met in their junior year at a football pre-game party and experienced love at first sight. They decided after graduation to settle in the suburbs outside of Atlanta and put down roots. Carrie received a job offer in a certified public accounting (CPA) firm where she would put her education to work in her chosen profession of accounting. Rick studied finance and got a job as a paraplanner in a mid-sized wealth management firm. They were married exactly one year and one month after graduation. They were just starting out and happy; life was good.

Two years later, Rick and Carrie were beginning to think about starting a family and getting a home. They were both making good money and had saved for a down payment. They had hoped to save more, but the cost of the wedding, the honeymoon, and two new car leases were consuming much of their cash flow. The housing boom was in full force in Atlanta, and prices were growing faster than they could save. The couple was worried about getting a house before the costs got out of hand. They figured if they had bought three years ago, the increase in value alone would have been worth it. However, they weren't sure how much they needed for a down payment and if they could afford a house in the neighborhood they wanted to be in. Making a home purchase work financially would be a stretch, plus there was now a little one on the way.

Another two years later, Rick, Carrie, and their young daughter, Katie, were living in their new Tudor-style home in the suburbs of Atlanta. Times were tight and the housing crisis was in full swing. The value of their home was plummeting, along with home values across the country. Everything was okay at Carrie's office, but Rick's job was in jeopardy. The housing crisis was having a significant impact on the financial markets, and Rick's firm was struggling. He knew that layoffs were inevitable if the economic situation didn't change.

With little Katie's arrival also came new expenses—clothing, medical, and childcare. But their biggest worry was their home. They both wanted to be in their neighborhood, and they had gotten into a bidding war at the time they purchased. To make the mortgage payments work, the banker told them to take an adjustable rate mortgage. Based on how the homes were appreciating, he explained they could refinance and take cash out to pay off the second mortgage they needed for the down payment and for some repairs when they moved in.

Unfortunately, their house was now worth 15% less than when they purchased it, and the adjustable rate mortgage payments became unaffordable a few months ago. Rick and Carrie knew that if Rick lost his job, they were in big financial trouble. They were both upset, and the financial stress caused by the house situation was becoming a source of conflict in their marriage.

They were angry and wanted to blame somebody. They were both smart business school graduates and worked in financial jobs. How could they have let this happen? They wanted to blame the bank, but that's not how they were raised. Yes, it was riskier than they understood, but they wanted it to work and ignored the warnings. In the end, they signed their names and didn't ask enough questions during the process, so they didn't feel right blaming others when they were also responsible. Most important, assessing blame wouldn't change their situation. Some of their friends in similar situations were simply walking away from their homes and declaring bankruptcy. But Rick and Carrie weren't raised that way, and for them, walking away wasn't an option. The bottom fell later that autumn when Rick lost his job.

Fast-forward 10 years, and it's now 2020. Back in 2010, Rick and Carrie had settled with the bank on a short sale and moved back in with Carrie's folks. Rick took a temporary job until the economy got better and took classes online at night to earn a designation of his Certified Financial Planner (CFP®). Rick then returned to financial planning with a new perspective. Carrie's CPA firm grew as the economy recovered, and she was in line to become a partner later in the year.

Katie, unfortunately, had grown up in a family environment filled with stress and fighting about money. She experienced what it was like to sell the house she grew up in and live in hotels for a while. She witnessed crying and sadness before the family settled back in her grandparents' home. She loved growing up with her grandparents around, but she knew her parents weren't happy with this situation. In 2014, the family moved into its own house again after a few years of living in a small townhome they rented. Katie didn't like all these changes in her life—moving and having to adapt to new places, new schools, and new friends. It wasn't easy for Katie or for her parents. Katie will be entering high school soon, and her home life finally seems to be settled.

Rick, Carrie, and Katie were all profoundly impacted by the economic environment of their time. How do you think Katie's money beliefs and future financial behaviors and decision-making will be impacted by what she experienced growing up? If Katie had a brother who was eight years younger, how do you think his money beliefs and perspectives would differ from Katie's? In another place and time, Rick and Carrie's decisions could have had profoundly different outcomes. The broader economy set the stage for their experiences, and these experiences will likely have a lasting impact on their child and any grandchildren.

THE BELIEF STEW

When it comes to shaping money beliefs and behaviors, which factors have the greatest impact? Is it your environment, your tribe, your ancestors, your parents, or your experiences? It would be difficult to tease apart these elements, which are so intertwined and deeply rooted in your subconscious. However, all of these factors contribute to your financial psychology.

We all have friends, co-workers, news programs, and/or social media whispering in our ears, giving us financial advice and stock tips. What advice you decide to hear, consider, and possibly act on may also have a great deal to do with your financial psychology. Many of us only hear and consider financial information consistent with our current beliefs (e.g., confirmation bias). Given all of our psychological baggage involving money, how can we learn to be open to new ideas and new ways of thinking to combat our status quo bias?

THE ANCHOR OF YOUR PAST

For many of us, our past acts like an anchor and hinders our ability to break new ground. Growing up constantly hearing "Nobody from this town ever made it big" or "No one from this high school ever got into Harvard" places serious doubts in your mind. For those who start in a lower middle-class or lower-class upbringing, this psychological anchor can be a source of constant drag against achievement. Every time struggle or conflict arise, that narrative can provide an easy out of giving up.

When we face this kind of psychological barrier, rewriting our story can be especially empowering. This is explored in detail in the coming chapters. When facing a psychological barrier, we can shift the narrative to something like: "I will be the first person from this town who...." This mantra can help us stay open to new possibilities and can replace the negative self-talk that keeps us chained to the ocean floor. Then, for those who follow in your path, you can be a role model. You'll show that if one person can make it, then others can as well. Don't be afraid to be the first or to do what others have yet to accomplish. Not having been done before doesn't equate to impossible, but merely a waiting opportunity for greatness.

YOUR CHOSEN ENVIRONMENT

Another aspect of our environmental influences on our financial psychology involves our chosen environment. The environment in which we live, the people with whom we surround ourselves, as well as the type of information we seek out—all make up our chosen environment. Most people tend to stay within the comfort zone of their existing beliefs and avoid information and opinions that run counter to their beliefs. As such, most will not examine or challenge their deeply held financial beliefs, which keeps them right where they are.

Social media brings the possibilities to construct our virtual environment in new and exciting ways. However, there are aspects of social media that can negatively impact our financial beliefs and behaviors. As we have the ability to connect to celebrities and personal influencers, we also get to see other aspects of their lives, whether authentic or contrived. This often creates a desire to be a part of their world and connect in any way possible. This can manifest in abusing credit and living beyond our means in an attempt to match the celebrity's social status with clothes, watches, or cars.

In fact, many Americans spend more than they make, and there is no end in sight to this behavior. Evidence abounds illustrating that our desires for materialistic satisfaction and instant gratification are causing many of us to spend more than we make. Social media only adds fuel to the fire, so we should choose our influences wisely. After all, if you were betting on who has more wealth, would it be the person who attempts to emulate the life of a celebrity or the person who follows Dave Ramsey—radio show host, author, and businessman? If your social media environment and viewing involves entrepreneurs and self-made success leaders, you have shaped your environment to provide inputs and beliefs of those whose perspective you desire.

Today, more than ever before, we have the ability to have more access to information and people than any generation before. It is a unique opportunity where we can have access to the real-time thinking of successful entrepreneurs through social media posts, YouTube videos, and podcasts. You have the ability to surround yourself with people whom previously you could have only read about in books. Choose your environment wisely!

WHO TAKES CARE OF YOU?

In times of need, who takes care of you? Our origins are tribal in nature. For hundreds of thousands of years of human existence, the answer was simple: Your tribe provided for your needs. In many respects, the tribe functioned as a mini-society. You played your role and contributed to the tribe, and the tribe took care of you through life, including being young, ill, and old. The tribe assisted in providing your food, security, shelter, and took care of you in times of need. In many tribes, respect and caring for tribal elders who provided a lifetime of service to the tribe was the reward for a life well lived.

The shift from hunter-gatherer and agrarian societies to urban living followed the Industrial Revolution. As machines and productivity began to take over, we left our farming tribal communities and headed for the cities, seeking the promise of a better life, materialistic possessions, and wealth. Gradually, many of our tribal benefits shifted to those provided by businesses and the government. For example, employer pension plans, also known as defined benefit plans, provided many of us a lifetime of income in retirement in return for our lifetime of work for the company. Social Security was brought into the mix, providing us the promise of later-life support from the federal government. With a company pension, a little bit of savings, and a Social Security benefit, we could be assured that a safe and secure retirement was in our future. In that way, the broader society took the role of the tribe, provided healthcare and retirement income, and took care of us in return for our service. We were more independent in many aspects of our life, but society had a foundation of health and financial care for us. The responsibility for planning for our retirement was taken care of by our employer and by the federal government. Our role was to work, consume, and raise a family.

However, in the past few decades, all the rules have changed. We now live in a world where most tribes are gone and employers no longer play protective roles in caring for us. These changes have been gradual and incremental, so just like the proverbial lobster in the pot, many of us have not noticed that we are being boiled. Essentially, society has shifted the burden of care back to us, while many of us no longer have the benefit of a tribal structure to assist.

For example, financial responsibility, risk management, and costs have been transferred from the employer to the employees. This has occurred in the shift from defined benefit to defined contribution employer retirement plans. Employer defined benefit plans guarantee the employee a specific amount of income at retirement, which is tied to their pre-retirement earnings. Therefore, the responsibility to save, invest, and manage the retirement funds are the responsibility of the employer, not the employee. Today, most of the defined benefit plans are gone. This has occurred for many reasons, primarily to benefit the company's valuation by discharging its liability of guaranteeing benefits to retired employees. These plans have been replaced by the defined contribution plans in which the employer only commits to the amount of the contribution it will make toward your retirement fund (e.g., the employer 401[k] match), if any. The responsibility of saving the right amount, choosing and managing the investments, and distributing the money in retirement to make sure it doesn't run out is now the employee's responsibility. Many employers still spend significant amounts on plan administration costs, and many offer employer matching contributions; however, the fact remains that the complex burden of retirement planning, savings, investing, and income distribution has been dumped into the laps of the employees. Often, employees are ill equipped to make these decisions and manage their money, don't trust their employer's plan representatives, or decide not to participate altogether. This is a clear and decisive shift in cost and responsibility toward the individual and away from society.

Another example of an environmental shift away from societal support can be seen in healthcare. If you are one of the approximately 150 million people who receive your healthcare from your employer, you have probably noticed some recent issues with it. The healthcare we have today costs more, provides less access to services, and is more complex for us to manage than what we had 20 years ago. The rising cost of healthcare has caused employers to seek ways to continue to provide benefits to employees at an affordable cost. For employers, the cost of employee benefits is one of the most expensive costs they face. If healthcare costs go up by 7% a year, then companies need to make 7% more each year just to break even. At this rate of increase, healthcare costs will double every 10 years. Employers need to find ways to continue to offer valuable healthcare to employees, so over time, these costs have been slowly transferred to employees.

Deductibles keep going up, co-pays are increasing, co-insurance has come into play, healthcare management has arrived, and our share of the premium keeps rising. The cost burden of healthcare has shifted dramatically to the employee. In addition, the healthcare plans themselves have shifted from a major medical model, similar to Medicare, to a managed care design. Also, employee incentives for high deductible healthcare plans (HDHP) and health savings accounts (HSAs) have emerged to try to help employees fill the gaps, if they are willing and able to take on more responsibility to manage their own healthcare. Regardless where you place the blame for what healthcare and healthcare fees have become in America, the costs and responsibility for our well-being have shifted from societal structures back to the now essentially "tribeless" individual.

Another important example of where responsibility for an individual's care has been shifted can be seen in the area of senior healthcare. In prior generations, the elders in society were kept at home or with the extended family to be cared for. The elders' roles included spending time with the younger generations, assisting with childcare, and passing down traditions, stories, and customs to the younger generations. In today's American society, most of our elders don't move into their children's homes but rather move into assisted living or nursing homes. The two-income earner "tribeless" family has made outsourced daycare for children and older adults a necessity. Even worse, as Millennials struggle to find gainful employment to pay off student loans and many even move back home, caring for older parents and their often complicated daily healthcare needs doesn't seem possible for them. The cost of children moving back home and caring for aging parents places enormous burdens on the family unit. Whereas the tribe used to care for elders, now the cost for assistance with daily healthcare and living, either at home or in a facility, is generally not covered by Medicare benefits and falls to individuals and their families. The monthly cost of a home healthcare or nursing home runs from $6,000 to $10,000 or more in many places in the country,[1] which is a significant amount of expense for the family unit to absorb.

Make no mistake, the burden of your future retirement, medical, and lifetime healthcare has clearly shifted in your direction. Are you financially equipped and ready to take on this needed responsibility, cost, and management? Ready or not, the responsibility is now on you for many of these expenses. Society is no longer watching over you. For most Americans, their ancestral tribal is no longer in place. You need to ask yourself as you get older: *Who Takes Care of You?*

Chapter 7: *Mammoth Mindset Insights*

1. We are wired to survive and adapt to the environment in which we live.

2. Your money beliefs and financial behaviors have a deep and meaningful impact on your life, and the ways in which these beliefs are formed are not always based on accurate information.

3. Different community environments impact your beliefs about money and norms around spending.

4. By the time you get to high school, your financial beliefs are likely well established. Social pressures of school may change perceptions of money and its role in social status and acceptance. Consider how the social pressures of your school years and environment shaped your beliefs about money.

5. Reflect on how the primary industries and jobs in your community shaped what feels normal to you when it comes to money.

6. It can be very useful to reflect on the economic context in which your parents, grandparents, and you were raised.

7. Despite all of our psychological baggage involving money, we must have an open mindset to new ideas and new ways of thinking to combat our status quo bias. Can you identify where/when you engage in status quo bias and when you have an open mindset?

8. When we face this kind of psychological barrier, rewriting our story can be especially empowering.

9. The burden of your future retirement, medical, and lifetime healthcare has clearly shifted in your direction. What mindset and preparation will you need to survive in the future environment that awaits you?

10. If you have children, what environments will they be (or were they) exposed to that will establish their money beliefs, influences, and behaviors?

NOTE

1. Scott Witt and Jeff Hoyt, "Nursing Home Costs," SeniorLiving.org, 2020, updated June 24, 2020, https://www.seniorliving.org/nursing-homes/costs/.

Your Financial Flashpoints

Mitsuno Koshitomo was standing outside the entrance to her bank, patiently waiting for it to open. It was 8:16 a.m. on August 8, 1945. We know this because a shadow of her, an effect of the moment of detonation of the atomic bomb dropped on Hiroshima created it. There were other shadows burned into history that morning also. One, on the asphalt of a street, an unknown man was pulling a cart. Another, the shadow of a steel valve, left imprinted on the concrete slab behind it. The flashpoint of the blast created these imprints. In a similar but less tragic fashion, the financial flashpoints of our lives create lasting imprints on our psyche and shape our relationship with money.

ANCESTRAL FLASHPOINTS

Logic would tell us that if something dramatic or tragic happened with our ancestors, certain psychological behaviors and behavioral reactions to such events would be passed down to us. That this was necessary for survival makes sense. Take, for example, the sight of a slithering snake. If we were to see this out of the corner of our eye, many of us would gasp and jump out of the way. We would do this even if we had never been personally bitten by a snake. We would do this even if our parents had never sat us down and warned us to watch out for snakes. Somewhere long ago in our ancestral past,

117

our ancestors learned that avoiding snake bites was beneficial to our survival and passed down this instinctive reaction to us, sparking our automatic alarm response and fight or flight instinct.

Dramatic and traumatic events that our ancestors experienced are now a part of our actual DNA. This instinctual response is much deeper than the level of thoughts, feelings, and behavioral adaptations. Scientists believe that these survival responses have been sewn into our genetic makeup similar to hair and eye color. These genetic changes are passed to succeeding generations like physical feathers handed down from our ancestors.

All cultures have their "flashpoints." Many people remember exactly where they were and what they were doing when they learned of the death of President John F. Kennedy; when the World Trade Centers were attacked by terrorists on September 11, 2001; when the news of the Berlin Wall falling reached them; when the deaths of John Lennon or Michael Jackson were announced; or when unexpected election results were reported. Both the memory of the event and our emotional feelings about it become locked in our subconscious.

Irish historian Oonagh Walsh has a theory about how the potato famine has had a lasting impact on the genetic code of the Irish. At a Science Week event at IT Sligo in 2013, Walsh discussed her theory that the Great Hunger triggered a higher rate of mental illness among later generations, both those who remained in Ireland and those who immigrated to other countries.[1] She believes that the severe nutritional deprivation between 1845 and 1850 caused "epigenetic change," a change in gene expression, making the population more vulnerable to mental illness. This does not necessarily involve changes in the genetic code, but effects may persist for several generations. Her argument was based on the dramatic increase of patients in asylums after the famine. Professor Walsh points out that according to the 1841 census, when Ireland had a population of 8 million, there were 1,600 inmates in district asylums, plus 1,500 in jails and workhouses. By 1900, when the population had halved to 4 million, there were 17,000 in district asylums and a further 8,000 "lunatics at large."

Patrick Tracey, author of the book *Talking Irish Madness,* calls *epigenetics*, which literally means around the gene, "the fascinating study of changes in gene expression: It gives us a glimpse of how 'nurture' gets written into the 'nature' of our DNA code."[2] He discusses the "three-legged-stool" of mental illness in the Irish. The first leg is in vitro starvation from those earlier, famine-ravaged generations, which has been carried through the generations of his family for 150 years. Two of his sisters' onset of schizophrenia was triggered in the mid-1970s, five generations after his ancestors immigrated to Boston in 1847. Tracey also attributes older paternal age to the increase in mental illness. At that time, it was inadvisable for men to marry until they inherited land from their parents. Therefore, men would wait until their parents died to marry, perhaps into their 50s, which corresponded with a doubled rate of schizophrenia in the next generation. Tracey believes alcohol to be the third leg of the stool, but much less of an impact than malnourishment and older fathers.[3] Michelle Casey, of the University of Cincinnati, cites the epigenetic changes theory from Walsh and the paternal age theory of Tracey and believes the third theory, based on her research, to be the tendency to suppress issues within themselves and the family to seem more "normal."[4] Epigenetic imprinting was not exclusive to the Irish. A preliminary study of pre-puberty victims who suffered from the nutritional conditions of the German famine of 1916–1918 was conducted by Gerard J. van den Berg and Pia R. Pinger.[5] They examined the extent that those conditions in one generation affect productivity-related outcomes in later generations. The study analyzed the impact of this famine on children and grandchildren of those exposed to the famine between the ages of 8 and 12. They found that paternal grandfather famine exposure is associated with higher mental health issues in third-generation sons, while maternal grandmother famine exposure has a positive effect on her granddaughters' mental health. The results provide further confirmation that adult mental health is affected by past nutritional shocks within the family.

FAMILY FINANCIAL FLASHPOINTS

The same phenomena is true for our experiences with money. Financial flashpoints are profound and memorable experiences we have regarding money.[6] The more emotionally intense the flashpoints are, the bigger their impact on our relationship with money. These can be direct experiences that we have had, and they can also be profoundly impacted by the financial flashpoints of our ancestors.

Consider the example of David, whose parents grew up in the Great Depression. He grew up hearing references about how awful it was, especially about men not being able to provide for their families, which caused death and devastation. As a little boy, he was determined to never let that happen to him. He studied the Great Depression in detail and learned that no matter how bad things were during the Depression, teachers could still provide for their families. They wouldn't necessarily get paid, but the parents of the students would provide food and lodging for the teachers.

So David chose his profession based on that information. He also grew up hearing the legend of how his grandfather single-handedly saved the family and the family farm by his dedication and relentless hard work. He learned that his grandfather wouldn't let one moment of time go by when he wasn't working. Given all the respect he had for his grandfather, it is no wonder that the seeds of workaholism were planted early and deep. Going into business for himself, working for a company, building in time for leisure and play were never options he entertained. David's approach to work and life were set at an early age and based entirely on the experiences of his parents and grandparents. He was trying to avoid having the experiences which they talked about so negatively.

YOUR FINANCIAL FLASHPOINTS

We are not only shaped by the experiences of our ancestors and the stories our family members pass down to us; we are also deeply influenced by our own experiences. You have had many flashpoints moments of your own. Events that you have witnessed or experienced directly leave an indelible shadow on your psyche. Your relationship with your parents, your experience at school, your first love, your first breakup, your first experience of death, the birth of your child—each of these incidents has shaped your thoughts, feelings, and behaviors in a profound way.

It is also true of your relationship with money. We have all had financial flashpoints that have shaped our relationship with money. The effects of these flashpoints are often held deeply in our subconscious. They create our beliefs about money, called Money Scripts®, which we discuss in detail in Chapter 9. Our Money Scripts®, in turn, drive our financial behaviors. Our financial behaviors, of course, determine our financial outcomes.

The sources of our financial flashpoints can be many and varied. The younger we are, the more likely we might walk away with a distorted sense of what happened, why it happened, and the lessons we learn from it. The more emotionally intense the experience, the bigger the impact it will have on us. For example, growing up in poverty can be a traumatic experience. Not having enough to eat, being homeless, losing housing, feeling ostracized at school because your clothes are worn or unwashed, seeing your parents stressed about money—all of these experiences can have a dramatic impact on our lives. Conversely, growing up wealthy can leave an imprint too. Perhaps you feel guilty because you have more than others or you never have to worry about money, or whenever you want something, you get it without any effort or concern.

When flashpoints occur, we try to make sense of them. This is especially challenging when we are children. We make up meanings; we blame ourselves. Sometimes we even make up conspiracies. In an attempt to protect ourselves from future pain, we make promises to ourselves: "I'll never do X again"; "I'll always do Y." Perhaps we decide to avoid certain situations, types of people, or places. We may try to control things and we may try to destroy things; these are all reactions to these impactful flashpoint moments.

So, just for a moment, think back to your most pleasant money experience. Now, think about your most painful money experience. Which experience came easiest to your mind—the most pleasant or the most painful? If you are like most people, it is easier to recall the most painful experience. If this is true for you, this suggests your relationship with money has a painful imprint on your psyche. What was your earliest experience with money? What did you learn from being a part of your family, specifically about money? It is very helpful to unpack these early experiences, even if you are doing so years or decades later.

If we are fortunate, we can articulate our thoughts and feelings about the situation. In an ideal environment, we have supportive adults around us who help us process our feelings and arrive at accurate conclusions about what happened and why. But for most of us, we don't have the opportunity to process these events in a healthy way. We end up trying to just cope with them, not think about them, and move on. Our financial flashpoints experiences have the biggest impact on us when they lie unexamined, hiding below the level of our consciousness. We may see the negative results of these financial flashpoints in our lives, but we remain unable to understand why we behaved a certain way, when we "know" we should have done something different.

CULTURAL FLASHPOINTS

In addition to our ancestors, our family, and our direct experiences, we are also impacted by our culture. Our culture is the sea in which we swim. Often we are not even aware of its impact on our beliefs and behaviors. Our culture creates images and directs our thinking in an attempt to influence our subconscious beliefs about money. Consider the popular nursery rhyme "Hush little Baby." In essence, the message is that if you're crying, don't worry, your parents will just buy you the right thing and you will be all better. If that doesn't work, they will just buy you something better.

We have discussed the impact of the Great Depression on a particular family and individual. But such events have a much broader impact on someone's relationship with money. Many people who went through the Depression ended up being anxious about having enough money. Many who lost their money in the banking industry's collapse had difficulty ever fully trusting financial institutions again. Many children of people who went through the Great Depression can attest to the anxiety and frugality of their parents.

A recent example of a cultural flashpoint can be seen with Millennials (people born between 1980 and 2004). They lived in a household impacted by the 2008 recession and housing crisis. Research surveys suggest that Millennials are generationally underrepresented when it comes to owning property or investing in stock markets. One hypothesis for this is that they lived through the crisis. Many saw their parents lose homes. Many saw their parents' delay retirement or return back to work as their retirement accounts sank in value. It is no wonder that they may be hesitant to get into real estate or invest in the stock market. After experiencing the financial devastation their family went through, with possible anxiety and fighting, it's no wonder this generation formed a negative impression of home ownership and the stock market.[7] While the messages might not have been overt, the feelings were registered harshly and deeply into the psyche.

But Millennials weren't the only ones profoundly impacted by the Great Recession. We conducted a study of financial planners in the wake of the stock market and real estate meltdown.[8] Over 90% of those we studied were experiencing medium to high levels of posttraumatic stress. They had difficulty sleeping; they were anxious; they had trouble concentrating; they were worried about the financial well-being of themselves, their clients, and their employees. The study also found that this intensely emotional experience was leading to cognitive changes too. Many were questioning the validity of what they thought they knew about how to help people and that the economic situation was evidence of a fundamental change in the rules of investing. In the years after the crisis, there was a significant shift from buy-and-hold strategies to more active investment approaches, suggesting that the emotional impact and cognitive changes led to behavioral changes in investment strategies. The cultural impact of the Great Recession has had a profound impact on beliefs and behaviors of consumers and professionals alike.

FILLING IN THE BLANKS

In each of the preceding cases, our psyche tries to make sense of what is happening. Essentially we "make something up" about how money works. We develop lists of "dos," "don'ts," "always," and "nevers" so that we can relive a good experience or avoid experiencing painful ones. What we make up is often NOT entirely accurate or the best conclusion about what happened, and we often end up engaging in responses that are not in our financial best interest.

Interestingly, two people experiencing the exact same event can arrive at totally different conclusions. Consider what happened to twin sisters Joni and Brenda. When they were 3 years old, they were told by their mother that she couldn't afford to take care of them and that they were going to be orphaned. Joni told us that she decided, at age 3, that she was going to survive, and she couldn't trust anyone but herself. So she approached her life on a quest to take care of herself. She is now 50 years old and has done extremely well financially. In taking care of herself and not trusting anyone else, she has avoided intimate relationships. She is single, has never had a committed relationship, has no children, and has few friends. Her sister, in contrast, walked away believing that the answer to protecting herself was to find someone to love her and take care of her. Her life has been one spent trying to figure out what other people want and give it to them so she is never abandoned again. Not surprisingly, her desperate dependence has led to her getting taken advantage of by people who say they love her. However, she has been used and abused many times, even to the point of severe injury. The signs of abuse were there, but she was too afraid to be on her own, all alone.

The story of Joni and Brenda illustrates how we can experience the same event and take away entirely different, often conflicting, lessons. You can see how each girl's take-away from her flashpoint caused her to think about relationships and money in different ways.

CORONAVIRUS FLASHPOINT

A recent flashpoint event is the 2020 COVID-19 pandemic. The virus and events surrounding its outbreak were a collective experience, which will have lingering effects. Some of these shared flashpoints happen suddenly, like the Kennedy assassination or the 9/11 terrorist attack. Other flashpoints and their effects unfold over time. Like the AIDS epidemic in the late 1980s, it took several years for society and the medical community to fully understand the disease and how it was transmitted. Initially, the disease caused a significant overreaction amid the chaos of lack of understanding. Magic Ervin Johnson retired at or near the height of his basketball career due to public pressure and ignorance. There was also a social backlash on those who were seen as "carriers" and "sources" of the disease fueled by fear and uncertainty.

The trauma, fear, and vacuum of credible knowledge in times of crisis can burn feelings of fear and panic into our subconscious. We are scarred, for better and worse, for having lived and experienced these moments in time. An important perspective to keep in mind is that, based on everyone's unique situation at the time of the flash-point event, we will experience the impacts, memories, and meanings very differently. So even though we may have all experienced the same event, its impact and meanings will be unique to each of us. The financial flashpoint will yield different beliefs, lessons, and subsequent behaviors. Those beliefs and behaviors shape a new financial reality unless they are explored and reasoned in healthy and holistic ways.

DEPRESSION FLASHPOINT

The Great Depression illustrates the lasting impact that can accompany a profound and widespread financial flashpoint. If you have ever known somebody who lived through the Great Depression, then you may have seen firsthand some of the lingering effects. Many Depression-era people remember what it was like having little money or food. They can recall stories of waiting in bread lines. They can remember mass unemployment and losing all of their money when the banks collapsed. Think about how panicked people got when Costco or Walmart ran out of toilet paper in the wake of Covid-19. Imagine having to wait in line for hours in the cold for a loaf of bread to bring home to your family for dinner. There was no work, no money, no food, and little hope for millions of Americans.

We noticed the impact on our parents and grandparents. We watched our grandmother take the extra packets of sugar and bread from the table when we ate out for dinner. We watched our grand-father never put a dollar in the bank again for the rest of his life. As children, these behaviors did not make much sense. Why were they hoarding food when they clearly had enough food at home? Why were they not using banks to store their money? Why is nobody else doing this? Imagine how profound the impact of that experience if it were to lead to decades of hoarding, insecurity about having enough food, fear of not having enough of many things, and a deep distrust of banks. Many of us as children and grandchildren are still living out the impact of this financial flashpoint, and many of us are unaware of it. We just carry around anxiety and fear about money. Or conversely, we spend more than we should because we don't want to deprive ourselves like we saw our parents or grandparents deprive themselves.

FLASHPOINT CONTEXT AND GROWTH

The coronavirus came out of nowhere to shut down society as we once knew it, cancelling sporting events and concerts, closing schools, and plunging the stock markets by over 20% in a matter of weeks. In the beginning, there was panic, confusion, fear, and wide public displays of irrational overreaction and fear of the unknown. After a few months, as we began to learn more about the disease, we slowly returned to a sense of a "new normal." In the middle of the uncertainty, however, we experienced the same types of catastrophic thinking our parents and grandparents experienced in previous events:

> *Will I lose all my money?*
> *Will the markets ever recover?*
> *This time everything is different!*
> *Will life ever go back to "normal" again?*

We will evolve to something that resembles what we used to do, but it won't be the same. As much as we may yearn for the way it felt before, the flashpoint changes us at the subconscious level.

Just like after 9/11, over time, we returned to a new normal, but life changed. We no longer travel by plane, move around in society, enter concerts or sporting events, or fly the way we used to. Not only do we have environmental reminders, such as longer security lines at the airport, on a subconscious level, we are aware of greater risk and a realization that our world is no longer as safe as it was in the past. We are more aware, our senses and emotions are heightened, and we just can't seem to be as relaxed or as comfortable during air travel as we once were. We change in the name of safety, privacy, and societal pressures. Flashpoints signal the change that is coming and the memory of the lives we are leaving behind. We are changed forever.

When you look back at our collective societal experiences pre-Covid-19, what will you remember and miss the most? Maybe you long for a time when you didn't know the meaning of the term *social distancing*. Perhaps you long for the day that you don't jerk your head around in public when you hear someone cough or sneeze. Just that trigger alone is likely to result in instant anger toward that stranger or fear that another pandemic is under way. Did you miss having the traditional sporting events that marked the change of seasons since you were a child? How will you reconcile your beliefs around the times we live in now? What lessons or beliefs will you pass down to children and grandchildren about the pandemic era? What lessons will you take with you regarding the stock market or your security in employment? What lessons will you take with you about small business risk? Flashpoints need thought. They need exploration and understanding. They need to be dealt with and reconciled in healthy ways to help you adapt and change in helpful ways, increasing your resilience. If you try to simply survive challenging times with a numbing sense of bewilderment and fear, moving with the herd, you will miss out on critical opportunities to evolve and grow.

CONCLUSION

A critical component of evolving your money mindset is being able to recall your financial flashpoints—the events and circumstances that established your relationship with money. It's important for you to identify the message about money your psyche arrived at, which is the focus of Chapter 9. Are you structuring your financial life based on accurate information or distorted conclusions? Are your conclusions helpful representations of what actually occurred or did you fill in the blanks with a message that's easier to understand or is designed to protect you from future pain? How have these conclusions helped you or hurt you in reaching your financial goals? Understanding your adaptations to these financial flashpoint events may not come easy and may require deep introspection to fully recall and comprehend. However, to optimize your financial life and stave off financial extinction, you must wrestle with your inner beasts and put them in their place.

Chapter 8: Mammoth Mindset Insights

1. Financial flashpoints are profound and memorable experiences we have around money.
2. The more emotionally intense the flashpoints are, the bigger their impact on our relationship with money.
3. What did you learn from being a part of your family, specifically about money?
4. Our financial flashpoints experiences have the biggest impact on us when they lie unexamined, hiding below the level of our consciousness.
5. Our psyche tries to make sense of what is happening at times of emotional financial crisis, and what we make up is often NOT entirely accurate or the best conclusion about what happened.
6. Understanding your adaptations to these financial flashpoint events may not come easy and may require deep introspection to fully recall and comprehend.
7. Recalling and making sense of flashpoints will take time. Use your Money Mammoth Insights journal notepad to capture your thoughts when they occur.
8. Are your conclusions helpful representations of what actually occurred or did you fill in the blanks with a message that's

easier to understand or designed to protect you from future pain?

9. Flashpoints need thought. They need exploration and understanding. Flashpoints need to be dealt with and reconciled in healthy ways that help our future selves adapt and change.

10. If you try to simply survive flashpoint times with a numbing sense of bewilderment and fear, moving with the herd, you will miss out on critically important opportunities to evolve and grow.

11. To optimize your financial life and stave off financial extinction, you must wrestle with your inner beasts and put them in their place. Only after you defeat those beasts can your Money Mammoth ascend to the top of the food chain and become dominant over your financial environment!

NOTES

1. Michelle K. Smith, "Did the Irish Famine Trigger Mental Illness in the Irish?," *Irish Central* (October 12, 2017).

2. Patrick Tracey, *Talking Irish Madness: Searching for the Roots of My Family's Schizophrenia* (New York: Bantam, 2008).

3. Patrick Tracey, "Famine Drives Madness for 150 Years," blogs, psychcentral .com/no-family-madder, 2014, last updated January 4, 2014, https://blogs .psychcentral.com/no-family-madder/2013/11/thanks-but-no-thanks-for-the-famine-that-drove-us-crazy/.

4. Michelle Casey, "The Prevalence of Mental Illness in Irish Americans: The Three Theories," February 27, 2017, libapps.libraries.uc.edu.

5. Gerard J. van den Berg and Pia R. Pinger, "A Validation Study of Transgenerational Effects of Childhood Conditions on the Third-Generation Offspring's Economic and Health Outcomes Potentially Driven by Epigenetic Imprinting," IZA Discussion Paper No. 7999, March 1, 2014.

6. B. Klontz and P. Klontz, *Mind Over Money: Overcoming the Money Disorders That Threaten Our Financial Health* (New York: Broadway Business, 2009).

7. H. Hoffower, "The Great Recession Created a Domino Effect of Financial Struggles for Millennials—Here Are 5 Ways It Shaped a Generation," *New York Times Business Insider*, August 11, 2019, https://www.businessinsider.com/how-the-great-recession-affected-millennials-2019-8.

8. B. T. Klontz and S. L. Britt, "Financial Trauma: Why the Abandonment of Buy-and-Hold in Favor of Tactical Asset Management May Be a Symptom of Posttraumatic Stress," *Journal of Financial Therapy* 3, no. 2 (2012): 14–27.

Your Money Scripts®

What we know we should do with our money and what we actually do are often two very different things. Put your hands up, about shoulder level, with your thumbs pointing toward your shoulders—like a referee signaling a touchdown in football. Looking at your left hand, imagine that your left hand represents what almost all of us know about money and what to do with it. It represents the "rules" to follow if you want to do well with money. The rules are relatively simple:

- Save money for the future.
- Spend less than you earn.
- Have a spending plan that reflects what is most important to you.
- Avoid emotionally driven financial decisions.
- Pay as you go; if you can't afford to pay cash for something, then wait until you can.
- Have an emergency fund.
- Anticipate future expenditures.
- As much as possible, avoid credit card spending and revolving debt.
- Buy used cars instead of new ones.
- Let trusted professionals invest your savings.

These rules are basic, well documented, and immutable financial *Best Practices*. Remember, your left hand represents all this "good" information about how to be successful financially. Those are the objective, unbiased financial "facts."

Now, look at your right hand. Imagine that it represents your actual financial behaviors. The gap you see between your two hands represents the distance in your behaviors between what you know you should be doing with your money and what you actually do with your money. We all have a gap. Sometimes it is a narrow one; sometimes, a wide one. Even though we know better, we don't always do better. Information about what to do and how to do it is seldom the problem. The basic philosophy is simple. Our actual behaviors are the problem.

What we know and what we do often don't match. Part of the gap exists because we don't realize just how controlled we are by our tribal instincts, which we have discussed in detail in previous chapters. But there is another powerful influence on our financial decisions—our Money Scripts®.

MONEY SCRIPTS®

Enter the field of financial psychology, which sheds light on the psychological underpinnings of our complex and often troubled relationship with money. For the past decade, we have conducted research on Money Scripts®, or those typically subconscious beliefs we have about money. They are passed down through the generations, learned in childhood, and drive our financial behaviors.

Money Scripts® arise from the experiences of our ancestors and from our own lives. We develop them in an attempt to make sense of how money and the world works. For example, consider the beliefs that "rich people are greedy" or that "money corrupts." You don't have to look far to find evidence that a rich person appears to be greedy or corrupt. Sometimes you have seen this directly, or these messages were passed down to you from your parents or grandparents who were mistreated by a wealthy person. We see stories in the news all the time highlighting the misdeeds of people who are wealthy.

These beliefs, like all Money Scripts®, have elements of truth. It is true that some wealthy people are, in fact, greedy, and many people have been corrupted by money. However, that is just part of the story. There are many examples of wealthy people who are generous and have done great deeds in the world. However, when we have settled on a belief about money, we pay special attention to evidence that confirms and supports our belief, and we tend to screen out, ignore, or discredit evidence that challenges this belief.

When beliefs arise from highly emotional experiences, they can be very difficult to change. For example, if someone grew up poor, it would make sense that he or she developed the belief that "there isn't enough money." If this person feels powerless, he or she might even hold the Money Script® that "there will never be enough money." Now, of course, when you include the word *never*, the belief becomes inaccurate. These types of Money Scripts® can be highly self-destructive. It could lead to people deciding that since there will never be enough money, why bother trying to get ahead? Or conversely, it could lead to people who are so anxious about "there never being enough money" that they can never enjoy their money even when they have acquired millions of dollars. Holding on to a Money Script® when it is not accurate, has lost its usefulness, or is passionately held is a driving force behind many self-destructive financial behaviors.

To make matters even more complicated, it is not uncommon to have Money Scripts® that seem at first glance to contradict each other. For example, it is common for people who have negative beliefs about money and the wealthy to also believe that their lives would be better if they had more money.

Financial success requires us to be open-minded and not rigidly stuck to a particular way of looking at money or the world. In a fast-moving and constantly changing world, flexibility in thinking is critical for us to be able to notice opportunities and abandon tactics that are no longer working. To achieve this open-mindedness and flexibility, it is important for us to identify our Money Scripts® and to modify them as needed to optimize our effectiveness.

THE KLONTZ MONEY SCRIPT® INVENTORY

There is a strong link between Money Scripts® and financial outcomes. The Klontz Money Script Inventory (KMSI), now in its second edition, was developed to help people discover their money scripts. It has been researched extensively, and scores on the KMSI have been found to be associated with income, net worth, credit card debt, socioeconomic status in childhood, financial behaviors, and other aspects of financial health. For many people, discovering and exploring their Money Scripts® are important steps in increasing their income, net worth, and financial health.

For a FREE test of your Money Scripts®, you can go to www .MoneyScripts.com. This test is the same one we have used in research with thousands of people. When you complete the test, your results will be automatically e-mailed to you. If you would rather take the test using paper and pencil, you can take it here:

KLONTZ MONEY SCRIPT® INVENTORY REVISED (KMSI-R)

Please indicate how strongly you agree with the following statements using the following scale:

1 = Strongly Disagree, 2 = Disagree, 3 = Disagree a Little, 4 = Agree a Little, 5 = Agree, 6 = Strongly Agree

	1 Strongly Disagree	2 Disagree	3 Disagree a Little	4 Agree a Little	5 Agree	6 Strongly Agree
1. I do not deserve a lot of money when others have less than me.						
2. Rich people are greedy.						
3. I do not deserve money.						

	1 Strongly Disagree	2 Disagree	3 Disagree a Little	4 Agree a Little	5 Agree	6 Strongly Agree
4. Good people should not care about money.						
5. It is hard to be rich and be a good person.						
6. The less money you have, the better life is.						
7. Money corrupts people.						
8. Being rich means you no longer fit in with old friends and family.						
9. People get rich by taking advantage of others.						
10. Things would get better if I had more money.						
11. More money will make you happier.						
12. It is hard to be poor and happy.						
13. You can never have enough money.						
14. Money is power.						
15. Money would solve all my problems.						
16. Money buys freedom.						
17. Most poor people do not deserve to have money.						
18. You can have love or money, but not both.						
19. I will not buy something unless it is new (e.g., car, house).						

	1 Strongly Disagree	2 Disagree	3 Disagree a Little	4 Agree a Little	5 Agree	6 Strongly Agree
20. Poor people are lazy.						
21. Money is what gives life meaning.						
22. Your self-worth equals your net worth.						
23. If something is not considered the "best," it is not worth buying.						
24. People are only as successful as the amount of money they earn.						
25. You should not tell others how much money you have or make.						
26. It is wrong to ask others how much money they have or make.						
27. Money should be saved, not spent.						
28. It is important to save for a rainy day.						
29. People should work for their money and not be given financial handouts.						
30. I would be a nervous wreck if I did not have money saved for an emergency.						
31. You should always look for the best deal before buying something,						
32. It is extravagant to spend money on oneself.						

SCORING PROCEDURES

In the following, place the point value on the line corresponding to the item. Add the points in each column and divide them by the number of items to determine the average score.

Money Avoidance	Money Worship	Money Status	Money Vigilance
1	10	17	25
2	11	18	26
3	12	19	27
4	13	20	28
5	14	21	29
6	15	22	30
7	16	23	31
8		24	32
9			

Total _____ /9 = _____ Total _____ /7 =_____

Total _____ /8 =_____ Total _____ /8 = _____

ANALYSIS

Our research has identified four categories of Money Scripts®: money avoidance, money status, money worship, and money vigilance. It is not uncommon for people to score higher in one or two areas, even if these areas seem to be in conflict. To see what each category means, you can read the following summaries. Use this key to score your responses:

1–2 = Your response style suggests that you do not endorse beliefs associated with these Money Scripts®.

3–4 = Your response style suggests that you may exhibit one or more signs of this Money Script®.

5–6 = Your response style is similar to a person who endorses these Money Scripts®.

Money Avoidance

Money avoiders believe that money is bad or that they do not deserve it. They believe that wealthy people are greedy or corrupt, and that there is virtue in living with less money. Because of their negative associations with money and wealth, money avoiders may sabotage their financial success and/or give money away in an unconscious effort to have as little as possible. Research has shown that money avoidance scripts can be associated with ignoring bank statements, increased risk of overspending, enabling others financially, financial dependence, hoarding, and having difficulty sticking to a budget.

Money Worship

At their core, money worshipers are convinced that the key to happiness and the solution to all of their problems is to have more money. At the same time, they believe that one can never have enough money. Individuals who score high on money worship scripts are more likely to have lower income, lower net worth, and credit card debt. They are also more likely to spend compulsively, hoard possessions, and put work ahead of family. They may give money to others even though they can't afford it and are more likely to be financially dependent on others.

Money Status

Money status seekers see net worth and self-worth as synonymous. They may pretend to have more money than they do and as a result are at risk of overspending. They often believe that if they live a virtuous life, the universe will take care of their financial needs. They may have grown up in a household that prioritized the financial aspects of social standing. Research has shown that people with money status beliefs are at greater risk of overspending, gambling excessively, financial dependence on others, and hiding expenditures from their spouses or partners.

Money Vigilance

The money vigilant are alert, watchful, and concerned about their financial welfare. They believe it is important to save and for people to work for their money and not be given financial handouts. Research has found that higher money vigilance scores are positively associated with higher levels of financial health. The money vigilant are less likely to buy on credit. They also have a tendency to be somewhat anxious about their financial futures, inspiring them to save. While they have a tendency to be secretive about their financial status with others, they are less likely to keep financial secrets from their spouses or partners. While money vigilance encourages saving and frugality, excessive wariness or anxiety could keep someone from enjoying the benefits and sense of security that money can provide.

CHANGING OUR MONEY SCRIPTS® CAN BE TOUGH

All life in any form, including viruses and bacteria, are gifted with lessons learned from previous generations. Because Sir Isaac Newton spent time watching and reflecting on the human implications of apples falling, now we don't need to. We can just take what he has taught us, expand on it, and apply it to our current situation.

However, other lessons "learned" by our ancestors can be grossly inaccurate conclusions about what they observed or can be accurate but no longer relevant. This can keep us stuck and unable to adapt to new situations. For thousands of years, scientific development was hindered because of our ancestors' insistence that the earth was the center of the universe. People who suggested otherwise were murdered or threatened with death to the point that they recanted what they knew to be true. George Washington, after all, bled to death because the doctors believed that bleeding out whatever was making him sick would make him well. Mental illness was at one point treated by drilling holes in a person's head to let out the "bad spirits."

We are born into a particular socioeconomic environment. And while money isn't everything, it certainly is in the middle of everything. Unfortunately, there is a taboo about talking about money, so much of what we learn is indirect. We learn, but from osmosis—absorbing what we see, hear, experience. Since money is one of those "taboo" topics in our culture, what we learn is not vetted by anyone. We observe things, we assume things, and our conclusions become our reality. These lessons were embedded so long ago that we are no longer conscious of how our current behaviors are linked to our childish beliefs. Until we examine our beliefs, we will keep getting the same outcomes.

REWRITING YOUR MONEY SCRIPTS®

Do you have the courage to take an honest look at your own Money Scripts®? How can you figure out what they are? Look at your behaviors, because your financial behaviors are directly related to what you believe about money. You are not inconsistent with your beliefs.

Take a close look at a financial behavior that you know isn't good for you. Perhaps you are overspending. Perhaps you are not saving enough. Perhaps you are making emotional investing decisions. You know you should not be acting this way, and it is not the result of a lack of knowledge. To shift these behaviors, you need to take an honest look at the beliefs driving them. For example, why would someone wrack up $20,000 in credit card debt? That makes no sense, right? So what Money Script® could explain such self-destructive behaviors? Perhaps your behavior is the result of one of the following beliefs:

- I would see myself as a failure if I couldn't keep my family happy, and give them the things and experiences that make them happy.
- I could lose my family if I can't give them what they want.
- I know how painful it is to grow up wanting things, and I don't want my children to feel that pain. I want to give them what I didn't have.
- I want my family to remember me as a generous person.
- What would my friends say if I had to pull my child out of private school because we really can't afford it?

These beliefs reveal a deeper and more powerful influence than what we know we "should" do. These types of beliefs could represent an underlying money worship or money status script. Your behavior suggests that you may be operating in the mythical world that says that money is the magic potion that can bring happiness; it can fix everything. While we might say, if asked, that we know that's not true in a logical sense, our behaviors suggest a much more powerful psychological force at play.

But what if it's not true? What if money can't make people happy? Certainly there is not a consistent relationship between money and happiness once we are able to meet our basic financial needs. There are many people who know this is true: people who have collected significant amounts of financial wealth and realize the folly of believing that money will solve all the problems inherent in human existence or that money will bring lasting love, peace, safety, and harmony.

Financial success requires us to get our financial behaviors in line with the financial reality of the modern world. This requires flexible thinking and being open to challenging our deeply held beliefs about money. We need to be open-minded and be willing to embrace the idea that we have it all wrong. To evolve and optimize our financial effectiveness, we need to have the courage to learn about ourselves and accept that our beliefs about money may be deeply flawed. We must be open to learning new ways of looking at money and relating to money.

Chapter 9: Mammoth Mindset Insights

1. What we know we should do around money and what we actually do are often two very different things.

2. Money Scripts® arise from the experiences of our ancestors and from our own lives. We develop them in an attempt to make sense of how money and the world works.

3. When we have settled on a belief about money, we pay special attention to evidence that confirms and supports our belief, and we tend to screen out, ignore, or discredit evidence that challenges this belief.

4. Money avoiders believe that money is bad or that they do not deserve it.

5. Money worshipers are convinced that the key to happiness and the solution to all of their problems is to have more money.

6. Money status seekers see net worth and self-worth as synonymous.

7. The money vigilant are alert, watchful, and concerned about their financial welfare. They believe it is important to save, and for people to work for their money and not be given financial handouts.

8. Take a close look at a financial behavior that you know isn't good for you.

9. Financial success requires us to get our financial behaviors in line with the financial reality of the modern world.

10. Flexible thinking and being open to challenging our deeply held beliefs about money is required.

Your Financial Behaviors

To evolve our money mindset, we need to take an honest look at our financial behaviors. So many of us are not paying close attention to them. To optimize our financial behaviors, we must first become keenly aware of them and understand their nature. Ultimately, this awareness is key to closing the gap between where we are now and where we want to be. However, something that significant and impactful rarely comes easy. For this reason, we must first develop our behavioral awareness skills.

FINANCIAL BEHAVIORS

A great place to start is making a list of financial behaviors you know you need to address. For example, this could include actions you should be taking, such as paying down debt, saving for retirement, or establishing an emergency fund. Or it could include actions you need to stop taking, such as overspending or loaning money to people you know won't pay it back. After you have made a list, it can be helpful to flag them in order of importance and tackle each one in turn. Next, identify the specific Money Scripts® and emotions contributing to the behavior. Your financial behaviors will make perfect sense when you identify the underlying Money Scripts® and where it came from. For example, it is not uncommon for people to have excessive debt when they have a Money Script®: "I will never be able to afford the things I really want in life."[1] This belief could easily emerge from growing up in a lower socioeconomic family. If you are experiencing poverty, of course you can't afford what you really want. With this belief, you might feel hopeless about being able to change your financial life. You may not look for opportunities to advance yourself, or may not recognize them when they are right in front of you. Given the situation seems hopeless, it makes sense that you would be vulnerable to overspending when you get access to credit, even if you know you shouldn't.

Once you have identified the behavior you want to shift and the money script that has been keeping it in place, it is helpful to identify the situations in which the behavior occurs, so that you can interrupt the pattern. For example, if you are vulnerable to overspending, you might notice that you are more prone to shop online when you are feeling sad, angry, lonely, or scared.

With practice, you can identify these triggers and replace your destructive behavior with a positive action. The positive action will be geared toward achieving a specific financial goal and disrupting the old behavior. Last, you can connect this new positive behavior to a reinforcement image and a physical totem or charm. For example, when you reduce your debt by a certain percentage or stick to your budget for a month, you can give yourself a reward. After you follow this formula several times with awareness and intention, your new financial behavior can replace your old destructive behavior and can become your new routine. In previous chapters, we have examined money disorders, including financial enabling and financial dependence. In the following, we explore several additional destructive financial behaviors.

It's important to note that several of these financial behaviors can be classified as disorders and are listed in the *American Psychological Association's Diagnostic and Statistical Manual of Mental Disorders* (*DSM-5*). The seriousness and importance of recognizing and correcting these destructive financial behaviors cannot be overstated. These conditions, which we will discuss in some detail, can be severe and cause significant financial, emotional, occupational, and relationship problems.

Financial Denial

While not a disorder in itself, *financial denial* is a common symptom of a troubled relationship with money. It often accompanies other money disorders. Essentially, it involves actively avoiding thinking about or addressing one's financial life. *Financial denial* has been defined as an " ... attempt to cope by simply not thinking about money or trying not to deal with it."[2] People engage in financial denial to avoid thinking about money and to avoid feelings of distress.[3]

Financial denial is a natural defense mechanism used to avoid feeling stress when we make bad decisions with our money.[4] While we get immediate psychological relief in avoiding uncomfortable feelings, we pay a price later on. By not allowing ourselves to feel that pain associated with our behaviors, we suppress an important internal warning, signaling to us that we need to be aware of something that needs to be addressed. Financial denial often leads to a compounding of financial problems and consequences. It takes courage to stare our finances in the face, but doing so is essential if we are to evolve our money mindsets and avoid financial extinction.

Compulsive Buying Disorder (CBD)

While the average American tends to be an overspender, *compulsive buying disorder (CBD)* is altogether different. CBD is an addiction to spending. It is characterized by an "obsessive, irresistible, out of control buying urges that lead to financial difficulties, feelings of guilt and/or shame, and interference with one's work or close relationships."[5] While CBD was not included in the most recent edition of the *DSM*, it can be classified as either an obsessive-compulsive disorder, an addiction, or a mood disorder.[6] CBD remains in the spotlight for many consumer researchers and has been shown to primarily impact women, beginning to manifest in the teenage years.[7] Clearly, the Internet and online retailers keep making it easier to shop, and CBD sufferers face a significant and growing challenge.

Here are some questions to help you determine whether or not you have symptoms of CBD:

- How much time per day would you estimate you spend shopping/actively looking at items for sale either online or in retail locations?
- How much time do you spend thinking about shopping?
- Do you get feelings of anxiety if you are unable to shop?
- How many days a week do you receive packages in the mail with items you have purchased?
- Do you buy something every time you shop online?
- Does your shopping session end after a purchase or do you just pause until you decide to shop again?
- Have you made promises to yourself or others to stop shopping?
- Do you feel guilty after shopping?
- Does shopping or thinking about shopping interfere with your concentration, work, or relationships?

If you worry that you might have CBD, we encourage you to seek the help of a mental health professional. To become more conscious of your spending, it helps to become aware of your feelings before, during, and after your shopping or buying activity. Track for an entire week how many times you start shopping online or in person for items that are nonessential. A necessity is something you need for your daily existence and not a new electronic gadget or something you wear; you know the difference.

It is also helpful to increase your awareness of what you are feeling while you are shopping. Are you feeling excited? Do you feel a rush of endorphins when you find something you like? Note your feelings during the shopping and searching process. Are you feeling happy? How do you feel afterward? Guilty? As you find the item you want to buy and place it in your cart, do these feelings persist? Are the feelings increasing? After you hit the "Buy" button and provide your method of payment, are you still feeling that buying rush or did you feel a pang of guilt or regret once you paid? How about when you get home and/or the package arrives: Do you still feel the purchase pleasure or do you have pangs of regret? Does the actual receipt of the item match the excitement of the shopping and buying process, or did you feel a letdown?

Finally, how do you feel when your credit card bill arrives? As you scan the charges and purchases you made for the previous month, are you happy with your purchases or frustrated by the amount you spent and what you bought? It's also important to note the average purchases you typically make both individually and monthly. Do your feelings of guilt or shame inspire you to return the items you have purchased?

If you believe you may have CBD, we again strongly recommend that you seek the help of a qualified mental health professional. By its definition, CBD is not just overspending or "retail therapy." If left untreated, it can wreak havoc on your mental health, financial wellness, and your relationships.

Hoarding Disorder

We have all seen the images on TV of hoarders with boxes and magazines stacked up to the ceiling in every room and hallway in the house. *Hoarding disorder* has also been identified as a mental disorder in the *DSM-5*. It has been described as "accumulation and having great difficulty discarding objects that most other people would consider useless or of limited value; having clutter so severe that it prevents or seriously limits the use of living spaces for which the space was intended; and cluttering, acquiring, or difficulty discarding causes significant impairment or distress."[8] When people feel regret or refuse to part with items that no longer have use, they are possibly denying to themselves the recognition they have made a mistake.[9]

Research on hoarding disorder has recently focused on the obsessive-compulsion aspects of this behavior in attempts to better understand the potential environmental factors that may contribute to this behavior.[10] Interestingly, advancements in research have shown compulsive hoarding as a function of money attitudes,[11] and there has also been evidence that suggests hoarding behaviors are often modeled by parents.[12] But hoarding can take on many different forms. For some people, money is the primary object that is hoarded and can result in being unable to enjoy the financial success they may have achieved.[13]

If you believe that you, or someone close to you, may suffer from a hoarding disorder based on the preceding descriptions, it is important to seek the help of a qualified mental health professional. The following are a few questions that may help facilitate self-awareness of hoarding behaviors:

- Are you emotionally attached to material things?
- Does the thought of getting rid of items make you anxious?
- Have people ever shared concerns with you about how much stuff you have?
- When you buy new things (e.g., clothes, tools, furniture, etc.), do you (always/sometimes/almost never/never) clear out or donate the old things?
- If you think about the clothing and shoes in your closets and drawers, what percentage of those items have you worn in the past 12 months? What about the past 2 years?

Why don't we get rid of the stuff cluttering up our homes and our lives? Studies have shown a significant link between hoarding and a history of trauma. Having the direct experience of not having enough led to an entire generation of hoarders after the Great Depression. Sometimes we hold on to items because we have trouble admitting to ourselves that we made a bad purchase and wasted our money. We may create excuses for keeping things we don't need like, "This is a collectors' item"; "This is a souvenir from a trip"; "I am going to fit into this one of these days"; or even, "This will come back into style one of these days." These excuses are often attempts to rationalize our hoarding tendencies and avoid the pain associated with the recognition of our behavior.

The inability to de-clutter is a major reason we hang on to things we will most likely never use again, if at all. Sometimes hoarding and CBD intersect as we buy in bulk, convincing ourselves it was "a really good deal" or "I saved so much buying this way." Sometimes this behavior makes sense, but when it becomes a regular buying pattern and begins to make your home look like a Costco warehouse, you may have some hoarding behavior present.

Workaholism

Workaholism is a destructive financial behavior, which has not been formally established as a disorder in the *DSM-5™*. However, it is an addiction that is considered to be similar to alcoholism.[14] *Workaholism* has been defined as "...an addiction wherein the workaholic is highly involved in work, feels driven to work because of inner pressures that make the person feel guilty or depressed when not working, and in which the person has low levels of work enjoyment."[15]

Workaholism has been characterized both positively and negatively in research where the focus has been on the motivation behind the behavior.[16] It can be a serious relational and mental health problem, which has been associated with depression, anxiety, stress, low self-esteem, family conflict, and lower job satisfaction.[17] Workaholism is one of those behaviors that people tend to be more aware of. There is a sense of working to excess and neglecting other important things in your life, like family and relationships. Workaholics also get reinforced for their excessive work by increased pay and promotions. However, in the end, it leads to lower life satisfaction and an inability to enjoy nonwork time. For optimal physical and emotional health, it is ideal for people to seek to strike a work-life balance.

If you believe that you are a workaholic based on the preceding descriptions and you have difficulty changing your behavior, it may be helpful to seek the help of a qualified mental health professional. Here are a few questions that may help facilitate self-awareness of workaholic behaviors:

- Do you find it difficult to work less than 50 hours per week?
- Have people close to you complained that you work too much?
- Have you missed important family events due to work (e.g., birthdays, recitals, holidays, graduations)?
- Do you have a difficult time enjoying time off from work?

- Do you have difficulty delegating work to others?
- Have you gone years without taking a proper vacation?
- Have you made promises to work less to yourself or others?

If you recognize you are a workaholic, it is important to set aside time and resources to pursue nonwork-related relationships and activities. For many people, though, this is much easier said than done. However, if the workaholism is difficult to change, seeking professional help may be required.

Gambling Disorder

When you imagine people who suffer from a gambling disorder, you might visualize someone who spends time at a casino or a racetrack, or someone who has loan sharks after them. However, the modern gambling addict will often gamble online, which has made the behavior even more difficult to challenge. *Gambling disorder* has been identified as a mental disorder in the *DSM-5* and is described as a "persistent and recurrent problematic gambling behavior leading to clinically significant impairment or distress."[18]

Addressing gambling issues has recently been a topic of interest for financial research due to the number of individuals impacted. Gambling addiction can take on many forms, including activities seen in Las Vegas as well as even some active stock market traders, many of whom are tempted to trade on margin. The expansion of technology, 24-hour access to information, and new gambling laws have created the ability to expand sports betting exponentially. The rise of seemingly harmless fantasy sports betting has hooked a whole new generation into online gaming. Gambling disorder is now found in a wide variety of populations and is diverse according to gender, age of onset, types of gambling, and attitudes toward gambling.[19]

- Have you gotten into financial trouble because of your gambling?
- Have you borrowed money to gamble?
- Have people close to you expressed concern about your gambling?

- Have you tried to stop gambling but were unable to do so?
- Has your gambling interfered with your work?

If you struggle with problematic gambling, it is important for you to seek professional help. Gambling disorder is a powerful addiction, and it can be very difficult to stop without mental health support.

FINANCIAL BEHAVIOR CHANGE STRATEGIES

Changing financial behaviors can be tough. In many cases where a money disorder is present, change may require assistance from a qualified mental health professional. However, many behaviors can be changed through self-help. Often it takes more than just the thought or commitment to change, and that's where some useful self-help tools come into play. The following are a few exercises you can use to tackle some of the pesky financial behaviors you would like to change.

The "Here I Go Again" Technique

This technique involves breaking the automatic behaviors. It can be useful for financial behaviors you would like to decrease, such as over-spending. It helps you increase your awareness of the activity. A great place to start is to identify what precipitates the behavior. Are you shopping out of boredom? Are you giving money to others out of a sense of guilt? Are you seeking an endorphin high? A week of journaling your activity will go a long way to help heighten your awareness as to when your urge to engage in the behavior kicks in. What follows are Five Mammoth Moves to help you break a behavioral pattern. We use the example of overspending to illustrate the technique:

1. When you are in the process of shopping, say out loud: "Here I go again, shopping for something I don't need." Saying this phrase will help you bring awareness to your compulsive buying behavior.
2. Recall the last time your shopping experience turned sour and how you felt. Hold that feeling in your mind and imagine sucking on a lemon. Did you feel a twinge on the back outside parts

of your tongue as you visualized and recalled the bitter taste of a lemon? The facial expression and taste memory can serve as an aversive sensory anchor.

3. Avoid the temptation to rationalize your need to shop. In the addictions world, this type of rationalization is called "stinking thinking." Stop making excuses. Remind yourself that you have other, more important financial goals you would like to achieve and hold that sour lemon face and taste in your mind. Do your best to anchor that sour feeling to each rationalization you make about your shopping behavior. If you need to fix this behavior faster, physically place a lemon wedge on a plate in front of you at the time you are typically tempted to start shopping. Before you hit the "Buy" button, put a lemon wedge in your mouth. This can serve as a fast and deep sensory anchor, which can be planted in your subconscious and work to help you break the pattern of this pesky disordered financial behavior.

4. Find a replacement for the shopping activity with another activity that can be equally as satisfying, more sustaining, and less financially destructive. For some, this could be a mental activity, like a puzzle, a favorite TV show, a craft or hobby, listening to your favorite reaffirming emotional song, time with a friend, or physical activity like a walk, run, or weight lifting. If you can tie the replacement behavior to a similar endorphin release, all the better. The key is to get away from the shopping environment and find a healthier way to get that emotional fix.

The Ping-Pong Ball Technique

This behavioral change activity harnesses the power of our emotional brain by making behavioral change concrete, visual, and kinesthetic. We illustrate it in addressing someone who has a tendency to hoard.

1. With hoarding, there is always an "intake process," which precipitates the hoarding behavior. In other words, before you can hoard things, you must first obtain them. This is why the

acquisition of hoarding items becomes the initial trigger for the behavior that follows. So, in order to address hoarding as a behavior, we need to stop the behavior that feeds the hoarding beast. We start this process with an easier and engaging entry point. Go to your hoarding stash; journey into your cave of treasures tucked away and accumulated. Then look at what you see as if you are seeing it for the first time. Write down the grouping of items you see by common themes. Examples might be shoes, magazines, children's clothing/toys, coats, or whatever you can see in common. Next, note the size or quantity of the relative groupings.

- What are the items, or types of items, you tend to hoard?
- Are there favorite items, or does your pattern of items seem random?

Where do you go to acquire this large grouping of common items? Do you go to a certain store or website? Journal about how you acquire these items. Try to recall your feelings as you go through the process. Can you identify when these feelings start to create stress or anxiety? If there are no patterns or items in common, then it could be that you are more focused on the hoarding aspects and less about the items being acquired. In this situation, your behaviors could be associated with overspending or CBD.

2. Now turn your focus toward your resistance to de-cluttering. You can start in one area or with one type of item, such as clothing, for example. Go through your closet and separate out items you haven't worn in the past year. Get several storage bins and place these items, sorted in any way you like, into the bins. You are NOT getting rid of these items, just setting them aside. Label the contents of each bin and place them in a storage location you can access, if needed. Over the next 6 to 12 months, note how many times you open these bins, looking for a specific item. If you take items out to wear, you can keep them out in your closet. After a year, repeat the same process with another set of bins and move the ones from last year into the garage or other storage area less accessible.

To help overcome the feeling of wasting money on bad purchases, find a worthwhile source to donate your clothes to others who truly need these items. Seek out an organization that supports a cause you are passionate about. That way, if you were to donate your clothing from the bins you could feel really good about these items and didn't just waste your money. Depending on the organization and the value of the clothing you donate, you may be able to get a charitable donation receipt, which can potentially help reduce your tax liability at the end of the year.

You can then repeat this step with other items in your home wherever they exist. The positive feelings of de-cluttering will help you break the hoarding cycle through reinforcement. The goal is to become aware of the hoarding behavior at the time of acquisition and break that behavioral cycle.

3. Hoarding behaviors fill an emotional need, which could include feelings of safety, loneliness, or comfort. The mere thought of getting rid of items can cause anxiety. That's why it is very important to find a replacement for the hoarding activity, perhaps one that is even more effective in meeting your emotional need. Perhaps in an attempt to meet these emotional needs, you could make a point of connecting with others. The key is to break the cycle and replace the acquisition and hoarding behaviors with a more effective way to manage your emotions and get your needs met. Take some time to journal about what emotional needs are being met for you by these behaviors and make a list of other possible ways to get these needs met. Hoarding behaviors are not easy for people to overcome, and many people need to work closely with a mental health provider to help. This is part of the Money Mammoth evolution: We must face our challenges to change and grow, but we don't need to do this alone.

4. For the hoarding financial behavior workaround, you will need a few supplies:
   - 1 one-pint, glass, mason jar with screw-on lid
   - 10 white ping-pong balls

- 4 non-smear color markers with the following color scheme:
  - Red Marker—Words that describe how you feel looking at your stuff
  - Blue Marker—How you will feel if you could have a fresh start with no regrets
  - Green Marker—What other purpose you could use the shopping money for
  - Yellow Marker—New hobbies or passions you would be free to pursue

Separate the balls into two groups of five. Place five of the balls into the jar and lightly screw on the lid in place. Take the other group of five ping-pong balls and write one-word answers for each of the four color marker questions on all five ping-pong balls. In other words, each of the five balls will have four different color words on them. Each ball should also have different words, meaning you will need five answer words for each color (five new hobbies, five fresh start feelings, five unpleasant feelings, etc.).

The goal is to replace the white balls in the jar with your Mammoth Mindset colorful word balls. For each behavioral milestone, you get to take a white ball out of the jar and replace it with a colorful word ball, for example, every time you accomplish an initial de-clutter of a particular room in your home. You can find a worthy charity or drop-off donation box and help others who have a greater need, and there is always an incredible need. However, if you acquire more items that become a new part of your hoard (like CBD), a non-necessity item that will not be consumed by your family in a near term, you must place a white ball back in. The only way to accomplish this is to remove one of your colorful ping-pong balls, because only five will fit. If you unwillingly acquire items again and don't want to remove one of your colorful balls, you need to strike a balance and help others with another meaningful donation. To win and maintain your Money Mammoth evolution, you must fill the jar with your five colorful Mammoth Mindset balls, and keep it filled!

Display your jar in a prominent place at home or at work, where you can see it on a daily basis. Another useful strategy is to briefly explain the meaning of the jar to anyone who asks. Your hoarding behavior is nothing to be embarrassed about: It is a behavioral habit, similar to overeating, smoking, gambling, compulsive shopping, abusing credit, or bingeing on sweet and salty snacks. These are all disordered behaviors that can be self-destructive and are habit forming.

When you are able to turn your jar colorful, and keep it there for several consecutive months, you will be well on your way to changing your behavior for good. Your Money Mammoth Mindset is evolving, and you are living the positive words contained within your jar. If you are willing to share your experience, your friends, family, and colleges can be your change helpers, and you may even inspire them to tackle a behavioral change challenge. Other supportive people can serve as your behavioral change cheerleaders, reminding you how important you said this was, and encouraging you to carry on and persevere. They will applaud your progress and determination, and they will celebrate your success.

Keep the jar as a reminder of what you accomplished. On the day you pull that last white ball out, plop drop in your final colorful ball, hear that beautiful final click of all five finally together and complete, and seal that jar for hopefully the last time. You may even consider using this tool to tackle another behavioral change challenge.

Chapter 10: Mammoth Mindset Insights

1. To evolve your money mindset, you need to take an honest look at your financial behaviors.

2. Make a list of financial behaviors you know you need to address.

3. Once you have identified the behavior you want to shift and the Money Script® that has been keeping it in place, it is helpful to identify the situations in which the behavior occurs, so that you can interrupt the pattern.

4. With practice, you can identify these triggers and replace your destructive behavior with a positive action.

5. The seriousness and importance of recognizing and correcting these destructive financial behaviors cannot be overstated.

These conditions can be severe and cause significant financial, emotional, occupational, and relationship problems.

6. It takes courage to stare our finances in the face, but doing so is essential if we are to evolve our money mindsets and avoid financial extinction.

NOTES

1. B. T. Klontz, S. L. Britt, S. L., J. Mentzer, and T. Klontz, "Money Beliefs and Financial Behaviors: Development of the Klontz Money Script Inventory," *Journal of Financial Therapy* 2, no. 1 (2011): 1–20.

2. B. T. Klontz, R. Kahler, and P. T. Klontz. "Facilitating Financial Health: Tools for Financial Planners, Therapists, & Coaches," National Underwriters (2016): 121.

3. A. Canale, K. L. Archuleta, and B. T. Klontz. (2015). "Money Disorders," in *Financial Therapy* (Boston: Springer, Cham., 2015), 35–67.

4. B. Klontz and T. Klontz, *Mind Over Money: Overcoming the Money Disorders That Threaten Our Financial Health* (New York: Broadway Business, 2009).

5. E. Horwitz, B. T. Klontz, and M. Lurtz, "Money Disorders and Other Problematic Financial Behaviors," in *Client Psychology*, CFP Board (Ed.), Wiley Publishing (2018), doi:10.1002/9781119440895.ch17.

6. D. W. Black, M. Shaw, and J. Allen, "Five-year Follow-up of People Diagnosed with Compulsive Shopping Disorder," *Comprehensive Psychiatry* 68 (2016): 97–102.

7. Ibid.

8. D. F. Tolin, R. O. Frost, and G. Steketee, "An Open Trial of Cognitive-Behavioral Therapy for Compulsive Hoarding," *Behaviour Research and Therapy* 45, no. 7 (2007): 1461–70, https://doi.org/10.1016/j.brat.2007.01 .001; R. O. Frost, G. Stekette, and D. F. Tolin, "Comorbidity in Hoarding Disorder," *Focus* 13, no. 2 (2015): 244–51.

9. Brad M. Barber and Terrance Odean, "The Courage of Misguided Convictions: The Trading Behavior of Individual Investors," *Financial Analyst Journal* 55, no. 6 (1999), SSRN: https://ssrn.com/abstract=219828.

10. A. C. Lervolino, N. Perroud, M. A. Fullana, M. Guipponi, L. Cherkas, D. A. Collier, and D. Mataix-Cols, "Prevalence and Heritability of Compulsive Hoarding: A Twin Study," *American Journal of Psychiatry* 166, no. 10 (2009): 1156–61, https://doi.org/10.1176/appi.ajp.2009.08121789.

11. B. Benson-Townsend and N. C. Silver, "Compulsive Hoarding" (2015), https://doi:10.15406/jpcpy.2015.04.00228.

12. D. F. Tolin, A. Villavicencio, A. Umbach, and M. M. Kurtz, "Neuropsychological Functioning in Hoarding Disorder," *Psychiatry Research* 189, no. 3 (2011): 413–18, https://doi.org/10.1016/j.psychres.2011.06.022.

13. A. Canale and B. Klontz, "Hoarding Disorder: It's More Than Just an Obsession—Implications for Financial Therapists and Planners," *Journal of Financial Therapy* 4, no. 2 (2013): 4, https://doi.org/10.4148/1944-9771 .1053.

14. W. Oates, *Confessions of a Workaholic: The Facts About Work Addiction* (New York: World Publishing Co., 1971).

15. J. T. Spence and A. S. Robbins, "Workaholism: Definition, Measurement, and Preliminary Results," *Journal of Personality Assessment* 58, no. 1 (1992): 160–78, https://doi.org/10.1207/s15327752jpa5801_15.

16. C. S. Andreassen, M. D. Griffiths, J. Hetland, and S. Pallesen, "Development of a Work Addiction Scale," *Scandinavian Journal of Psychology* 53 (2012): 265–72, https://doi:10.1111/j.1467-9450.2012.00947.x.

17. Klontz, Kahler, and Klontz, (2016). Facilitating Financial Health: Tools for Financial Planners, Therapists, and Coaches, National Underwriters Co.

18. American Psychiatric Association, *Diagnostic and Statistical Manual of Mental Disorders* (2013), 585, https://cdn.website-editor.net/ 30f11123991548a0af708722d458e476/files/uploaded/DSM%2520V.pdf.

19. E. Blanco, H. Shen, and M. Ferrari, "Principles of Nanoparticle Design for Overcoming Biological Barriers to Drug Delivery," *Nature Biotechnology* 33 (2015): 941–51.

YOUR EVOLUTION

Your Transformation

To successfully evolve, you must change your beliefs and behaviors. In fact, as you expose yourself to new ideas, you are already immersed in the process of evolving. Research has shown that behavioral change follows a six-step process.[1] Psychologists have verified this change process across many domains, including behaviors such as the cessation of smoking, gambling, alcohol abuse, and eating disorders.

SIX-STEP PROCESS OF CHANGE

Becoming aware of the stages of change and understanding the change process can help you accomplish two goals: 1) identify where you reside within this process, and 2) accelerate your movement toward change. Once you know the path, you will be able to get to your change much easier. The six stages of change are as follows:

Stage 1: Pre-Contemplation

In this stage, you are in denial. You have little, if any, understanding of the problem and no acceptance or ownership for the solution. You may believe that it is no big deal or that it doesn't really matter. However, there may be an underlying feeling that life or some areas of life aren't ideal, but you have no interest in making a change or you are against the whole idea of changing.

Stage 2: Contemplation

In this stage, you have some recognition of a problem and an under-standing that your situation needs to change. You can identify some of the negative consequences of continuing your behavior and are tak-ing responsibility for some of what's happening. In this part of the change process, if change is going to occur, it is typically within the next 12 months.

Stage 3: Preparation

In this stage, change is anticipated within the next one to three months. You are getting ready to make the change, seeking informa-tion and gathering strategies to change. Rather than resisting change, your focus has shifted to formulating solutions and a plan of attack. At this stage, you are creating a vision of how you want a situation to be, which can help fuel your intrinsic motivation for change. During this point in the process, you may seek advice and guidance from experts.

Stage 4: Action

During this stage, your plans are put into action and implemented. You are actively engaged in making the change. Trying to get people to change before they are in the Action phase typically fails. For example, when people feel pressure to set a New Year's resolution to stop smok-ing, eat healthier, or start exercising, most of them fail to take sustained action. Often they are in the Contemplation stage, knowing they need to make a change, but they have skipped over the Preparation stage and have failed to adequately research and develop their strategies for sustaining their desired change.

Stage 5: Maintenance

In this stage, your new behavior has become a regular part of your routine. Depending on the change you made, this step can take three months or longer to achieve. Setbacks are common and should be expected during this phase. Having the support of a trusted friend, partner, advisor, or counselor can go a long way in helping you sustain your new behavior. Having a keen awareness of the indicators and triggers of prior negative behaviors is also very important to sustaining change.

Stage 6: Termination

Now the new behavior is fully integrated and becomes the new way of life. There is little temptation to revert back to prior behavior. Continued awareness and vigilance to protect against slipping back to negative behaviors are always a good safeguard.

CHANGE IN ACTION: RESULTS OF A FIELD TRIAL

Change can be tough. If you are predisposed toward financial denial and the thought of money matters makes you feel sick, a financial transformation can be especially challenging. Maybe just buying this book was a significant step for you, a spark to ignite change. As you read, have you been taking a mental inventory of what you need to do differently? If so, you are well on your way to transformation.

The iconic business best-seller *Good to Great*, by Jim Collins, was based on his research work with graduate students implementing regression analysis software to look for patterns of "exceptional company growth" using historical stock performance. The qualitative study on Level 5 Leadership was a spinoff study using the same research. *Money Mammoth* is based on two groundbreaking, published, academic peer-reviewed research studies, examining the effectiveness of financial psychology in the transformation of financial lives. The good news is that financial change is possible. In fact, our studies have shown that it can occur quite quickly.

For example, we conducted a study of employees in three companies, examining their involvement in their employer's 401(k) plan.[2] Employees were classified into two groups: 1) those who were already "engaged" in their 401(k) plans and 2) those who were "unengaged," and not contributing at all. After a one-hour employee retirement plan meeting, approximately half of these employees made a significant step and changed their financial behaviors. The following chronicles this study, which focused on creating financial change. It serves as a great example of how connecting your passions with your financial goals can make significant change a reality.

THE EMPLOYEE RETIREMENT PLAN MEETING DILEMMA

The research began when a major insurance company was looking to redesign its 401(k) employee retirement plan meetings in its workplace. The head of the Retirement Plan Division, we'll call him Jim, was a long-time veteran of the employee benefit marketplace. Jim had worked for several leading retirement plan companies for the past few decades. He had seen and tried almost everything relating to employee 401(k) retirement plan meetings. He was convinced that, after decades of trying to reach employees with the traditional educational approaches with marginal success, there must be a hidden influence impacting employee behavior. After all, 401(k)s make sense, and contributing to them is in the best interest of most employees. Jim, like most financial professionals, believed that if people had the right education they would behave in the right ways. However, after decades of well-informed trials, testing, and failures, there was still a significant number of employees in every employer group that simply could not be reached.

Jim read the available books, articles, and research on how beliefs, heuristics, and behaviors impact financial decision-making. He wanted to understand why employees continued to not engage in their employer-sponsored retirement plans when it was clearly in their best interest to do so. After his deep dive into the research, he was convinced that the solution to his problem was to redesign the employer's approach to the employee retirement plan meeting. However, Jim knew he needed to find experts to help guide their understanding of the employee's psychology so that they could develop a tailored-made solution.

Ask the Experts

Jim compiled a list of leading behavioral finance academics. He conducted a series of interviews over several months, looking for a solution. Jim described his desire to create a unique employee retirement plan meeting that would connect with these unengaged employees and get them to act in their own best interest. More specifically, Jim believed that insights from behavioral finance should be used in this new approach so they could address the employees' beliefs that were creating the unengaged behavior.

What Jim discovered was both surprising and frustrating. While these academics were adept at reiterating their research finding and describing the nature of the problem, they had very little, if anything, to offer in terms of solutions. In fact, many reverted to the typical approach of education, based on the assumption that if employees became aware of what was creating their unengaged behavior, they would change. Other researchers tried to bend the employee retirement plan meeting direction to more closely fit their current research projects, telling Jim that he was asking the wrong questions. As a result, Jim came away from these experiences doubting whether all this academic research on behavioral finance was simply a theoretical endeavor with little hope for practical application with his clientele.

Jim characterized these meetings by the following analogy. He saw the unengaged employees similar to people who were drowning because they didn't know how to swim. The experts, he said, could only talk about the fact the person was drowning due to the inability to swim, and described the many reasons that swimming lessons were not made available to people. Other experts described various methods by which people may avoid the risks of drowning, and some even suggested he focus on the education system in general because no one was teaching swimming in school. Jim observed:

All along, people were drowning. We were looking for the life preserver to throw these employees and help save their financial future, while all the experts kept describing why these people were drowning. It was like all they could do was wait for them to die and preside over the autopsy.

Jim recalled this experience as one of the most frustrating he had encountered.

"We really thought these experts were going to be able to help find our solution and that we were on the right path," he told us.

Jim now realized that the books and research he had read about behavioral finance were not applicable to helping individuals change their behavior. They were helpful in identifying problematic financial behaviors after the fact, but offered little to no value in actually changing people's financial behaviors. In essence, he found them useless to his pursuit to actually help improve the lives of these employees.

In the fall of 2014, Jim reached out to us in his quest for a solution. He said he had exhausted his options and wanted to hear our thoughts on his struggles to find a solution. After a series of meetings, we agreed to assist Jim and pursue a project to redesign his 401(k) employee retirement plan meeting in an attempt to engage the non-participating employees.

Understanding Money Scripts®

The first step with Jim's team members was educating them on the fundamentals of financial psychology. This centered around understanding heuristics and Money Scripts® that drive financial behaviors, and applications of financial psychology to facilitate behavioral change. Topics covered included a detailed training on Money Scripts® and the research that shows how they predict financial behaviors and outcomes. There was much discussion and a Q&A. One of the challenges was getting the team to recognize its own biases toward the way people make financial decisions—specifically, the belief that more education would be the answer.

Based on our research, we understood that the majority of their unengaged employees already knew they needed to save for retirement. In fact, it is hard to find an adult in the United States who doesn't "know" he or she should be saving for retirement. So more lecturing about the need to save for retirement was not likely to be effective.

The importance of understanding that other people may not think and make decisions the same way we do can't be emphasized enough. This is especially true of individuals who have money vigilance scripts or have financial backgrounds. These individuals believe that financial decision-making is an entirely logical process based on best practices. Therefore, they assume that if people just understood the importance of taking certain financial actions, then they would act on it. But that is just not how humans operate. For example, consider the obesity epidemic in the United States. People already know they should eat less and exercise more. As such, more education around eating and exercise is not likely to be helpful. What is needed is a psychological shift. Unfortunately, people who work in the financial services tend to think that just more education will be sufficient to shift behavior. After several weeks of education meetings, discussions, and dialogue, John's team was ready to dig into its first task: the development of *financial psychology avatars.*

Financial Psychology Avatars

The development of the financial psychology avatars involved a creative and collaborative session whereby the team began to identify behavioral patterns within its general population. They used the four categories of Money Scripts® as a starting point and created several hypothetical employee profiles based on hypothesized beliefs about retirement. The team was free to create these profiles based on what members believed about the way people thought about retirement. After much discussion, the team refined these avatars and gave each a name: *Suzy Status, Lonnie Lunchbucket, David Denial,* and *Vigilant Vicki.*

Interviews

The next step involved testing these avatar profiles. To this end, the team conducted over 75 in-person interviews with actual employees, asking questions about their financial beliefs and behaviors. This proved to be an invaluable process as the team emerged from these interviews with valuable firsthand insights. The team began placing each of the 75 interviewees into the avatar profiles by sharing their stories with the group and then voting. During this process, team members were able to better refine the avatar groups and modify their characteristics to more closely match their prospective marketplace of employees. More important, they began to see each of these individuals through the lens of their financial psychology. Collectively, they began to understand why their traditional education and information approaches had failed.

Key Conclusion 1: Messaging

With the financial psychology avatars well defined, the team began to discuss the types of messaging and approaches that might best resonate with each. More specifically, the team considered *why* these groups either engaged or avoided engaging in their employer-sponsored 401(k) plans. Through a series of financial psychology exercises, beliefs and motivations for participation were explored through the eyes of each avatar group. The team reached its first key conclusion, which was used as the basis for the formation of the employee retirement plan meeting.

The team felt the reason specific employee avatar groups failed to fully engage in their employer plans was due to the fact they were not properly motivated to save for retirement. In other words, they simply couldn't see or believe in retirement for themselves, and as such, participation in the 401(k) was just throwing money away that they needed now. This was the key in understanding those who would not engage.

When financial service companies come to this crossroad, most have decided to turn down the path of information and education. The rationale is that if people just understand the logical reasons why they should save and plan for retirement, participation would follow. We now know this is a largely ineffective approach to reach those in financial denial. Rather, the team realized the key was to focus on motivation for the desired behavior, which is inspired emotionally, not logically.

However, this decision brought with it a new set of challenges. How would the team incorporate an approach with specific messaging for the unengaged that didn't alienate the existing participating employees? The team went back to their interview files to identify foundational messaging that would resonate across all groups. The team also believed that the money vigilant employees were already locked in and committed to their retirement participation and were unlikely to be negatively impacted by this new approach. The research team identified this as an important variable that needed to be tracked and measured as well. The team then moved forward to focus on developing the approach that would motivate unengaged employees to action.

Key Conclusion 2: Motivation to Change

After being educated on the key ingredients of behavioral change, the team identified a second component needed to help shift their clients' behavior: motivation. The financial services industry has always believed, as with most salespeople, that it was *their responsibility* to motivate a client's behavioral change. In fact, the opposite is true. This was another example of an enormous wrong turn the financial services industry continues to make.

Research on behavioral change demonstrates that sustained change is only motivated intrinsically. In other words, for lasting change to occur, the motivation to change must come from within ourselves. Other people cannot motivate us to sustain long-term change. When we feel external pressure to change, whether it is from a spouse, a boss, or a high-pressure salesperson, any changes we make are likely to be temporary. In this case, only the employees themselves could create the motivation for lasting change. The challenge was clear: How could we design an innovative, emotionally focused approach for employees that would create the motivation to participate? Traditional educational and informational approaches had already proved ineffective for this group.

Key Conclusion 3: The Status Quo

As the development of the new employee retirement plan meeting took shape, the team needed to better understand the psychology of the unengaged employees. What was driving their lack of participation? One of the barriers to change is that change can be tough. It takes energy and can be uncomfortable. Ultimately, people tend to seek comfort and pleasure and avoid discomfort and pain. Saving for the future requires some immediate pain. You need to spend less now. It also requires effort to do something different. We are psychologically wired to prefer the status quo—to keep things just the way they are now.

Clearly, the engaged employees were willing to sacrifice pleasure today, enduring the discomfort of lower take-home pay in return for a secure retirement in the future. In other words, engaged employees placed more value on the anticipated pleasure of their future retirement than the pain of less take-home pay. In contrast, the unengaged employees were unwilling to make that sacrifice. They were not sufficiently motivated by their concept of retirement, and the thought of sacrificing and saving for it was a nonstarter. The question was clear: How do we build intrinsic motivation in the unengaged employees sufficient enough for them to overcome the status quo and actually change?

TELL ME A STORY. PAINT ME A PICTURE. SHOW ME!

The team then turned to delivery approaches with a focus on psychological techniques that have been found to be effective in shifting financial beliefs and behaviors. The team decided to utilize specifically designed, experiential, sensory-based approaches, including visualization techniques. In the meeting, employees would be invited to visualize their ideal retirement and create physical representations of what their retirement lifestyle would look like during the one-hour meeting. The approach turned out to be simple and powerful. In essence, the techniques allowed the employees to see what was possible for them, thereby creating the intrinsic motivation for creating this lifestyle. Best of all, the visualization exercise was fun. There was absolutely no discussion of numbers, graphs of investment instruments, or any other financial concepts or education. It's worth noting that the meeting approach was a dramatic shift from the traditional 401(k) signup meeting. This project would have never moved forward without an open-minded team that was willing to trust us and take significant risks.

The Facilitation Script

The final steps involved creating the language for the meeting, in which the new approach would be incorporated. It was important to present the meeting properly as its elements were likely to be quite unexpected for employees who were accustomed to traditional PowerPoint presentations. This is where specific attention was given to the messaging language of the meeting. We needed to pull the employees into this new approach for the diverse groups of employees who would be attending. Special attention was given to specific language that would appeal to the engaged and unengaged employees alike.

Second Thoughts . . .

After the intervention was designed, concerns began to emerge. This new approach was so radically different from the traditional meeting method used that the team worried if it would actually work. What would employers think of this new approach, and would they be willing to try this new meeting style with their employees?

The Study

The program was tested with three companies: 1) a regional bank, 2) a custom auto manufacturing company, and 3) a construction company. There were over 200 employees across the three companies that were studied. We classified employees who were currently participating in the employer 401(k) retirement plans as *Engaged* and those who were not participating as *Unengaged*. We tracked the effectiveness of the approach to see if it would: 1) decrease the number of unengaged by getting them to enroll in the plan and participate with payroll-deducted voluntary 401(k) plan contributions; 2) increase contribution rates in employees who were already contributing; and 3) increase the number of employees that requested and attended a follow-up meeting with a financial advisor.

The Intervention

The one-hour employee 401(k) retirement plan meeting had several elements designed to wake-up Unengaged employees while reinforcing savings motivations for currently Engaged employees. There was a specific focus to not include financial information in the presentation. There was no talk of investments, fund choices, historical performance charts, or even examples around the cost of *not* saving for retirement. The intervention used a specially designed visualization technique, a version of which is explored in detail in Chapter 13. The visualization exercise was designed to create a wakening and enhanced desire for the employee's ideal retirement lifestyle. The meeting incorporated a variety of sensory elements to encourage openness and creativity to set the stage for discovery and the creation of a detailed vision of an ideal retirement. As a final step, participants were provided with a totem or symbol with specific meaning and as a reminder of their motivation for savings.

The following story about one of the construction company employees illustrates how powerful the totem can be to help motivate achievement. Months after the employee retirement plan meetings were concluded, we were driving in the city where the company was located. At a stoplight across the intersection was a large gravel hauling truck also waiting for the light to change. Through the windshield of the truck, we could see the driver and steering wheel. There, on the dashboard of the truck, prominently displayed, was the totem this employee selected in the meeting. The driver seemingly keeps the totem in the truck as a daily reminder of the vision he is working toward and the sacrifices he is making toward reaching those goals. Totems can serve as useful tools to help override impulsive spending behaviors and serve as a daily reminder as to why delaying immediate financial gratification is so important. Whether a stuffed animal, a picture, a piece of jewelry, or some other representational reminder, we strongly encourage you to find a meaningful totem, one that reminds you of what's most important to you and why you are saving in the first place.

The Results

The results were quite remarkable. Among the three employer groups tested, the new employee retirement plan meeting resulted in a

38% reduction of the unengaged employees. We also observed a significant increase in contribution rates for the employees who were already engaged and participating. Finally, 86% of the employees who attended the meeting followed up and met with financial advisor representatives to discuss their retirement lifestyle visions that they had created.

The results of this new approach were inspiring. We had found an effective way to reach Unengaged employees and inspire them to become active 401(k) plan participants. The intervention was able to overcome avoidance and inspire savings behavior. For the most part, you already know what you need to do when it comes to money. That is why more education and information is NOT effective for you. We are emotional beings. To change our financial lives, we need to ignite our passion. Like the individuals in this study, the way to ignite our passion is by having a clear and exciting vision.

SUMMARY

One of the themes we have explored about human nature in this book is our instinct to seek pleasure and avoid pain. Our desire for the future state is needed to lower our perceived pain associated with the sacrifice of saving. The stronger our desire to attain the financial lifestyle we want, the more pain and sacrifice we are willing to endure to make it a reality. Ask yourself how well established in your mind is your future vision and how passionate are you in making that vision a reality. We explore how to firmly establish that complete vision in your mind in the next chapter.

Chapter 11 Mammoth Mindset

Reflection/Journaling Exercise

1. Can you recall a time in your life when you faced a significant challenge that required you to change your behavior (i.e., sports competitions, making a team, losing weight, passing a key exam)?
2. Do you remember your motivation to reach your goal?
3. Can you recall seeking out information and learning about your change?

4. Do you recall creating a plan, schedule, or routine for your new behavior?
5. What sacrifices did you make or challenges did you overcome?
6. Can you recall feelings of wanting to give up or quit? What kept you going, how did you persevere?
7. Can you recall, and try to journal in as much detail as possible, the moments and feelings you experienced as you achieved your goal?
8. Can you recall if that experience gave you the confidence or motivation to achieve another major goal after that?
9. **Key Mammoth Bonus Question:** What lessons and experiences can you take away from your past success story, which may help your transformation?

As you recall stories of your past successes, let this fuel your confidence that you can continue to transform your life and achieve the goals you seek. Using past success to drive motivation is a form of visioning used by prehistoric tribes before a hunt as well as coaches giving locker room speeches. Try to capture as much of your story as you can.

NOTES

1. J. Prochaska and J. C. Norcross, "Stages of Change," *Psychotherapy: Theory, Research, Practice, Training 38*(4) (2001): 443.
2. E. J. Horwitz, B. T. Klontz, and F. Zabek, "A Financial Psychology Intervention for Increasing Employee Participation in and Contribution to Retirement Plans: Results of Three Trials," *Journal of Financial Counseling and Planning 30*(2) (2019): 262–76.

Your Vision

Before you can get where you *want* to go, you need to know *where you are*. And to know where you are, you need to know *who you are*. Knowing who you are and where you want to go are essential elements of building your vision, which gives you the horsepower to get to where you want to go. It is critical to building intrinsic motivation.

AVOID THE "WHEN-THEN" TRAP

Avoiding beliefs like following will help protect you from one of the bigger money myths out there, known as the When-Then trap:

- "*When* I make more money, *then* I will be happy."
- "*When* I get that promotion, *then* I will spend more time with my family."
- "*When* I have $1 million, *then* I will be rich."

The problem, of course, is that the "Then" typically never arrives, which is part of the human curse. Psychologists call this the "hedonic treadmill" because we are wired to forever be dissatisfied. We are programmed to always want more, to never rest on our laurels. Ask any honest wealthy person and he or she will admit the following: "Make no mistake, having money is great, but it doesn't magically make you happy."

Now, of course, you don't believe this. Even if you have read all the studies you think to yourself: "Well, it might not make YOU happier, but it would definitely make ME happier."

Hey, look, we aren't going to judge. We get it. You are human and the hedonic treadmill is drilled into your subconscious. So go ahead and keep on moving. Set your goals and go after them. The fact is that after you are making enough money to meet your basic needs, more money won't magically make you happier. Your best predictor of your future happiness is your current level of happiness. So your job is this: Find the right mental attitude to maximize your feelings of happiness today. Right now. NOT tomorrow.

DISCOVERING WHO YOU ARE

If you want to evolve your money mindset, you need to know who you are—what you value most, whom you love, and what energizes and restores you. It is very important for you to find ways to act on those values TODAY and not wait until you have enough money to prioritize them. The key is to design your life to experience those values today. That's really the magic. If you don't have a clear picture of what gives you joy now, you will have difficulty ever achieving it. The challenge is that you are the only one who can find that place within yourself. For some people, this understanding is easily discovered, while for others, it's more elusive. It really depends on how in touch with yourself you are. Knowing who you are may take some time and reflection, but in the end, the more time you devote to the search, the more in tune to yourself you will become.

The more you can discover about what makes you happy today, the more effective you will be in creating a vision that is consistent with what you value most. This self-knowledge gives you the benefit of practicing happiness today and creating a future that contributes to and expands that sense of excitement, gratitude, and abundance. The search and understanding of who we are can be a winding and elusive journey. The path to reaching those answers lies within each of us. We are in the best position to identify and truly understand what areas, activities, people, places, passions create life energy for us. Engaging in/with these, and even talking to others about our favorite things, creates excitement and energy. Our brains can release endorphins when we are thinking about or engaged with our favorite people, places, and things.

Do you know who you truly are and what really matters to you? It helps to become aware of the times when you feel the most fulfilled, content, at peace, and joyful in your daily life. Be in the moment, and be aware of your feelings and moods as your emotions start taking over. Why are you experiencing this pleasure? Note what is occurring and try to tie it to the reason you are having these feelings. Try to put your finger on exactly where your joy is coming from. We are looking for the source of the feelings and what is the thing, action, activity connecting with you. A great place to start is to reflect and journal on what gives you the most joy in your daily life. What is it for you? When you are feeling the most connected, passionate, and alive, ask yourself the following questions:

- What am I doing?
- Where am I?
- Who am I with?
- What is so wonderful about this experience for me?

Likewise, painful or uncomfortable experiences are very important too. It is important to reflect on these also. Why are you feeling this way? A likely answer is that you are in a situation where you are doing something you do not like. This awareness tells you that this direction and/or activity is not a great fit for what you want. These feelings indicate a gap between who you are and what you are doing. When the gap between who you are and what you are doing becomes too wide, you will feel a sense of dis-ease, pain, or discomfort. Those feelings are your psychological alarm warning you that you are not living your best life. Your evolution requires you to be traveling along your ideal path. Don't mistake who you are with what you are doing. You owe it to yourself, your family, and your ancestors to tighten the gap between who you are and what you are doing.

When you have a clear picture of *who you are*, you can turn your attention to discovering *what you want*. Your vision for what you want is your opportunity to align who you are with what you want. In Chapter 11, we saw that employees failed to engage in their retirement plan savings because they lacked the motivation to save. However, once the employees connected with their ideal vision for retirement, the motivation to begin saving came almost instantly. That is an example of how powerful connecting what you want with a picture (or pictures) can be. When you can tie a vision-building exercise with your own pictures, the results can be very powerful.

ACHIEVING YOUR FINANCIAL GOALS

In a recent study, we used the power of knowing what you want to significantly improve people's chances of achieving their financial goals.[1] Our team tested whether positive emotions could be harnessed to improve financial decision-making. More specifically, we designed a double-blind, randomized control experiment to see if we could use people's emotional attachment to a nostalgic item to increase their emotional engagement in their savings behaviors and potentially improve their financial habits.

We randomly assigned participants into one of two groups: 1) a control group, and 2) an experimental group. Both groups were surveyed before the experiment, immediately after the experiment, and three weeks following the experiment. The experiment was a double-blind study, meaning that neither the participants nor the presenters knew which group they were in (experimental or control), nor were they aware of what was happening in the other group.

When participants arrived at the study location, the control group received a standard financial education presentation. This presentation focused on educating participants on the importance of saving, the power of compound interest, and various savings strategies, with time for questions and answers. In contrast, the experimental group participants did not receive an education on savings. Instead, they experienced a presentation that focused on immersive, emotion-based exercises designed to evoke positive memories and feelings. With these positive emotions evoked, the presentation shifted to naming these emotions and the underlying values, and how these values and emotions relate to their future savings goals. Three weeks after the study, both groups were contacted and reported back on their savings behaviors. The results were dramatic.

WHAT WE FOUND

Both groups significantly increased their rates of savings as a percentage of gross income. However, there was a significant difference with regard to the magnitude of these increases. While the control group participants increased their savings by 22%, the experimental group participants increased their savings by a whopping 73%—an increase three times greater. If maintained over the course of the year, this change could represent an average of $10,020 in annual savings for the participants in the experimental group, compared to their average of $5,838 in annual savings prior to the study.

A variety of savings beliefs and behaviors were also positively impacted. The experimental group participants showed statistically significant increases in their readiness to save, confidence toward saving, and their financial health from pre-experiment to post-experiment.

WHAT THIS MEANS: SEVEN STEPS TO ACHIEVE YOUR FINANCIAL GOALS

We hypothesize that the experimental group participants were able, through positive, emotionally charged visualization, to develop a deeper emotional incentive for saving money. The exercises they engaged in may have enabled them to more viscerally relate saving money to their family, life values, and goals that mean the most to them.

You must engage your emotional brain—your Money Mammoth—if you want to change your financial behaviors. If you want to improve your financial health, try some of the same exercises the experimental group participants experienced in the study to increase their own savings behavior. These seven steps can massively improve your chances of achieving your financial goals. Put these seven steps into action, and you will be able to get what you truly want.

Step 1: Choose Three Financial Goals.

To harness emotions and gain financial confidence, come up with an exciting vision of what you are saving for by asking yourself the following questions: What would saving for the future get you? What is it you truly want? Get specific: What does it look like? How would it feel to have it? Who might you enjoy it with? Where are you? What do you see, feel, experience? Identify at least three financial goals. A house, an early retirement, a vacation, a new car—what is it? If you're having trouble with this step, just sit back, close your eyes, and try to picture your ideal life 5, 10, or 20 years from now. Where are you? Whom are you with? What are you doing? Where do you live? What are you driving? How does it feel?

Step 2: Passion Test Your Goals.

For these financial goals, we want to make sure you really, really want them. You've got to be passionate about them. You've got to be hungry for them. When you think about your financial goals, we want you to be pumped! So look at each goal. If you can't give it a 9 or 10 on an excitement scale of 1 to 10, with 10 being the most exciting, then pick a different goal. So now that you have your three top financial goals—goals that absolutely thrill you—you can move on to the next step.

Step 3: Name Your Goals.

There's nothing more boring than a "savings account" and cutting out joy to fund it. Do you want to go out to eat or save $40? Umm . . . go out to eat. Do you want to save $5 or get a latte at Starbucks? I'll take the latte, please. How about putting $30 in the savings account or playing a round of golf? Is that a trick question?

Savings accounts suck, well, at least the name does. It is too boring, too nonspecific! Savings accounts are nothing to get excited about. We need to give our financial goals NAMES—specific, exciting names. We need give them names that conjure up images and feelings that thrill us. So instead of having a vacation goal, name your goal a Family European Vacation. Instead of a vehicle goal, how about a four-wheel-drive Toyota Tacoma? Instead of a retirement goal, call it your Financial Freedom Fund. Link your passion and excitement to the financial goal by naming it something exciting!

Step 4: Timestamp Your Goals.

Now, go back to your goal and add a date by which you want to achieve it. So your "Family European Vacation" goal could be your "2022 Family European Vacation" goal. Your "Financial Freedom Fund" could be your "Financial Freedom at 50 Fund."

Step 5: Picture Your Financial Goals.

Now, when we say "picture," we mean an actual picture, and this is where the activity gets fun. Remember, our research subjects who did this actually increased their savings rates by 73%, so you have to find a picture! For this part, we want you to imagine that you're back in kindergarten and it's time to have fun. We want you to find a way to create visual reminders of your savings goals. In our study, we had people use a poster board and draw words or pictures, or cut out pictures and tape or glue them. If you're serious about achieving your goals, it's worth a trip to an arts and crafts store to pick up a poster board and complete the step. Take some time to create visual representations of your financial goals. Cut out words and pictures; draw pictures; have fun. Spend some time with this.

Now create a visual motivator. For example, cut out a picture from a magazine depicting your goal and tape it to a mirror or hang it on a wall. Better yet, put a picture of your goal as your screensaver or smartphone wallpaper, where you can see it several times a day. Once you are done, keep this visual reminder close to you; carry it with you. These visual reminders are so powerful in helping to keep you focused on what matters most to you. They keep you passionate, motivated, and focused.

Step 6: Create Subaccounts

In this step, you're going to create specific savings or investment accounts for each of your financial goals. This technique is based on your natural tendency to separate your money into separate mental accounts. In this case, it will help you achieve your goals because a general "savings account" is easy to draw from; but "robbing" your Financial Freedom at 50 Fund for an impulse purchase is less likely to happen. Creating subaccounts is easy for investments like IRAs or 401(k)s that have their own account names. But you can also do this for other financial goals too. Many banks now let you divide your savings account into subaccounts you can name, and you can direct specific amounts of money to go to each one every month. So set these up and give them the names and dates you created in Steps 3 and 4.

Step 7: Automate Your Success.

Now that you've got a clear vision of what you want, a picture that you can carry with you, and you're passionate about getting what you want, capitalize on this clarity and passion to automate direct transfers from your checking account to your subsavings accounts. Stop reading and go do it right now. You may not be able to save all that you want to save right now, but you can revisit these and increase them as your income increases. If you set payments to pay for what you want most first, you'll surprise yourself as you quickly and easily adjust your lifestyle to get what you want.

Automation capitalizes on what we call the "status quo" bias, meaning because we have a natural tendency to just keep things the way they are, once we set up an automatic transfer, we will keep it going because it takes extra effort to stop it. So use the motivation you feel right now to set up automatic payments. Seriously, put the book down now, log into your bank account, and set up automatic monthly transfers from your checking account to your savings accounts. If your goal is an early retirement, research your options, like a 401(k) or IRA, and set up automatic payments, many of which can be taken directly from your paycheck. You can adjust to your new income shifts in no time, and before you know it, you will have made major progress toward your goals.

BONUS TIP: SOCIAL PRESSURE

Think of a supportive person in your life; this person could be your spouse, your partner, a close friend, or even your financial planner. Send him or her a message right now and let them know you want to tell them your new strategy to achieve your financial goals. Then set up a call and tell them about it. This will help you take action and stay on track. If you execute these seven steps, you're going to have a blast and these POWERFUL psychological motivators can massively increase your ability to achieve your financial goals. So let's make it happen!

SUMMARY

If you are like many Americans, you realize that you may need to save more for the future to reach your goals. But how can you bridge the gap between what you know you should do and taking the time and effort to make it happen? If your goal is to motivate yourself to save more, consider activating your emotional brain using one or more of the steps previously described. When we have a clear picture of what we want to save, when we can identify why it matters to us, and when we can experience on a deep, emotional level how great it will feel to reap the rewards of our efforts, saving more becomes not only possible—it becomes fun.

Chapter 12: Mammoth Mindset Insights

1. The most powerful visions are those we share with a loving and supportive partner.
2. To fully connect with your passion, your shared vision must be firmly established.

3. If you want to evolve your money mindset, you need to know who you are—what you value most, whom you love, and what energizes and restores you.

4. When you have a clear picture of *who you are*, you can turn your attention to discovering *what you want*.

5. Revisit your shared vision periodically, perhaps even once a year. You will likely see areas you want to add or remove, and the specifics may change along the way.

NOTE

1. B. T. Klontz, F. Zabek, C. Taylor, A. Bivens, E. Horwitz, P. T. Klontz, . . . and M. Lurtz, "The Sentimental Savings Study: Using Financial Psychology to Increase Personal Savings," *Journal of Financial Planning* 32, no. 10 (2019): 44–55.

CHAPTER 13

Your Relationship

Since disagreements around money have such a profound impact on relationships, we have dedicated an additional chapter to the topic. The ability to communicate with your spouse or partner about money is directly related to the health and quality of your overall relationship. One way to look at it is that the single biggest financial threat to someone is divorce. If you have witnessed it or experienced it yourself, cutting your net worth by 50% can be devastating. Many people never fully recover. Prioritizing frequent and healthy communication is not only good for the emotional well-being of you, your spouse or partner, your family, and especially any children you may have, it also has a fabulous return on investment!

In the following, we present 10 principles we believe are essential to making the most of our intimate relationships. These principles, or habits, apply to all forms of committed relationships in which the participants are striving to create, maintain, or enhance intimacy. This includes not only romantic relationships but successful business relationships, partnerships, and friendships.

1. ASSUME 100% RESPONSIBILITY FOR YOUR 50%

In any relationship conflict or impasse, it really helps to embrace the mindset that each party is equally responsible for the situation.

This responsibility lies in the dynamics of interaction, as problems do not arise in a vacuum. We do not believe there are any innocent bystanders. Period. We believe each person contributes to the impasse. The most productive action a couple can take is for each to reflect on his or her own individual contribution to the conflict.

The concept of being equally responsible for any particular relationship interaction is very difficult for many people to see at first glance because, in many incidents, it seems like there is an innocent victim and a guilty perpetrator. Almost always, we feel like we are the ones being victimized. In our experience, the couples that do the best are the ones that are able to take a *time out* when the discussion gets heated, replay the situation mentally, and identify things they might have done differently.

This requires each person to put on the hat of a relationship incident detective. In practice, when a couple gets to an impasse, we suggest they take a 20-minute cooling off period, relax, and reflect on what they could have done differently to change the situation. Was it my timing, a particular word or phrase I used, was I misplacing any anger, was I using humor inappropriately, and so on.

After this period of self-reflection, the couple comes back and each person shares his or her discoveries, quite often making amends. Each person suggests changes that he or she would like the other to make to prevent the same thing from happening again.

We share the concept of assuming 100% responsibility for your 50% early on in our work with couples. One woman recently told us: "If I have to agree to this concept in order to work with you, I will. But in all honesty, I can't think of one thing that I do that contributes to the problem." Now she is quick to recognize many of the ways that she negatively impacts not only her primary relationship but also all other important relationships in her life.

2. SPEAK YOUR TRUTH

You may have heard the saying "Don't Sweat the Small Stuff." Well, when it comes to intimate relationships, we disagree. Speaking your truth about the small stuff is just as important as addressing the bigger issues. Ignoring smaller irritants in a relationship can be just as problematic as the cowhand who ignores a small pebble lodged in his horse's hoof. This small pebble has the potential of permanently disabling the horse.

Like a good cowhand who cleans the debris from the horse's hoof, successful couples know it is the unspoken words, thoughts, and irritations, the unkept commitments that, like the pebble in the horse's hoof, can disable a relationship.

Silence erodes a relationship's foundation. We ask couples to recognize that if one of them has a complaint about the relationship, then they both accept that there is, in fact, a problem. This stands in stark contrast to the typical reaction of arguing whether or not there is a problem to begin with. In this scenario, we teach couples to speak their truth and listen to the complainer as if the relationship is at stake—because it is.

If irritants, big or small, are not treated as important issues, they have the potential of threatening the long-term health of the relationship itself. Intimate relationships require both partners to speak their truth, listen, and be willing to act when either member of the relationship identifies a problem.

3. LISTEN NOW OR PAY LATER

You may have heard the quip: "We have two ears and only one mouth because it's twice as important to listen as it is to talk." Though we don't actually know if this is the reason we look like we do, we do believe that, within the context of relationships, listening is at least twice as important as talking.

Many of us appear to be listening when another is talking, but in reality we are not truly listening. Instead, we are preparing our own response, our own arguments or rebuttals to what is being said. In relationships that work well, especially in times of struggle and conflict, it is critical, in that moment, for at least one member of the couple to drop into a reflective listening mode.

When this process is done correctly, a person can feel truly heard. They are also much more likely to be able to listen to you. If people feel heard, they feel safe. Safety is the foundation of intimacy.

In many situations, the simple act of listening, which allows someone to get the sense that they are finally being heard, immediately de-escalates the situation, and the conflict moves from impasse to resolution. Even if it does not lead to instant resolution, the energy of a conflict is frequently changed. Active listening deepens each partner's understanding of the other.

There is something magical about a person hearing information three times. The reflective process allows this to happen by having 1) the speaker share, 2) the listener reflect back what was said, and 3) the speaker then clarifying. These three components are at the heart of the reflective listening process.

We also encourage couples to listen with what we call the "The Beginner's Mind," which facilitates deeper listening and understanding and comes from meditative traditions. It teaches couples to see each moment as a unique and novel opportunity. It allows both people to be present in the moment for the actual experience, instead of judging, analyzing, and comparing it to situations that have occurred in the past.

If people are able to listen with a Beginner's Mind, they are able to let go of all assumptions and judgments about what they think their partner is meaning or saying. At this moment, there is no analysis or interpretation. To teach the concept of the Beginner's Mind, we ask people to pretend that instead of listening to their partner, they act as if they are meeting a stranger for the first time. We ask them to imagine they don't know the meanings of words, phrases, or concepts being spoken.

A hidden benefit of this type of listening is that being heard like this actually helps the speaker become clearer, not only with his or her partner, but even more important, with themselves.

4. KNOW THE ODDS

Noted relationship researcher Dr. John Gottman suggests that successful couples have a ratio of five positive interactions for every one negative interaction.[1] This 5:1 ratio is necessary for a relationship to maintain positive momentum.

A number of years ago, a popular counseling approach, called Transactional Analysis, led to an awareness of categorizing communication as being either a "warm fuzzy" or a "cold prickly." A warm fuzzy message or interaction makes people feel just that—warm and fuzzy. A cold prickly leaves them feeling bad. These types of transactions can be verbal, such as statements like "I love you" or "I am disappointed in you." They can also be nonverbal, such as a touch, hug, or a roll of the eyes.

With anything less than a ratio of 5:1, the relationship will not feel safe, and the partners will become conditioned to hear the negative and ignore the positive. A ratio of less than 5:1 leads to the loss of ability for one partner to influence the other, and when a positive statement, look, or touch comes, it is easily dismissed by the recipient. Expecting to hear something negative, he or she tends to shut down emotionally when the other partner starts talking. Dr. Gottman warns that negative interactions such as criticism, defensiveness, stonewalling (or going silent), or demonstrating contempt are especially corrosive to relationship intimacy.[2]

On the other hand, with a 5:1 ratio, a negative interaction, because it is relatively unusual, has none of the power that it does when the ratio is less than that. This ratio of positive to negative interactions provides what we call "money in the relationship bank." These deposits are available for withdrawals when the relationship is faced with significant difficulties.

5. LOVE IS NOT ENOUGH

Falling in love is a temporary chemical and spiritual event. The "falling in love experience" is to intimacy what an automobile's starter and first gear is to long-distance travel. Without it, you couldn't get moving, but it wasn't designed and cannot gather momentum, get very far very fast, or be able to shift a relationship to a higher and more satisfying level of intimacy. In other words, "falling in love" provides the potential promise of intimacy but is not intimacy itself.

Falling in love is actually a selfish act. That is, the person we are falling in love with is not only our partner, but ourselves. For example, we often find and learn to love our poetic selves, our playful selves, our creative selves, our giving selves, our funny selves. These "selves" often emerge in ways that are normally hidden until we meet our lover. When lovers in this phase of a relationship are separated from each other, they feel great torment and agony.

The staying-up-all-night conversations, poetry, pre-occupation, and not eating phase cannot be sustained for long. Scientists have discovered that the chemicals being released in the brain during this phase of a relationship are similar to those that are released when someone uses heroin. These chemicals go to the part of the brain responsible for attachment, connecting the individual to a person or substance in a similar manner. Perhaps this is nature's way of binding us together to increase the likelihood of successful pair-bonding, conception, and childrearing as a family unit.

Individuals can fall in love repeatedly, although at the time one is in love, they often feel that this particular lover is their one and only soul mate. Relationship disorders can involve an individual who is addicted to this initial chemical event, and seeking it exclusively, despite the consequences. Again, our contention is that falling in love is not intended to sustain the relationship in the long term, but a relationship grows in terms of intimacy over time. Intimacy is possible when two people make the commitment, have pertinent information about how to be intimate, and practice intimacy skill-building tools.

6. LOVE THYSELF

The quality of any relationship will be limited to the quality of the relationship we have with ourselves. In other words, we are limited in terms of how much love we can actually accept from another, how much we can allow in, based on our own belief of how loveable we believe we are. When expressions of love from others exceed the level of our own belief of our lovability, we will reject it. You cannot allow someone to love you more than you love yourself, just as you are limited in how much you can love another by your own sense of your lovability.

Want a quick assessment of the degree of love that you have for yourself? The next time you find yourself locking your keys in the car or making some other mistake, pay careful attention to the words you call yourself. Listen to your judgment of your actions right after you have walked from one end of the house to the other, arrived at your destination, only to find that you forgot what you went in search of.

Don't be surprised if these are some of the same words you find yourself thinking or using to describe someone else if they make similar mistakes. Actually, the words we ascribe to other peoples' actions and motives are the same as we unconsciously ascribe to ourselves. It is with the same degree of gentleness or cruelty that you will eventually treat your partner, and for that matter, your friends, your coworkers, even your children. The very best thing you can do to improve the quality of any relationship you have with others is to improve the quality of the relationship you have with yourself. Remember, no one can love you to a degree that is greater than that to which you love yourself.

7. NO CARRY-ON BAGGAGE ALLOWED

It would make sense that whatever skills we have developed, whatever our historic relationship experiences have been, the wounds, the victories, all of it will follow us into our next relationship. It is unavoidable. We all have a relationship history. From the moment we came into this world we were in relationships with others, and we bring all that history into the here and now, mostly subconsciously. Baggage is what keeps us from being able to see what is actually happening in the moment, hear what is actually being said. It puts others voices inside our heads and hearts and into our partner's words and actions. It is baggage that we were gifted by being children of our parents.

The key is to know ourselves well enough to understand what is coming into the relationship in the moment is about unfinished history or business triggered by a current event. The challenge is if we are not aware of the past being triggered, but believe the current situation is the cause of the current pain, nothing done can fix the underlying problem.

Slowly then, the initial feelings of love begin to fade. Partners who are not aware of their past and how it affects their current relationships lack the ability to distinguish between an issue that is current in origin and one that represents an unfinished piece of history. Most know this by its more familiar term of *emotional baggage*. Any unfinished emotional issues with parents, grandparents, grief, loss, trauma, and so on emerge and present themselves, disguised in the current relationship as a current event. Baggage like this can keep a person from being unable to actually hear, see, or speak in the here and now because it is all filtered through the old messages that the baggage includes.

The Carry-on Bag Story

One husband reported that early in their relationship his wife asked him to help her hang a picture on a wall. After getting prepared, he asked her to hold the picture up where she wanted. This seemingly simple request resulted in a fight.

Upon reflection, what had happened when he asked her to hold the picture while he pounded the nail in, triggered an emotional memory (not a conscious memory) of when, as a small child, she would ask her dad to help her do something. Instead of him showing her how to do it, he would do it himself and ask her to hold whatever she had asked him to help her with. Since the dynamics in her family were that you kept all upsets to yourself, this unfinished business came roaring into view decades later and completely took over the moment. Without this couple reflecting on what had happened, this piece of baggage would have had the potential to continue to be negative energy in the relationship.

How Complete Is Your Set of Luggage?

We pick up more baggage as we grow into adulthood, and the later baggage is piled on top of that from our childhood. The baggage shows up when someone tells us he or she loves us, and we wonder what this person really wants from us, what his or her hidden agenda is. Emotional baggage is what makes us recoil from a loving touch. It breeds "yeah-buts"—four-legged, little two-eared things that can overpopulate the lawn of our relationship. Falling baggage has crushed many a relationship, so there is no room for baggage on the relationship ship. Messages about money are just one category of lessons learned while growing up.

8. BEWARE OF INVADERS

Invaders are people, things, ideas, and beliefs that have the capability of coming between, impeding, interfering, taking energy from, eroding, and, if left unaddressed, destroying an intimate relationship. Symptoms of an invader existing in a relationship include if one of the partners complains about the time and/or energy the person or activity takes from the relationship, when secrets are kept about the activity, when a partner feels like he or she has to defend the activity, and if one uses the activity to relieve tension within the relationship.

Successful couples are able to put the partner and relationship as THE priority. This means the partner and relationship come before friends, parents, children, school, work, and, yes, even tennis. Successful couples make agreements to make the relationship one of the safest places on earth for them. They agree to not talk about, except in glowing terms, each other with other people without permission.

Interaction with all other aspects of the world is done collaboratively, rather than independently. If there are children, parenting is done after collaborative talk. Children are not permitted to collude with one parent or the other. Children know they cannot play parent against parent because the couple works as a unit. Family, friends, work, play, hobbies—everything, including finances—is dealt with from the position of the couple's collaborative efforts. Once there is a commitment to a relationship, there is no longer a focus on one or the other. The focus is on the relationship. Like birthing a child, the couple creates a new entity.

9. CHILDREN NEED NOT APPLY

Little kids don't have adult relationships. A successful relationship occurs between two adults. A child sees or hears something and reacts, often in an emotionally flooded way. He or she may fight, run away, freeze, or surrender in times of trouble. A child may also engage in name calling, throwing objects, slamming doors, going silent (the adult version of the childhood technique of holding one's breath), running away, tattling, or hitting. Self-soothing in inappropriate ways are adult versions of childish reactions. If children hear "No," they immediately go to "they don't love me" rationale. Kids are egocentric.

Fully functional adults under the same conditions are able to take a moment to choose from a number of possible responses, not the most immediate reaction. Adults should know who they are, how to discover what they want, how to ask for what they need, and can see the big picture; they have the ability to put things in context and know how to negotiate. Adults should know that no one can make them feel responsible for their feelings.

There is a wonderful place for childlike reactions in an adult relationship. This is the space occupied by unconditional love, wonder, play, and delight. These are the very best aspects of childhood. While little kids believe the world revolves around them, adults see that they influence and are influenced by a bigger picture.

10. SAFETY FIRST

A successful intimate relationship, for one thing, means that it is a safe one. In order to have a safe relationship, we need to build in safety devices. When engaging your partner, you need to make sure that your timing is right. Rather than ambushing your partner when you have something important to talk about, simply asking the question, "I need to talk to you about something important, is now a good time?" is hugely beneficial. If the answer is "Yes," it is helpful to remind your partner of your intent. For example, "I want to talk about this before it turns into something bigger than it is." It is important for couples to delineate "fair and foul" territories in the way they engage with each other. Using phrases like "You always" or "You never," interrupting the other person, changing the subject, ignoring the other person, walking out of the room during discussions, and not keeping commitments are examples of things we suggest couples put on the list of "foul" behaviors.

Couples need to have the skills to defuse a tense situation. Time-outs, methods of self-soothing, and negotiation skills are among those important skills. It is essential for the individuals in a relationship to know when they need outside help. Statistics show the average couple that needs professional intervention waits seven years before they seek help, and even more astounding, only 1% of them ever do.

EXERCISE: CREATING YOUR RELATIONAL FINANCIAL VISION

A financial lifestyle vision does not exist in a vacuum. The most powerful visions are those we share with a loving and supportive partner. To fully connect with your passion, your shared vision must be firmly established. The following are the essential elements for a solid vision of your future:

1. **Shared:** between partners
2. **Clear:** in your minds' eye
3. **Articulate:** how it makes you feel
4. **Sensory:** describe using ALL senses
5. **Compelling:** makes you want to be there now
6. **Source of Happiness:** puts a smile on your face
7. **Sacrifice:** something worth saving for

THE SHARED VISION PROCESS

A great place to start is to build your visions separately. Set aside time and commit to several hours to complete this process. Make sure your working environment is clear of stress and potential distractions. For this process, you will need a device that allows you to access your photo library and the ability to create new folders and place copies of photos in those new folders. The photo program you use for this exercise should also allow you to create a quick slideshow from the photos in the new folders you will create. Note: Most smartphones have this capability.

Step 1: Find separate spaces where you can take your device and access your favorite photos. Find a place that is relaxed and allows you a comfortable place to work.

Step 2: Establish a time limit you would like to initially work apart on your visions. Usually 45–60 minutes is a good start. Set an alarm, and at the end of that time, check in with each other and see if you are ready to share or if you need more time.

Step 3: Identify five lifestyle categories that appeal to you. Here is a list of possibilities, but of course, you can create your own:

- Location: Where you want to live.
- Family: I want to be close (proximity and/or emotionally) to the following family members.
- Friends: I want to be surrounded by the following circle of friends.
- Pets: I want to have my pets close to us.
- Type of Home: I want to live in a place like this....
- Alone Time: When I spend time alone, I want to be doing this....
- Together Time: When we spend time together, I want to be doing this....
- Fun Time: I want to make sure we have plenty of time to have fun.
- Family Activities: My favorite thing to do with our family is.../

- Friend Activities: When friends and family visit, I want to do this....
- Travel: I want to go to....
- Food: Here's what we love to eat....

Step 4: Create five files, one for each lifestyle category you have selected.

Step 5: Review your photos and begin placing the ones that represent your ideal retirement lifestyle into the designated folders. If you can't find a photo that represents your goal, try to find one on the Internet. In the interest of time, you may want to limit the photos to 10–15 per category. Identify/mark your favorite photo from the 15 in each group.

Step 6: It's time to share your visions. Decide who will share first and who will listen. The presenter will go through each category and briefly describe why this group is important to include in their Top 5. The presenter will go through the pictures using a slideshow format, using the background music of his or her choice. At the end of each group, the presenter will reveal his or her favorite photo and explain why it is so loved. The listener's job is just that: listen. Do not talk, comment, interrupt, or make remarks during the presentation. Smiling and laughing are permitted, crying too. Look closely at the pictures and seek to understand the emotional connection they have, and see if you can understand the motivation underlying your partner's connection to these images.

Step 7: Switch presenter and listener roles and repeat Step 6. Notice the similarities and differences in groups and even pictures.

Step 8: After both people have presented, each person can discuss his or her favorite parts of the other's vision. Again, one person talks uninterrupted and the other listens. Then change roles and share again.

Step 9: Identify areas of overlap and discuss them. How can you work together to flesh out what these retirement lifestyle choices will look like? Sometimes this involves negotiation; sometimes it involves compromise. You may even want to combine your overlapping groups into one shared vision folder, and combine pictures within groups if you selected similar categories.

Step 10: Identify areas that are different. Perhaps your partner identified an area that you forgot but is also very important to you? Or, perhaps, it doesn't relate to you at all. When this occurs it is quite normal. In your planning, you can look for ways to support your partner's dreams and desires, even if you do not share them.

Step 11: Reflect on your shared vision. Is this vision of your future compelling to you? Is it exciting? Do you want to begin living this lifestyle as soon as you can? Are you willing to make savings sacrifices to make this vision a reality? Do you want to explore in more detail how much you might need to save every month to make that lifestyle, or something close to it, a reality? If you answered "Yes" to these questions, you have created a compelling vision to fuel your passion.

Chapter 13: Mammoth Mindset Insights

1. Assume 100% responsibility for your 50%.
2. If irritants, big or small, are not treated as important issues, they have the potential of threatening the long-term health of the relationship itself.
3. Intimate relationships require both partners to speak their truth, listen, and be willing to act when either member of the relationship identifies a problem.
4. In many situations, the simple act of listening, which allows people to get the sense that they are finally being heard, immediately de-escalates the situation, and the conflict moves from impasse to resolution.
5. With anything less than a ratio of five positive to one negative interactions, the relationship will not feel safe, and the partners will become conditioned to hear the negative, and ignore the positive.
6. The very best thing you can do to improve the quality of any relationship you have with others is to improve the quality of the relationship you have with yourself.

7. Emotional baggage can keep a person from being unable to actually hear, see, or speak in the here and now because it is all filtered through the old messages that the baggage includes.

8. Invaders are people, things, ideas, and beliefs that have the capability of coming between, impeding, interfering, taking energy from, eroding, and, if left unaddressed, destroying an intimate relationship.

NOTES

1. J. M. Gottman, *Why Marriages Succeed or Fail* (New York: Simon & Schuster, 1994); J. M. Gottman, J. Coan, and C. Swanson, "Predicting Marital Happiness and Stability from Newlywed Interactions," *Journal of Marriage and the Family* 60 (1998): 2–22.

2. John M. Gottman, James Coan, Sybil Carrere, and Catherine Swanson, "Predicting Marital Stability and Divorce in Newlywed Couples," *Journal of Marriage and Family* 60, no. 1 (February 1998): 5–22.

Your Plan

This book is not intended to give you specific financial advice. Everyone's financial situation is different, and financial advice needs to be shaped to your particular needs and circumstances. However, you don't know what you don't know. As such, we wanted to flag some areas of critical importance to your overall financial health and share some foundational financial best practices. As a disclaimer, the information that follows is not necessarily right or appropriate for you and your specific circumstances. However, it is based on the collective wisdom and generally accepted practices of financial experts. To examine your specific situation, we strongly recommend that you meet with a financial planner who is qualified (e.g., a Certified Financial Planner, CFP®) and is also someone who puts your interests before his or her own and does not withhold important information from you.

To develop your plan, you need to combine two elements: 1) your vision for your desired future (e.g., your financial goals) and 2) the path you need to take to achieve it. In other words, you need to know what you want and how to make it happen. While the psychological aspects of managing your financial life are critical, you must combine them with a practical, strategic approach to achieving your goals. A vision without an actionable plan is nothing more than a pipe dream.

To harness the power of financial psychology to achieve your goals, you need a plan.

ARE YOU READY TO TAKE ACTION? (IT'S OKAY IF YOU'RE NOT)

As you may recall from the behavioral change process in Chapter 11, it's going to be challenging to make changes unless you are firmly in the *Action* stage of change. This is when you are fired up to make changes happen. Your desire and motivation for change becomes greater than your fear of or resistance to change. If you feel you are not there yet, the thought of developing a plan of action may seem like more trouble than it's worth. You may sigh or groan at the thought of all of the effort it is going to take.

Don't worry, this means you are currently in the *Contemplation* or *Preparation* stage of change and need a little more time to get ready. Specifically, we encourage you to go back and do some more work on your vision. Try to make your vision more real for you, more exciting. Spend time thinking about what gives you joy and drives your passion for learning and doing. Imagine that you have one day a week right now that is totally yours to enjoy—no other responsibilities or obligations. What would you do with it? Where would you go? Who would you spend time with? What would you like to learn more about?

Continue to build your vision with details—the more the better—and try to picture yourself in that environment. How does it make you feel? How can you make it even better? Paint a mental image of what you most desire. If you can't picture what you want to accomplish, you will have a very tough job of making it happen. In fact, this lack of vision and fear and uncertainty around it is a major reason that many people sabotage themselves. If you have forgotten who you are and what you love, you may need to explore this in more detail with a counselor or therapist.

Once your vision becomes exciting and compelling, you will build your intrinsic motivation to make it happen. Your desire to make your vision a reality will overshadow your reluctance to take charge of your financial life. Your fears will melt away, and you will embrace a mindset of accomplishment and success. You will be in control. Don't be afraid to seek financial security, wealth, independence, freedom, and the means to help others. Don't you and your family deserve that?

MONEY MAMMOTH EVOLUTIONARY PATH

Vision => Motivation => Planning => Action => Transformation

The preceding Money Mammoth Evolutionary Path is unlocked through a deep understanding of your true self—knowing your motivations, biases, Money Scripts®, personal past, and triggers. A passionate vision creates motivation and energy to plan. The speed at which you reach your goals is up to you.

START HERE: BUILDING YOUR MAMMOTH FOUNDATION

We believe the best way to think about your plan is by looking to best practices. What follows is a framework designed around foundational personal finance elements. This is meant as general information and areas for you to consider, not as financial advice specific to your situation. Given that we are college professors in finance, among other roles and experiences, we would be remiss to pass on this opportunity to share some baseline financial education. For those of you who are more financially experienced, this may be a refresher or review of pragmatic and effective best practice. Even the most experienced individuals may notice an area in their financial life that needs more attention.

An important point is that there are many considerations and personalized calculations associated with a well-constructed and comprehensive financial plan. While it would be ideal for every American to seek a comprehensive financial plan developed just for them, the reality is that many are not accessing this service. As a result, many are left holding the responsibility for their financial well-being without education in basic personal finance. To help fill this gap we are going to provide you with a few basic financial concepts and practices needed for a solid financial foundation.

While many financial problems can appear seemingly complex, oftentimes the solutions to fixing them are sometimes quite simple. When you look at most of the personal financial challenges Americans have, they come down to just a handful of issues: lack of liquid emergency savings, too much personal debt, spending beyond one's means, and compulsive wasteful buying that robs personal net worth. By understanding the fixes associated with these financial pitfalls, you will be more than well on your way to establishing a solid financial Money Mammoth base from which to expand and grow your financial plans.

These components are presented in three segments: 1) survival, 2) hunting and gathering, and 3) adaptation versus extinction.

SURVIVAL

There are several areas you will need to address to ensure your basic financial survival. Many people who have faced financial catastrophe have failed to adequately address one or more of these areas. This is not meant to be an exhaustive list, as everyone's financial situation is different. However, these are areas we commonly see that have gone unaddressed and can cause significant problems. Based on your unique financial situation, you can best decide the order in which you address these areas. You will likely need to establish or update your will and financial and healthcare directives; address guardianships; and establish any needed trusts. You will also likely need an emergency fund to float three to nine months of expenses. You need to get any personal debt under control and try to avoid revolving credit card balances. It is also very helpful for you to establish a monthly baseline for expenses, which can be done by tracking your household expenditures and income. Last, you will want to make sure that your assets, income, and family are adequately protected. We will dive deeper into several of these areas of financial best practices in the following, including explaining some critical elements and some industry jargon you may come across.

Establish Will, Healthcare Directives, Guardianships, and Trusts

Many people do not have a will or have wills that are out of date. With simple will kits, online legal document preparation resources, and local estate attorney offices, there are many ways to accomplish this important Mammoth Move. If you have children and/or dependents, you will need to address guardianship and expenses for raising your dependents until they are of legal age. Additionally, depending on your specific situation, establishing and funding trusts may be in order.

Our recommendation would be for you to establish a relationship with an estate attorney who can help you get the legal advice you need. Most financial planning firms have relationships with estate attorneys they use and could help make a referral for you. Medical and financial powers and directives are equally important to have in place. At some point you could be in a serious accident or illness that makes it impossible for you to make financial and medical decisions. If you do not take steps to set up financial and medical directives now, you may be leaving the people you love most with a terrible mess in the midst of perhaps the hardest time in their lives.

These directives allow a person you designate to make medical and financial decisions on your behalf when you cannot. Ideally, you would discuss your desires if these situations were to arise with your designee to make sure your wishes would be carried out in the manner you desire. Also, you should let the person know you would like him or her to be your designee instead of surprising the person later at the time of the crisis. Medical and financial powers and directives can be handled along with wills, trusts, and guardianship matters through a good estate attorney. Many of these directives lay dormant and "spring" into action if you become incapacitated.

NOTE: Never give anyone a general "power of attorney" unless you have consulted with an attorney you have hired to represent you.

Track Your Income and Spending for Three Months

Ugh! We know. Sorry! Unless you are an engineer-type personality, chances are you hate the thought of doing this. However, this can be a very transformational exercise. Often, when you do this, change requires very little effort. Most people are shocked when they see where their money is actually going. Getting a clear picture of what is happening addresses this simple concept: You can't manage what you don't measure.

To better understand your monthly spending, you need to see where your money is going. You can either keep track in a notebook or you can find an app you like. There are several helpful apps for managing your household budget, such as "Mint" and "Wally." Many banks are now providing apps for tracking income and expenses. In fact, these apps will do much of the heavy lifting for you. You just turn them on, link up your accounts, and they will track your income and expenses for you. You may need to go in and make sure their system is correctly classifying your expenditures into the correct categories, but they will give you an excellent start.

Month 1

Whatever system you decide to go with, start at the beginning of the month. Note all your fixed household expenses (e.g., rent/mortgage, utilities, etc.) and other purchases (using cash or credit). For this month, focus on capturing as much of your income and expenses as you can to determine your *net monthly cash flow* as accurately as possible. You will use this as your baseline and track the next month's income and expenses the same way.

Month 2

Now that you have captured your monthly cash flow, create two categories: 1) "ND" for non-discretionary and 2) "D" for discretionary. ND expenses are items you are committed to by contract or obligations, and D represent expenses you decide to make each month. For example, a mortgage, car payment, utility bill, and property taxes would be ND expenses, while clothing, grooming, gardening, and dinners out would be D expenses.

Month 3

In the third month (and beyond), notice patterns in your spending. Sometimes becoming conscious of your spending will lead to immediate and effortless shifts in your behaviors. Look for patterns in your spending. Do any of your expenditures surprise you? Are they in line with your values? Are there areas easy for you to cut or reduce to improve your net cash flow? If a surplus doesn't already exist, work to create one by cutting back your spending or increasing your income so you can meet your goals in the next section, which includes setting aside adequate money to meet your savings, retirement, and other financial goals.

Establish Your Emergency Fund

Financial planning best practice indicates that you should have three to six months of household living expenses saved for emergencies. Many people who blew off this personal finance gem suffered significantly during the societal shut-down that accompanied the Covid-19 pandemic. In general, single income households are recommended to hold six months of expenses, while dual income households should hold at least three months. Emergency funds should be placed in liquid accounts in cash (e.g., savings accounts) or near-cash equivalents (e.g., certificates of deposit, money market funds).

Emergency funds should be used only for unexpected household emergencies like a broken appliance, medical emergency, or temporary job loss. When these situations arise, these funds can be accessed if no other funds are available or you would otherwise need to use credit card debt. Emergency funds are to be held sacred and are *NOT* to be used for vacations, clothing, gadgets on sale, or concerts. You should establish savings accounts for these other goals, but in a different account. It was recently reported that over half of all Americans couldn't pay for an unexpected emergency of $400 without using debt, meaning that 50% of Americans have absolutely no liquid savings or emergency funds.[1] Of all the financial information we see reported in the news relating to how bad of a job Americans generally do regarding personal finance, this statistic is the most troubling. You need to look at your monthly household budget and find a way to save as much as you can toward your emergency fund until it is fully funded. This should be one of your top financial priorities.

Take Control of Your Personal Debt

Payments on monthly credit card and other consumer debt are a cancer to your financial health. To build wealth, you need to shift more income to savings. To shift more income to savings, you need to create more free cash flow through reduction in debt service payments. Once you get a clear picture on your monthly expenses and cash flow, you will be able to identify areas for reduction in discretionary expenses. Then you can tackle paying down credit card debt, starting with the highest rates first. Technology can be helpful for this also, with apps such as "You Need a Budget" that can help you manage debt. For this strategy to work, you will need to be committed to limiting future credit card purchases to only those you can pay off in full each month. Once you hit a tipping point where your balances start to fall and your payments begin to get smaller, you will have more monthly income to help pay down debt. As a result, the pay-down of debt accelerates. However, this strategy only works if you can stop your overspending. We have provided tools and techniques in previous chapters to help you understand and address financial behavior problems. Use your tools, use your vision for motivation, and follow your behavioral trigger work-arounds from your journaling. If you get stuck, then seek professional help. You can do this. We believe in you. Make your personal debt elimination one of your top priorities. It is critical to your financial survival.

Protect Yourself

Knowing all the types of insurance coverages you need, as well as the right combination of benefits and amounts, is an overwhelming task for anyone. However, you need to know enough to make sure you aren't buying policies you don't need and to make sure you have what's important. To that end, we provide some simple explanations of some key insurance coverages and what each protects. We also include and define some of the jargon you will run across, as the insurance industry is full of unusual terms, which only adds to laypeople's confusion. Additionally, we provide a few tips that may help you avoid mistakes and save you money. This is *NOT* an exhaustive list of insurance coverages, and we may not address something that is critically important for your individual situation. As such, we strongly encourage you to work with an insurance professional for coverage specific to your individual needs.

Understanding Insurance Survival

Let's begin with a few basics and terms. The purpose of any insurance policy is to compensate you for a financial loss you have suffered or for which you are held responsible (aka to "indemnify" you). In essence, insurance is designed to put you back in the financial position you were in prior to the loss. The purpose of insurance is not to fully indemnify you for all costs or expenses or to help you profit from the situation. The use of deductibles and co-pays are used to discourage people from taking advantage of insurers as well as help keep costs down through a small amount of personal risk retention. For any risk you are taking for which you do not have insurance, you are thought to be "self-insuring."

Asset and Property Protection
Homeowners and Renters Insurance

Your personal assets, your home, and potentially some of the other structures on your property are typically protected under a homeowners or renters policy. Almost all insurance will have a list of *perils* (aka the causes of a loss) and actions/events that are *excluded* from claim. It is important for you to find the list of Covered Perils and Exclusions under your policy or ask your insurance agent to point them out to you. Read them carefully and make sure there isn't anything on that list you feel you would need protection from based on your specific circumstances. Many people who are frustrated with insurance claims are upset when something isn't covered, and on closer examination, the specific peril was clearly either not covered or excluded in the policy.

Most homeowners policies have several sections related to various areas of coverage. Typically, Coverage A is your dwelling and Coverage B is for detached structures. If you have your dwelling covered at levels equal to or greater than 80% of the home's *fair market value* (aka the price to which a buyer and selling would agree in the current market), you will typically have replacement coverage for your home and detached structures. Detached structures are usually covered for 10% of the coverage amount for your dwelling, while your *personal property* and contents (Coverage C) are covered at 50% of the coverage amount for your dwelling. It is important to note that *personal property* is typically covered on a current market value basis for that item and *not* a replacement cost basis (the cost of buying it new), but you can purchase a rider for replacement cost coverage if desired. Finally, Coverage D is for *loss of use,* which is typically covered at 30% of the coverage amount for your dwelling, and covers indirect expenses incurred while a property was damaged. For example, if a fire destroys your home and your family needs to rent another house while your home is being repaired, those expenses would represent a *loss of use* claim.

Renters and condominium owners policies are similar to homeowners policies, but with some differences. For example, a renters policy covers the renter's property and contents but has no coverage for the dwelling and detached structures since the person is renting. The condo owner's policy is similar but provides a small amount of coverage for detached structures since shared common areas often exist. All three types of policies, homeowners, renters, and condos, have similar coverage for *liability risks,* which is discussed in the next section.

Auto Comprehensive and Collision

Auto insurance is another common area of coverage. Comprehensive and collision is the section of the auto policy that covers damage to your own car. The damage can come from *collision* with something or damage caused by something else (*comprehensive*). Glass breakage, theft, hit and run, vandalism, and collisions with animals are all covered under the *comprehensive* portion. These coverages have several deductible amounts from which you must choose. Make sure to compare the different premium costs for increasing your deductibles. Remember, if you have a good emergency fund established, you can self-insure with higher deductibles and lower premium costs. This can help boost monthly free cash flow and help accelerate your savings.

Sublimits and Riders

Assets like electronics, jewelry, and collectibles are typically limited to maximum loss amounts between $1,000 and $2,500 each. Similarly, all electronics that are not permanently attached or dealer installed in your vehicle (i.e., radar detectors, GPS) are typically excluded from coverage. These would have to be covered under your homeowners policy and would be subject to the sublimits. After deductibles are paid, you may get little or nothing back.

If you own assets that exceed these limits, you may decide to *schedule* (aka list) these assets as a *rider* (aka addendums or endorsements) to your policy. You can purchase a rider or *endorsement* that changes or modifies various aspects of your policy, such as asset valuation at time of loss. Exploring riders and endorsement is an important part of getting the right coverage, so have your agent quote this separately so that you can see the costs associated with each and make an informed decision.

Scheduling Property

Scheduled items are typically for a specifically stated value (aka agreed value) based on an appraisal or receipt. Unfortunately, this type of property coverage can be expensive, but losses of these items typically do not require the payment of a deductible. The good news is that the insurance company breaks out the cost of scheduled item coverage so you can clearly see what it costs. Once you see the cost you can decide if you want to include that coverage. If it's an item like jewelry, you may decide a home safe or safety deposit box provides adequate risk protection against theft or fire.

Samples of Valuation for Property Loss

Another area of importance is how your asset will be valued at time of loss, known as its *valuation*. Payment and indemnification for losses on covered property items are valued in different ways. The following list is a basic list of typical valuations on types of property.

Asset Type	Typical Valuation (Unendorsed Policy)
House and Attached Garage	Replacement Cost*
Detached Structures	Replacement Cost*
Scheduled Property**	Stated, Agreed, Appraised Value
Personal Property and Contents	Current (Fair) Market Value***
Car/Boat/Motorcycle/ATV	Current Market Value

*Typically requires that home is insured for at least 80% of current market value.
**Scheduled property typically doesn't pay policy deductible for losses.
***Certain asset types may be subject to sublimits (i.e., jewelry, electronics).

Claim Loss Example of Valuation

The valuation of an asset will determine the amount of your claim. For example, let's say you had a TV stolen from your home that you purchased last year for $1,200. Assuming your policy had a $1,000 deductible and the theft would be covered for the TV, how much might you receive? First, you would start with the valuation of the TV, which would be depreciated for one year of use, or approximately $500. Next you would apply any sublimits for electronics, but the $500 valuation is below the sublimit level. Last, the deductible of $1,000 would be applied and you would end up receiving $0 ($500 – $1,000). In fact, based on the value of the TV, you would likely not bother filing a claim unless other items were taken or other damage was done. What this means is that you are self-insuring or retaining the first $1,000 of claims of covered losses.

Proof of Loss

The last area to highlight under the "Asset and Property Protection" section is *proof of loss*. To establish that there was indeed a loss, you typically must first prove you owned the item. To do this you would need receipts or some other way to verify that you purchased or owned the item. Another problem can arise when there has been a substantial loss, like from a major theft, flood, fire, or hurricane. Could you even remember all the items you own if everything was lost?

One solution is to take some time to lay out as many valuables on your bed as possible and take pictures on your phone (and keep a backup somewhere). Next, walk around your home taking a video to film all the details and possessions in your rooms. While it's not as good as receipts, insurers will often accept dated pictures as a form of proof of ownership. Moving forward, take photos or save electronic receipts of meaningful purchases in a backed-up file as well. A little extra time when you buy something can be very helpful. While many credit card companies keep detailed records of past purchases, the records seldom provide details of the items purchased.

Liability Protection
Liability Insurance Coverages

Another important type of insurance coverage is liability insurance. A *liability claim* arises when someone *alleges* that they were harmed based on your actions or inactions. The insurance policy typically swings into action when there is an allegation of liability; actual responsibility *is not required* to trigger a claim. Additionally, the insurer may provide for some or all of the legal expense to defend you.

The damages caused are typically classified into three areas: 1) *bodily injury* (BI), 2) *property damage* (PD), or 3) *personal injury* (PI). BI is when the person was physically injured, and can include expenses relating to medical, rehabilitation, loss of future income, ongoing additional required expenses (*compensatory damages*), and the cost associated with pain and suffering (*punitive damages*). PD is when you cause damage, destruction, or loss of use to someone else's property. PI is when there is damage caused to a person's reputation, freedom, or when mental trauma is caused. PI liability claims can include issues like defamation of character, false imprisonment, slander, or libel.

Liability Coverage Under Homeowners/Renters/Condo Policies

The liability sections under most homeowner and renters policies are fairly standard. Coverage limits are typically expressed in amounts of $100,000. Liability coverage is typically provided for BI and PD caused by an insured, which can include all resident relatives' actions. The actions that lead to injury or damage need not occur at home to be covered by a homeowners policy. For example, if you hit a golf ball that causes damage to someone else's home along the golf course, it would most likely be covered under your homeowners policy. In addition, liability claims often are not required to pay policy deductibles.

Liability Coverage Under Auto Policies

The liability section of most auto policies works in a similar way, but uses something called *split limits* to show liability policy coverage. For example, an auto policy may have split limits of 100/300/50. For these limits, the 100 represents a maximum of $100,000 of BI coverage that can be paid to any one individual injured in an accident. The 300 represents a maximum amount of $300,000 that can be paid for the entire event for BI expenses. The 50 represents a maximum of $50,000 of PD that can be paid for any one event or accident. Remember, liability covers damage you cause to others and their property. For damage you do to your own car, that's a different section of the coverage.

Personal Umbrella Liability Policy (PUP)

A critical and commonly overlooked insurance coverage for many higher net worth individuals is personal umbrella liability policy (PUP). PUP offers higher limits of liability protection for BI and PD above what you have in your homeowners and auto policies. It is designed to work with your other liability coverages to provide *drop-down* coverage. Drop-down coverage means that as long as your liability coverage on your homeowners and auto policies meet the minimum levels (established by your insurance company and typically $100,000 to $250,000), the PUP will provide seamless integration for liability claims.

So, a liability claim exceeding the limits on your underlying policies (home and auto) will be covered by the PUP up to the policy limits. A PUP policy also covers liability claims alleging personal injury (PI) as well. Remember, PI claims are not covered under your homeowners or auto liability policies.

Here's a potentially huge insurance savings tip for you when using the PUP. Many people feel the liability protection on their auto policies are inadequate to cover the potential claims and damages associated with expense litigation today. As a result, people increase their liability limits to $250,000, $500,000 and even $1,000,000 under their auto policy to cover this risk exposure. As an alternative, consider purchasing a PUP and lowering your liability limits to the insurance company required minimums for drop-down coverage. This can allow you to get $1,000,000 or more to total liability protection and significantly lower your auto premium costs.

This can create more free cash flow that can be used for savings or to address personal debt elimination. Insurance companies may not make this liability savings strategy well known. Agents sometimes aren't so forthcoming to help facilitate this three-policy integration since it can substantially lower premiums and commissions. However, a good property and liability agent will be up to speed and willing to help you coordinate these coverages.

Disability Insurance (DI)

Disability insurance (DI) is one of the most important and often overlooked forms of protection. One of your most important assets is your future lifetime earning potential. One of your greatest risks, therefore, is your inability to earn income based on an accident, injury, or illness. DI covers your replacement of income if you become unable to earn an income.

If you become disabled, your bills keep coming in, and if you can't work, it won't take long to become financially overwhelmed. Also, if you become disabled, it's likely that your household expenses will increase for your needed care. This is a recipe for disaster that can wipe you out fast. Over 50% of working Americans will encounter an accident, sickness, or injury that will require them to miss work for 90 days or more sometime during their working years. In fact, you are much more likely to become disabled in your working career than dying unexpectedly. Despite the importance of this type of insurance protection, very few working Americans own their own individual disability insurance policy. Even many people who have life insurance fail to understand that *their risk of disability is significantly higher than their risk of premature death.*

Due to the nature of DI, the underwriting process can be extensive because it involves both health and financial aspects. When considering a DI policy you will need to consider several options and features.

Benefit Period

The benefit period is the length of time that benefits will be paid to you under a qualifying disability. Benefit periods can range from one year until retirement age. The longer the benefit period, the higher the cost. The benefit period is a very important consideration. A best practice is to select the benefit period you want coverage for *first* and *then* select the amount of monthly benefit you need and can afford.

Benefit Amount

The benefit amount is the amount of maximum monthly payments you can receive. Typically, you can buy a DI policy to protect approximately two-thirds of your gross salary (which could possibly include commissions and bonuses). Some policies can be purchased to replace up to 100% of your salary, depending on your occupation.

Definitions of *Disability*

The definition of *disability* is the contractual language that triggers the ability to receive benefits under the policy. Definitions of disability revolve around your ability to perform the *material* and *substantial* duties of your job. Under an *own occupation* definition of disability, you may be considered disabled if you are unable to perform those duties and responsibilities of your specific occupation, based on your experience, education, and training. This is the easiest definition under which to qualify, and as such is also the most expensive.

It is more difficult to qualify as disabled under the *any occupation* definition of disability, and as such, this option is the least expensive. Under the *any occupation* definition, you only qualify as disabled if you are unable to perform the duties and responsibilities of ANY occupation you can perform, based on your experience, education, and training. For example, let's say there was a surgeon who lost the ability to expertly use her left arm from a mild stroke, but decided to teach at the medical school of her university hospital. Under an *own occupation* definition of disability, she would be considered *totally disabled* and would receive full benefits under the DI policy, *plus* the full income from teaching. Under the *any occupation* definition of disability the surgeon would not be considered disabled because she would still be able to perform the duties and responsibilities of an occupation based on her experience, education, and training.

There is also a *modified own occupation* definition of disability that starts as an *own occupation* definition for the first two or three years, then converts to an *any occupation* definition. This provides the policy owner a few years to transition and prepare in case of a total disability, and is priced in between the two other definitions of disability options.

Riders

There are several riders that are offered on most DI policies that are very important to consider. The residual disability benefit rider provides partial payment of the monthly benefit amount when returning to work following a period of total disability. The waiver of premium rider applies during a period of disability and suspends the payment of premiums due. Otherwise, you would still be responsible for paying your premiums while you were disabled, which can be more challenging. There are also cost of living adjustment (COLA) riders that will automatically increase your monthly benefit amounts annually to keep pace with inflation and guaranteed purchase option (GPO) riders that allow you the option to increase benefits annually for a cost. These riders are very important and should be considerations as you weigh the costs and potential benefits when designing your policy. Most people choose to layer DI policies and purchase increments throughout their working career based on their incomes and what they can afford at the time.

Long-Term Care Insurance (LTCI)

Because of the complex nature and features of comprehensive long-term care insurance (LTCI), the discussion of specific policy recommendations are not possible. However, a general education on the need for LTCI will help in your overall understanding. LTCI is a form of asset protection insurance. To illustrate this point, consider the average cost of a long-term care skilled nursing facility. The all-in cost per month can range from $8,000 to $15,000 (or more) per month,[2] depending on your location and the services you require. For simplification purposes, let's assume a $10,000 average monthly cost for our example. For each year you are in a nursing home, it will cost you approximately $120,000 per individual (and $240,000 per couple). At those rates, how long would it take for you to go through all of your savings and assets?

If you're thinking Medicare will pay for these costs, you are most likely wrong unless it follows an extended hospital stay and in concurrence with your physician. However, Medicare does not cover custodial care, which is daily assistance with activities such as eating, bathing, dressing, toileting, transferring, and continence. If you need help with these activities of daily living (ADLs) at home or in a care facility, Medicare will most likely not cover these expenses. These expenses require private insurance or cash. If you are thinking Medicaid will cover these costs if you have depleted all of your assets, you may be partially correct. You would first have to spend down almost all your assets and possessions as well as satisfy a waiting period. If you did qualify for state Medicaid care, it's important to keep in mind that the beds for LTC needs are scarce, it may be far away from your family members, and it's likely that you wouldn't get the highest quality of care. The bottom line is that unless you are willing and able to self-insure (e.g., pay out of pocket for your own care), the only way you will have any control over where you go, the quality of the facility you live in, and the quality of your care is if you have private LTCI.

Long-term care insurance policies work similarly to DI. There is a benefit period, a benefit amount, a waiting or elimination period to satisfy prior to receiving benefits, and riders like annual cost of living adjustments (COLAs), guaranteed purchase options (GPOs), and waiver of premium riders. Benefits can be paid for healthcare services provided in a home setting, in an assisted living facility, at a skilled nursing home, and even at a hospice facility. The difference between LTCI and DI is in how you qualify for a claim. For LTCI, a physician needs to certify that you are unable to perform two of six ADLs, and you are expected to be unable to perform them for the next 90 days. At that point, your waiting or elimination period would begin prior to receiving benefits.

While there are many plans, you might want to see if your state has an LTCI partnership plan option. These plans have been approved by design specifically by your state of residence and designed to work with your state's Medicaid plan to allow for a shared spend down of assets and Medicaid assistance. Many different insurance companies in your state will have state partnership LTCI plans to consider. You should also look into "shared pool" LTCI plans as well, which allow for spousal/partner sharing of benefits. This can be valuable as LTCI premiums are expensive based on the potential benefits paid, and is a plan that you use or lose. This means if you die in the hospital or at home of a heart attack or stroke, your premiums paid and benefits will go unused, like auto or homeowners type of insurance. That's why a shared pool approach gives both spouses access to the benefits and increases the odds of the plan being used. Your LTCI representative who sells state partnership plans is required to present you with a buyer's guide and outline of coverage for you to compare plans. Look into plans that use a "days of illness" method of satisfying the waiting period because of their ease to understand and simplicity for planning when home healthcare expenses are involved.

Life Insurance

There are many schools of thought when it comes to determining the proper amount of life insurance needed to protect yourself and your family. Financial best practice suggests a needs-based approach to determining the amount of life insurance you need. Due to the often complex nature of financial calculations and inputs required, many choose to have this work done by a life insurance risk and underwriting professional (e.g., CLU, CFP®). However, for those who are looking for best practice guidance, here are the elements you should consider.

For the analysis, you should start by determining your final expense needs at death. These would include the cost of a funeral, estate fees, paying off all personal debt, paying off the mortgage(s), and establishing money to help with the surviving family members' adjustment. Additionally, you should calculate the educational needs for any children and costs like wedding expenses you would wish to pre-fund. You should also calculate the amount needed at death to replace your income as if you were still there for your family, which could also be used to fund educational and retirement needs for your surviving spouse. There are many additional considerations, including rate of interest, inflation, and tuition rate increases. If you are not very savvy with a financial calculator or Excel spreadsheet, there are some useful financial calculators and planning tools available online.

Since we don't know your financial situation, we can't give you specific advice. That said, some general best practices are worth consideration. If you don't have any dependents (e.g., children) or anyone relying on your income (e.g., a spouse/partner), you may not need life insurance. However, if you anticipate having dependents in the future, you may notice that it is cheaper to get a policy when you are younger and in good health. If you are under 40, have a spouse, and children, you would want to consider having a minimum of $500,000 of a 20-year *term* policy. Of course health and other factors could easily increase or decrease this amount.

To put it bluntly, please don't be a deadbeat parent or partner. At a minimum, get this insurance protection in place for the income earning spouses in the family. Don't forget the monetary value of a stay-at-home partner. The replacement costs for childcare and household management can be quite significant. Term insurance is relatively inexpensive for what you get and what it provides for your family and is more than adequate for most life insurance needs. Simply stated: It's the right thing to do, and everyone will remember you for how you took care of your family after you were gone. It really is the ultimate gift of care and love a parent and/or partner can use to protect the well-being of his or her family. There are other forms of life insurance, including many excellent permanent life insurance plans. However, these plans are designed to serve specific family financial needs and should be recommended by a professional as a part of an overall comprehensive planning process.

HUNTING AND GATHERING

With your survival plan in place, let's focus now on hunting and gathering. In essence, this is where you begin to go on offense. Your focus is on saving, investing, and wealth accumulation. While the amount of savings needed will depend on your specific financial vision, we can look to best practice here as well for guidance. You may have heard that you should save 10% of your income for retirement. The specific number is up to you. The question is really this: How wealthy do you want to become and how fast do you want to get there? It is not unusual to see highly motivated wealth builders save 30–50% of their income. You will need to plan on taking advantage of accelerating your retirement wealth accumulation after age 50. Your plan also needs to look at which vehicles are most efficient for accumulating savings for specific goals like education and retirement funding. As you near your transition to your desired vision in retirement, you will need to make changes to your portfolio allocations and risk profile as well as planning for taxation from different potential income sources. In the hunting and gathering phase, you should also identify plans to address out-of-pocket healthcare expenses.

Hunting and Gathering—Highlights of Financial Best Practices
Tax Advantaged Savings

The importance of optimizing your most tax-effective means for retirement savings, your employer-sponsored retirement plans (e.g., 401[k], 403[b]), cannot be overstated. If this option is available to you, we strongly suggest you take advantage of it. The ability to save on a pre-tax basis reduces your taxable income, possibly with employer matching contributions, and tax-deferred growth stands as one of the best ways to save for retirement. At a minimum, you should be contributing to the level where you take full advantage of all possible employer matching contributions. This is free money, plain and simple. For example, if your employer matches your contributions $1 for $1 up to 6%, by contributing 6% of your pay on a pre-tax basis, you will in essence double your money before any investment earnings. This is an incredible retirement savings advantage.

If you are saving for your children's or grandchildren's education, the Section 529 plans and Roths can both be excellent ways to save and fund for educational needs. Both plans offer tax advantages for accumulating money to specifically address educational funding and distribution needs. Section 529 plans are offered by many states to help fund education to both local and nonlocal educational institutions. Your accumulation typically grows tax deferred, and access to funds for qualifying educational expenses can be withdrawn tax free as well. Specific plan rules and state tax laws apply, so as always, we recommend that you consult with a financial advisor before you decide which accounts to use, and check with a CPA to consider tax implications. There are also ownership and transfer considerations you will need to build into your plan as well.

Diversification and Income Planning

Financial best practice dictates the need for diversification. This includes diversification in the asset classes you hold, which is discussed in the following, but also in the types of accounts you have. As such, it can be helpful to have long-term savings/investments in a combination of qualified (pre-tax) investment accounts (e.g., 401[k]s and traditional IRAs) and nonqualified (or after-tax) investment accounts (e.g., Roth IRAs, trust, or brokerage accounts). That way, when you go to distribute your savings and turn it into income, you will have a mix of different tax options. It's hard to anticipate the tax rates in the future when it comes time to start liquidating your funds for income. Having a mix of taxable and nontaxable accounts can allow you to take income according to your needs and prevailing tax rates at the time. In terms of how best to approach this in your specific situation, as always, we recommend you consult with a financial planner and/or CPA.

Planning for Healthcare Expenses

The cost of healthcare is on the increase. There are several best practice tax preferred savings vehicles that allow you to pay for out-of-pocket healthcare expenses on a pre-tax basis. In fact, after you establish your emergency fund, you may be able to take advantage of a high-deductible healthcare plan (HDHP) if your employer offers one. The HDHP can be combined with a health savings account (HSA). An HSA allows for tax deferred growth and can roll over year after year. Your HSA funds can even be used to pay for out-of-pocket Medicare expenses after age 65 as well. All of these areas of savings, investing, and wealth accumulation are worth consideration.

Investing

Many people struggle with investing. In fact, making bad investing decisions is a popular way for people to sabotage their financial lives. People waste incredible amounts of time fiddling with their investments and portfolio of stocks or funds, more than they can ever expect to get back in added return. In fact, all the fiddling actually ends up hurting their returns. Studies have clearly shown that the more trading people do, the lower their returns. That time and energy could be much more effectively applied to the other financial issues we discussed, including focusing on increasing your income or growing your business. Often, people obsess about their portfolios and what's happening in the markets because it makes them feel financially smart and proactive. In reality, they are doing more harm than good to their net worth. As a reminder, this information is not meant to be financial advice. To make appropriate investment recommendations specific to you, a financial planner would need to know the details of your financial situation, your risk tolerance, your risk capacity, your financial goals, and much more. So what follows is for educational purposes only based on established financial education principles. For your specific investment decisions, we strongly recommend you meet with a Certified Financial Planner (CFP®).

Index Investing

Perhaps you have heard about studies showing that over time (e.g., a 15-year period), index funds beat professional stock pickers 95% of the time. While we will not be giving you specific investing advice, we thought a discussion about index investing might be useful. Index equity (aka stock) funds currently account for approximately 50% of the assets invested in the United States through mutual funds and exchange-traded funds (ETFs). However, to understand the power of index investing, the 50% (approximately) figure overstates these funds' impact on the marketplace as a whole. Vanguard estimates that stock index funds and ETFs account for less than 5% of trading volume on U.S. exchanges.[3] So while they account for nearly half of the volume of funds and ETFs, they only account for 5% of the activity. This means that those who own indexed investments do not "trade" them and therefore seem to truly understand the goal of the long-term investor and the power of the indexing itself.

To illustrate how confident financial experts are in the performance of the index over time, here's a story from Warren Buffett. If you haven't heard of him, Warren Buffett is thought by many to be the most successful investor in modern history. Once, Mr. Buffett offered to wager $500,000 (for charity) that no investment professional could select a set of five hedge funds that would match the performance of an unmanaged S&P 500 Index fund. The bet was to last 10 years, and Buffett picked Vanguard's low-cost S&P 500 Index fund as his contender. Ten years later, Buffett claimed victory with his S&P 500 fund delivering an average annual return of 8.5% compared to the fund-of-funds' average annual gain of 2.4%.[4] So, in other words, the S&P 500 trounced all of these teams of Wall Street experts over time.

Here are some of Warren Buffet's additional quotes about low-cost index funds.[5]

When trillions of dollars are managed by Wall Streeters charging high fees, it will usually be the managers who reap outsized profits, not the clients. Both large and small investors should stick with low-cost index funds.[6]

Huge institutional investors, viewed as a group, have long underperformed the unsophisticated index-fund investor who simply sits tight for decades. A major reason has been fees: Many institutions pay substantial sums to consultants who, in turn, recommend high-fee managers. And that is a fool's game.[7]

Retirement Date Funds

Another popular alternative to individual index funds are *retirement date funds*, also known as target date funds. These funds solve the problem of which index funds to pick and in what percentages to make sure you have a diversified portfolio. Many employee-sponsored retirement plans (e.g., 401[k]s) have these funds-of-funds available as investment options.

There is an investing rule-of-thumb that you take the number 100 and subtract your age, and that's the percentage you should allocate to equities (aka stocks) within your retirement portfolio. Of course, with any best practice, the advice is generalized and simplified for the broadest application. As we have stated, we are not giving you financial advice. That said, the concept is rooted in sound thinking. As we age and near retirement, there is less time to recover from the inevitable cyclical downturns and market contractions. As a long-term investor nearing retirement, it therefore makes good sense to reduce your exposure to riskier investments (such as equities) as you age and shift your allocation to historically less-risky investments (aka cash-equivalents, Treasuries, and bonds). While in retirement, some exposure to equities could still make sense as your savings is spent down and there is a need to protect your remaining nest egg from the impacts of inflation.

Retirement date funds work on the same Rule of 100 concept, where exposure to equities within the fund is reduced as you near retirement age. These adjustments are made automatically. So rather than do-it-yourself investors needing to worry about rebalancing and adjusting their various index fund investment percentages, the adjustments are made for you. Typically, there are different funds established where you pick the fund that has a date corresponding to your anticipated retirement date. For example, if you were planning on retiring in 2025, you might select a Retirement 2025 Date Fund. The same type of analysis can be done for historical performance, fees, and other charges for the different funds offered. You can find several lower cost and fee retirement (target) date funds just like with the index funds.

The reviews and press on retirement date funds has been mixed. For example, when asked if target date funds are really adding value, Warren Buffett replied:

> *No, probably not. The S&P 500 Index Fund is the one to use. That's the one I used in that bet I made for ten years. It's the one I've told the trustee for my wife to put 90% of the funds I leave her in. One of the pitfalls of target-date funds is the fees.*[8]

However, according to Morningstar's 2019 Target-Date Landscape Report (2020), the average asset-weighted expense ratio for target date funds was 0.62% as of 2018.[9] These asset-weighted expense ratios don't seem to be too far away from those of index funds, and you can probably seek out those with below average expenses. Despite the debate, retirement or target date funds are becoming increasingly popular with invested assets reaching an all-time high of $1 trillion in 2017. The popularity of these retirement date funds has increased in the past decade, attracting more than $40 billion in assets per year.[10]

How Do I Get Started?

There are many reputable companies that offer index funds and/or retirement target date funds and ETFs. In the example of retirement target date funds, many hold similar index funds within them at similar percentages. While we do not recommend one place over another, the three largest asset managers in the world are BlackRock Inc., best known for its iShares brand of exchange-traded index funds, which has $7 trillion under management; index fund pioneer Vanguard Group Inc., which has $5.6 trillion; and State Street Corp., which manages $2.9 trillion. Together, these companies hold about 80% of all indexed money. As of 2020, approximately 22% of the shares of the typical S&P 500 company sits in their portfolios, up from 13.5% in 2008.[11] Many popular trading platforms, like TD Ameritrade and E*Trade, have research tools that allow you to compare the funds and ETFs for these and other companies, and examine past performance, fees, and expenses.

We strongly recommend that you seek the counsel of a Registered Investment Advisor (RIA) or Certified Financial Planner (CFP®) for help in determining the proper asset allocation and savings amounts to meet your specific retirement vision. As your net worth grows, so does the complexity of your financial situation, and a qualified expert can help you execute your plan and bring critical issues to your attention. In addition, the biggest mistakes people make investing are behavioral. Even people who invest in index funds, for example, do significantly worse than the funds themselves because they are often trading in and out of them as they are emotionally responding to market conditions. When it comes to investing, just like all other aspects of our financial lives, we are our own worst enemy.

However, for those who are just starting out and are confident in using online tools to assess their risk tolerance, there's no reason why you can't get started on your own. A decade ago, the marketplace, sources and access to information, and online tools were not as robust as they are today. We live in an increasingly online world, and in the midst of the Covid-19 pandemic of 2020, many of us got even more comfortable doing things online. Our collective comfort with virtual meetings, online banking, savings, investing, and budgeting is increasing. People who want to take charge, become self-educated, and get started on their own now have everything they need to be empowered at whatever level of engagement they desire.

ADAPTATION VERSUS EXTINCTION

Once you are a proficient hunter and gatherer, your biggest concern will be adapting to avoid extinction. As you close in on making your retirement vision a reality, you need to make some adjustments. Your planning will need to consider the advantaged opportunities that become available at age 50. You will also need to adjust and reallocate your investments and consider the appropriateness of taking a more conservative overall risk profile. It also may be a good idea to plan on what amount of Social Security benefits you will receive and plan on the timing of when you would like to begin taking them. As you age, healthcare and associated expenses become more of a potential burden. Specific planning to address these increased needs will be beneficial. Finally, as your wealth grows, there will be additional estate considerations. One of the best parts of having wealth is your increased ability to use it to help others. If that's a desire of yours, you will want to include some estate gifting and planning to your list. As you make your desired vision a reality, you will plan for what could be the best years of your life.

Adaptation versus Extinction—Highlights of Financial Best Practices

Retirement Savings Acceleration and Allocation

If you are getting a late start on taking charge of your financial life, you may need to make up for lost savings time. That's exactly how the current tax law has been set up. It allows for increased contributions into many qualified retirement savings after age 50. Just like the target date funds discussed previously, financial best practice suggests that risk profiles should shift allocation toward a more conservative approach, which often includes a reduced exposure to equities.

Planning Social Security Income

When it comes to planning your retirement income, there are several best practices to consider. If you are eligible to receive Social Security income benefits (aka, you have attained *fully insured* status; typically 40 credits), you will need to project your retirement benefits and determine at what age you wish to begin receiving them. You may be eligible to elect *early retirement* and begin receiving a permanently reduced benefit at age 62. If you wait until *full retirement* age (e.g., 67 for those born after 1960), you will receive 100% of your benefit amount. You could also wait and take *late retirement* at age 70 and receive a permanently increased benefit. Currently, you receive about 8% more in benefits for each year you defer taking income after age 62 and until age 70. That's an important consideration to keep in mind as you plan your retirement income. If you go to SSA.gov, you can find a Social Security benefits estimator, which can help with your planning projections.

Income Tax Planning

To plan the best strategies to fund your retirement, you will want to consult with a financial planner. He or she will help you evaluate your accounts and their taxable distribution rules to determine your net after-tax amount and the interest each earns if you delay taking income from them. Efficiency in tax and income planning is very important at this stage. As you near your retirement age, you can adjust your projections and plans based on the current distribution tax laws.

Planning for Healthcare Expenses

With the cost of healthcare rising, we are likely to experience the increased burden of higher out-of-pocket costs. If you are on a fixed income in retirement, then healthcare costs can pose a challenge. Once you go on Medicare, typically at age 65, the out-of-pocket expenses include monthly Medicare Part B and D premiums, deductibles, co-pays, and noncovered expenses. About two-thirds of Americans chose to trade those unknown expenses for a known monthly cost through the purchase of a Medicare Supplement plan. These standardized plans are offered through private insurance companies. As you get closer to age 65, you will begin receiving information on your Medicare options and Medicare supplement choices.

There will be other healthcare expenses for services Medicare doesn't cover, such as eyeglasses, dental care, hearing care, and long-term care expenses. If you can take advantage of a HDHP with an HSA, you can accumulate additional funds you can use after age 65. If this option isn't available to you, you might want to consider adding an additional after-tax savings account identified for healthcare expenses and premium funding for later in life. This is one area where it's hard to know how much you are going to need. Over-saving in this type of account shouldn't be a concern, and excess funds can always be used to generate additional income if needed.

Estate Distribution and Gift Planning

Last, since you can't take it with you, you should consider doing some estate gift planning. There are many estate tax advantages available for gifting, trusts, and charitable donations. Sometimes, you can even make charitable donations of assets, which may have significantly appreciated over time on a tax preferred basis versus a cash donation. Planning as to how your estate will be distributed and how the funds will be received by those who receive them should be given careful considerations. Working with a good estate attorney, trusts can be established to provide for others very generously, but with provisions that decrease the likelihood that they will mismanage the money or lose their drive for accomplishment. It is not uncommon to see lives destroyed when inheritors receive large amounts of money from large wealth transfers without any of these behavioral provisions built in.

PROGRESS MEASUREMENT TOOLS

We have laid a lot of information on you. This is a chapter you will likely want to revisit as you progress. We leave you with a few standard financial health measurement tools to help you chart your progress. As a reminder, this chapter is meant to give you a basic grounding in standard financial planning information. It is possible that some of this information does not apply to your financial situation. As such, do not take any of what we have written as financial advice specific to you. Your best bet is to consult with a Certified Financial Planner (CFP®) who can help you develop and implement a plan specific to your unique needs and circumstances.

Financial Health Measure 1: Your Financial Strength Is Your Net Worth

Net Worth (Assets – Liabilities)
Assets = All your stuff
Liabilities = All you owe
Your Goal: Grow Your Net Worth

Financial Health Measure 2: Your Free Cash Flow

Free Cash Flow = Your Net Income – Your Total Expenses
   Net Income = What you bring home (income after taxes)
   Total Expenses = Everything you spend
   Your Goal: Increase your free cash flow to accelerate your savings/investing

Chapter 14 Mammoth Mindset Insights

1. Don't spend more than you earn.
2. Break your addiction to materialistic shopping endorphins.
3. Develop savings and wealth endorphins.
4. Be aware of your money behaviors and break bad habits.
5. Stay focused on your vision/goal for your desired lifestyle.
6. Be the Money Mammoth and live in your new environment.

NOTES

1. Report on the Economic Well-Being of U.S. Households in 2018-May 2019, Board of Governors of the Federal Reserve https://www.federalreserve .gov/publications/2019-economic-well-being-of-us-households-in-2018-dealing-with-unexpected-expenses.htm.
2. Author's calculated figure based on compiled information and expertise in the area.
3. Alex Bryan, "Most Arguments Against Index Investing Aren't Compelling: A Closer Look at the Merits of Common Arguments Against Index Investing," Morningstar, November 22, 2019, https://www.morningstar.com/articles/ 957419/most-arguments-against-index-investing-arent-compelling.
4. Julia La Roche, "Warren Buffett's Bet Against Hedge Funds Had an 'Unforeseen Investment Lesson,'" *Yahoo Finance*, February 24, 2018, https://finance .yahoo.com/news/warren-buffetts-bet-hedge-funds-reveals-investment-lesson-everyone-135500243.html.

5. Mitch Tuchman, "5 Warren Buffett Quotes for Anyone Who Thinks They Can Pick Stocks and Get Rich Like He Did," *Barrons Market Watch*, August 11, 2017, https://www.marketwatch.com/story/the-5-times-warren-buffett-talked-about-index-fund-investing-2017-04-28.

6. Warren Buffet, Reuters online, February 25, 2016, https://www.reuters.com/article/berkshire-hatha-buffett-indexfunds-idCNL1N1GA07S.

7. Warren Buffet, "Promoting Innovation and Managing Change," CNBC.com, 2014; Warren Buffet. (2015, March 2). "These Investments Are a Fool's Game," CNBC.com, https://www.CNBC.com/2015/03/02/Buffett-These-Investments-Are-A-Fools-Game.html.

8. Julia La Roche, *Yahoo Finance*, February 24, 2018, https://finance.yahoo.com/news/warren-buffetts-bet-hedge-funds-reveals-investment-lesson-everyone-135500243.htm.

9. Morningstar's 2019 Target-Date Landscape Report, 2020, https://www.morningstar.com/lp/tdf-landscape.

10. Karen Wallace, "What Are Target-Date Funds? Investors in Target-Date Funds Can Set Up a Diversified Portfolio and Maintain a Sensible Asset Allocation for Decades Without Breaking a Sweat," Morningstar, April 4, 2020, https://www.morningstar.com/articles/808120/what-are-target-date-funds.

11. David McLaughlin and Annie Massa, "The Hidden Dangers of the Great Index Fund Takeover, The Big Three—BlackRock, Vanguard, and State Street—Are the Most Important Players in Corporate America. Whether They Like It or Not," *Bloomberg BusinessWeek*, January 9, 2020, https://www.bloomberg.com/news/features/2020-01-09/the-hidden-dangers-of-the-great-index-fund-takeover.

CHAPTER 15

Your Success

Perhaps you have noticed a pattern in your life: Things change; the rules change; the environment changes; bad things happen; our best laid and well-thought-out plans fail. There are countless examples of these patterns happening in human history and probably in your own life. Every economic crisis involves some unforeseen event that triggers a threat to our financial survival. One of the most critical aspects to surviving as a species has been our ability to adapt and evolve. Now, of course, not all of us survive a crisis let alone thrive in and after it. Those of us who do best in a crisis have certain psychological traits that have been found to be associated with success. These include open-mindedness. To survive and thrive in a changing world, we need to be open to learning. We need to be flexible in our beliefs and open to challenging and changing them to adapt to changing circumstances.

The pandemic-related market turmoil, as well as the financial crisis of 2008, the tech bubble of 2000, and countless previous examples, all represent changes in the financial environment that require us to adapt. We don't know for sure when the next threat to our financial survival will emerge. Whether a threat is personal to us or one with much larger societal implications, the occurrence is not a matter of *if* but *when*. As such, we need to have a survival guide to help us navigate the crisis.

YOUR FINANCIAL SURVIVAL GUIDE

You have done everything right: You have the needed insurances; you have been working hard; you have an emergency fund, and you are saving for your short- and long-term goals. You have been investing wisely and are following the recommendations of your CPA, your estate planning attorney, and your financial planner. But, despite all of these efforts, the financial crisis hits.

When you perceive a threat, your brain floods your bloodstream with hormones such as adrenaline, which prepare you to protect yourself. While this works great if you were being chased by a predator, your survival response can wreak havoc on your financial situation. You must keep in mind that our animal instincts are the primary reason we are vulnerable to engaging in self-destructive financial behaviors. When we are emotionally flooded, we become rationally challenged. When we are scared about the economy or our finances (or excited, for that matter), our animal brain takes over, and we are vulnerable to financial self-destruction.

Often, our most critical financial decisions are made under pressure—pressure to bid on and purchase the right home, pressure when to buy a car by the dealership and salesperson using high-pressure tactics, and pressure when unexpected expenses hit. Such pressure may make you question your approach to personal finance in general, or rattle your confidence in your financial decision-making ability. So, what can you do when you are terrified about money and your emotions may be making your financial decisions for you? The following are seven optimal *Money Mindsets* to help you navigate your next financial crisis, engage in rational financial decisions, and emerge from the threat better than ever before.

Money Mindset 1: Put Time Between Your Impulse and Your Action

Financial decisions made when we are emotionally flooded are almost always ill advised. It is essential to calm down and get your rational brain back online. A great way to do this is to turn off the news, find a quiet place, and take a few deep breaths. When we are stressed, we take shorter, shallower breaths. Taking several slower deep breaths can initiate a relaxation response.

As you exhale, repeat in your mind a comforting word or phrase, such as "Relax" or "Take it easy." When we are upset, it takes about 20 minutes of calming thoughts to allow the rational brain to take control again. Even then, we can still be swayed by our emotions, so consider seeking financial advice from an objective professional before making any big financial moves.

Money Mindset 2: Avoid Catastrophic Thinking

"The markets may never recover."
"I'm going to lose all my money."
"This time it's different."

If you have had any of these preceding thoughts pop into your mind in the middle of a financial crisis, you are not alone. In fact, do you remember the terror you felt in the early months of the Covid-19 pandemic or back in 2008 or 2000? Chances are you had some or all these thoughts each and every time. Did you act on them? Did doing so help you or hurt you? We have these thoughts every time we experience a market crash. These beliefs can become viral and highly infectious too, as we watch pundits have panic attacks on screen and read endless media warnings about the coming apocalypse from which we may never recover (despite the fact that to-date humanity has survived precisely *every* challenge and has emerged stronger as a result).

Just because a thought pops into your mind doesn't mean it's true. You need to notice your internal chatter and take time to write down these automatic thoughts. It is critical that you spend some time evaluating the accuracy of your thinking. Approach each belief as a scientist would approach an experiment. What is the evidence that supports this thought? What is the evidence against it? Is there a better way to look at this? What is the worst thing that can happen if your assumption proved true? Could you live with that? What is the most likely thing that will happen? What advice would you give a friend who was having a similar thought? A fabulous technique is to find someone to consult with, someone who knows more than you do about whatever is worrying you. Depending on your particular thought, this could be a financial planner, a therapist, or some other expert.

Money Mindset 3: Harness the Power of Mental Accounting

When we see on the news that the market is down 20% or more, we can become terrified. But take some time to think about what "the market" is. For example, most investors do not have 100% of their money invested in the Dow Jones Industrial Average or the S&P 500, which are common market indicators in the news. As we have discussed previously, we have a natural tendency to put things into mental buckets. Sometimes this tendency hurts us, such as when we spend a bonus check or tax refund in ways we would never spend our paycheck. However, we can harness this tendency to our benefit.

In the middle of a market tumble, take a moment to look at the asset allocation in your portfolio. For example, you may notice that you have 50% in stocks and 50% in bonds or cash. In this scenario, your stock portion may be down 20%, but the other parts of your portfolio may be down much less or not at all. The red charts and downward arrows on the news may not be a direct reflection of what is happening in your portfolio.

Money Mindset 4: Expand Your Frame of Reference

In the middle of a financial crisis, times will be very tumultuous. Market volatility may be at an all-time high. Your friends may be engaging in quite dramatic behaviors, such as going all in or out of the market. If you are not careful, you will get caught up in the panic as your brain is wired to run with the herd.

We have experienced many fast and dramatic drops in the markets, and we will experience many more in the future. It might feel like your portfolio has fallen off of a cliff. In fact, if you look at a one-week, one-month, or three-month chart of the Dow Jones Industrial Average (DJIA), that's exactly what it may look like. However, prudent investors are in it for the long haul.

Short-term market fluctuations are likely to have much less of an impact on your financial health than you think. If you are a long-term investor, don't focus on a narrow frame of reference. Try to expand out the DJIA or S&P 500 charts. For example, look at the DJIA for the past 3, 5, or 10 years. Just for fun, look at the 100-year DJIA chart. What do you see? When you expand your frame of reference, you will notice that what is happening right now looks much more like a pothole than a cliff. If you are a long-term investor, then a narrow frame of reference is not only unhelpful for your state of mind and your impulses, it is probably irrelevant to your financial health.

Money Mindset 5: The Worst-Case Scenario Exercise

When you are in the middle of a crisis, the struggle is real. As bad as the situation is, the experts will tell you that it will get worse before it gets better. This can be terrifying news. We worry about our futures; we worry about losing our business or our job; we worry about losing our retirement savings; and we may even worry about depleting our emergency fund and being unable to pay our bills. Our brains interpret these events as life-threatening, and they may be for some. However, for most people, these types of market events are *not* life-threatening. The problem is that your stress around your fears *can* be life-threatening.

This following exercise helps you arrive at that conclusion. It is a form of exposure therapy, which is the most effective way to lower anxiety. Quite simply, you take some time to think through the worst-case scenario.

Are you worried about losing your job? If you did, what would happen next?

If you couldn't pay your rent, what would happen next?

If you lost your home, then what would happen?

For this exercise, you just keep going down the rabbit hole of the worst possible outcomes. Often, at the end of the line, you realize that while there will be disruption, stress, and discomfort, it is not life-threatening, and eventually, you will get back on your feet. For example, if you lost your job, then maybe you couldn't pay your rent. If you couldn't pay your rent, you may lose your apartment. If you lose your apartment, you may need to move in with your parents, with a sibling, or with a roommate. You might need to file for unemployment or for bankruptcy. While these events are quite painful, they have happened to many people. These events can make you stronger and wiser. You can rebuild and move on to higher levels of success.

Money Mindset 6: Your Future Self

Another powerful strategy is to focus on being the person today that you will feel proud of tomorrow. Financial markets are cyclical: they go up and then down and then up again. So the financial crisis will pass. They always do. Picture yourself on the other side of the crisis. Looking back on how you handled it, how do you want to feel about yourself? Of course, you will have had your low points of doubt, anxiety, and fear. But overall, wouldn't it be great to look back and see how you were a source of support, help, and inspiration for others? Wouldn't it be nice to know that even though you were rattled, you didn't act impulsively? All things shall pass and the crisis you're going through now will end. Paint a picture of how you would like to look back on how you handled it and make a point to weave some of the money mindsets and behaviors into your daily life during the crisis.

Money Mindset 7: Where Is the Opportunity?

There are opportunities all around us all the time: opportunities to improve our relationships, make new friends, increase income, and enhance joy. However, when we are mired in negativity and fear, it is very difficult for us to notice these opportunities. In fact, we may focus instead on what isn't working well. Just like a plant that is watered, whatever you pay attention to in your own life grows. It is very important to acknowledge pain and grieve our losses. You need to spend time doing that; we all do. But you don't need to stay in that space. In the midst of a crisis, practice asking yourself this question several times a day: Where is the opportunity?

Have you made a bad investment decision? Now is the opportunity for you to learn from your mistake. Did your business crumble? Now is the opportunity for you to find out what you could do to improve your chances of success with your next venture. Lose your job? Now is the opportunity for you to find one that is a better fit for your passion and skills. Stuck at home in the middle of a pandemic? Now is the opportunity for you to learn a new skill, start a side hustle, improve your marriage, or spend more quality time with your children. Is all hope lost? Now is the opportunity for you to develop a spiritual practice and learn to let go of the things you can't control. See how this works? The "where is the opportunity" mindset is quite powerful at any time in your life, but especially in a crisis.

YOUR EVOLUTION

In an ever-changing and often unpredictable world, it is important for us to continue to evolve both as a species and as individuals. This is equally true in the financial world, where technology, jobs, and opportunities are in constant flux. To support you in your financial evolution, we have covered three primary success themes critical to your evolution in this book.

Success Theme 1: Your Financial Outcomes Are the Product of Your Money Scripts®

Your early experiences and those of your ancestors resulted in specific beliefs about money. You may have learned them from direct conversations with your parents, by observing how people interact with money, or through genetic transfer. Your financial decisions are the product of generations of beliefs inherited from your family and/or your culture. Some of these Money Scripts® may be helpful and some may be harmful. Some may have worked very well in the past but may be destructive now.

Your Money Scripts® are further shaped by your own experiences and financial flashpoints and drive your financial decision making, for better or worse. They are held in your subconscious and drive all of your financial decisions. To optimize your financial life now and maximize your future financial survival, you must become aware of your Money Scripts®. You must learn to recognize them. You must spend time analyzing them. You must change the beliefs that are no longer working for you. For a FREE test of your Money Scripts®, you can go to www.MoneyScripts.com. This test is the same one we have used in research with thousands of people. After you complete the test, your results will be automatically e-mailed to you.

Success Theme 2: You Need a Clear and Exciting Vision of What You Want

Success takes effort and sacrifice. Without a clear and exciting vision of what you want, it will be very hard to stay motivated. The more abstract your definition of *success* (e.g., retirement), the less likely your inner Money Mammoth will take you there. Human beings are wired to conserve energy. We need a passionate purpose to get moving. Once this vision is created, you will become unstoppable. Self-exploration and vision construction are critical to creating intrinsic motivation to pursue and achieve your goals. With a clear vision in mind, fueled by your passion to make it a reality, the development of a realistic plan for savings and financial management becomes relatively easy. Without the vision, it can feel disheartening and laborious. When you can picture, feel, and taste your goals, you will be much more likely to achieve them. Remember, our research has found dramatic behavioral changes (e.g., 73% increase in savings) after just 60–90 minutes of creating a detailed vision of your financial goals. Make sure you have taken the time to use the exercises in this book to create *your* vision.

Success Theme 3: If You Want Different Results, You Need to Change Your Behaviors

By understanding the behavioral change process, you can prepare for success. Behavioral change isn't always easy, and some people just don't think it is worth the effort. A critical component of success is knowing what it will take to get there. You need to understand what actions you need to take and how to make changes stick to ensure your success. Replacing counterproductive or maladaptive financial behaviors with financial best practice behaviors can have a significant impact to help turn around your financial position quickly. Remember that you do not need to do this alone. Our research has found that one of the biggest differences between middle class and ultra-wealthy people is that middle-class people are significantly more likely to feel like they need to do it all themselves. In contrast, ultra-wealthy people are significantly more likely to consult with people who know more than they do. Push past the idea that it costs too much to seek professional mentoring from coaches, financial planners, attorneys, and CPAs. Often, just a few hundred dollars paid to one or more of these professionals can save you thousands and make you tens of thousands in the long run.

BECOMING YOUR MONEY MAMMOTH

The mammoth was chosen as our visual representation for this book for several reasons. The mammoth was a huge creature and embodies its name. The mammoth was big, solid, stable, steady, massive, and strong. It represents the financial foundation for any individual or family. The phrase *Money Mammoth* elicit images of mighty financial power, strength, safety, and stability. When a mammoth was excited or scared, it would have been unstoppable. The key is to harness the energy of a mammoth and point it toward your financial goals. Creating an exciting vision fuels your inner mammoth, and it will push you toward your financial goals. However, the mammoth is also a warning. The mammoth was unable to survive environmental change and became extinct. Similarly, if we are not able to change and evolve to match our changing environment, we will be in danger of financial extinction.

IT IS YOUR TIME TO EVOLVE

When bad things happen, it's our response that determines our adaptability. Reflect now on how you and your family were impacted during the recent COVID-19 pandemic. Was it a time of financial stress for you? Looking back, what financial safeguards do you wish you had in place before the crisis? Try to resist the urge to throw up your hands and argue that it was all totally out of your control and there was nothing you could do. By luck or design, some people entered the crisis in much better shape, for example, with large emergency funds and multiple sources of income. Others started businesses (e.g., online businesses) in the middle of the crisis and increased their income by thousands of dollars a month. What can we learn from those thrivers to help us evolve our money mindsets?

Looking back, would having a larger liquid household emergency fund of six to nine months of fixed monthly expenses been helpful? How about your personal debt: Were there any purchases in the months leading up to the crisis you wish you hadn't made? Do you wish you could have paid down more personal debt beforehand? What about from a housing situation: Were you in a strong financial position and got your home refinanced at or near record low interest rates? What things could you have done differently? Do not let this crisis go to waste. Do not miss out on the opportunity to learn, adapt, and grow. What doesn't kill you can make you stronger if you take the opportunity to evolve.

There is no guarantee that another financial crisis won't occur. In fact, another one *will* occur. It is also true that you can't predict what will happen since each crisis is different. Most people only consider meaningful change in their lives following a crisis. Even then, most do not take the opportunity to change their beliefs or behaviors. Often, people take steps to explore change, including doing some research and listening to experts; however, when the crisis is over, they have little motivation to change. Yet, if you continue to learn, grow, and improve your financial health, learning from your mistakes and the mistakes of your ancestors, you will be in a much better position to avoid financial extinction. That's really what our message is all about: connecting your mindset with behavioral awareness and sturdy financial legs.

Evolving your money mindset involves two key components: 1) the money and 2) the mindset. The money is the simple part. Much of personal finance is fairly simple and straightforward. The mindset is where the magic or disaster happens. Your money mindset predicts your financial outcomes. When you have the right mindset, success follows. It is really that simple. With the right mindset, there will be no way of stopping you from reaching goals. Your Money Mammoth will charge ahead at full speed, and the effort needed to change will become inconsequential. Success will be a foregone conclusion.

The modern economic environment is always changing. The economy is turbulent, and likely always will be. We go through cyclical economic times of up and down. When the seas are rough, we are filled with anxiety and stress. Personal financial responsibility has never been more important. The days of denial and ignorance around personal financial matters need to end. The world has changed, and if we want to enjoy financial success, it is entirely our personal responsibility to make it happen. Living in the wealthiest society in history at the most affluent time in history while having record-high levels of personal debt and half of the country with under $500 in liquid savings for emergencies is totally unacceptable.

As a financially independent society of responsible individuals, we have failed. We have become totally financially dependent and vulnerable, and most of us live our lives with no financial safety net. There is simply no logical reason for us to behave this way, especially when the solutions to build a good financial foundation aren't difficult to understand. In the future, a lack of personal financial responsibility and failure to implement foundational best practices will result in financial extinction. The next financial Ice Age will be here before you know it. Will you and your loved ones be prepared?

THE BLUE PILL OR THE RED PILL

This is your last chance. After this there is no turning back. You take the blue pill, the story ends, you wake up in your bed and believe whatever you want to believe. You take the Red pill, you stay in wonderland, and I show you how deep the rabbit hole goes. Remember, all I am offering is the truth, nothing more.

—Morpheus to Neo, *The Matrix* (Warner Bros., 1999)

Unlike Morpheus, we are not asking you to take a pill or drink any Kool-Aid. But we have offered you the truth and nothing more. In essence, this is your chance to start taking control of your financial future. Time is running out and working against you. Your mission is to make time work for you.

The keys to wealth are actually quite simple: work hard, save aggressively, and invest wisely. If people start early, even if they have a modest paying job, there is no reason why they shouldn't be able to achieve millionaire status if they follow these three principles. However, most do not, and it is rarely due to a lack of financial knowledge. Instead, it is due to their unexamined pasts, their sub-conscious Money Scripts®, and their difficulties taming their animal brain. Instead of doing what we need to do, many of us end up doing something stupid. For example, in recent years, the practice of day trading has caught on again. Many are trying to get-rich-quick by "beating the market." The vast majority will fail. Instead of using the simple wealth-building formula, they fall prey to the fantasy of fast success. There are countless examples of poor people who work hard, save their money, and then blow it by falling prey to the fantasy of fast success and easy money. That is just not how people become wealthy, and in fact, it is how many families stay stuck for generations, with each new generation falling prey to a different form of the lie.

Just like Neo, you have a choice to make. This book is nearly finished and our time together is drawing to a close. When you turn the final page of *Money Mammoth*, you'll have a choice to make. Will you put the book down and go back to business as usual?

Will you let the Money Scripts® in your subconscious fuel you with excuses to maintain your status quo?

- "Personal finance is too hard."
- "I have too much debt to ever get ahead."
- "There HAS to be a way for me to get wealthy fast."
- "I could never succeed so why bother trying."
- "Unless you're born wealthy, you really don't have a shot."

Are you going to continue to run with these self-fulfilling prophecies, or are you ready to say enough is enough? Are you sick and tired of being stuck, or do you need to experience more pain and suffering until you hit bottom? Are you going to take action, or are you going to set this book down, give it a five-star review on Amazon.com, and just go on with your life as if nothing has happened?

Or perhaps you are one of the 20% of people who are in the action phase of change, and you are fired up to transform your financial life. Perhaps you have hardened your resolve during our time together and are ready to hunker down, cinch it up, and dig down deep for what lies ahead. Now is the time to summon your passion for your ideal life and embrace your inner resolve, and take action. Perhaps you have had enough and you no longer want to live your life with the constant fear of money and the nagging feeling in your gut that you're not doing what you should be doing financially. Trust us on this point if nothing else: The effort you will go through to get your financial house in order is nowhere near the chronic pain you will feel by continuing a life of financial chaos, knowing something is wrong, that you and your family are at risk, but that you are doing nothing to improve your life. The knowledge that you are not in control of your financial fate, that you are vulnerable, or that you are dependent on others for your survival can be agonizing.

Regardless of where you come from and where you are now, you have a decision to make. You will either choose to live a life of financial stress or you will take charge of your financial future. If you decide to take charge, you can get a clear and exciting vision of what you want and harness the power of your inner Money Mammoth to make it happen. When you set your intention and pour your passion into achieving that outcome, nothing can stop you. You will be like a charging mammoth: unstoppable. It's that simple. You get to choose A or B. Are you going to take the red pill or the blue pill? The best time to get your financial house in order was yesterday. The next best time is today. You can take action today to start setting things right. This is your chance. Now that you know what you know, there is no turning back. You must evolve your inner Money Mammoth or face financial extinction!

Index